JOHN MACQUARRIE'S N<

John Macquarrie's Natural Theology
The Grace of Being

GEORGINA MORLEY

ASHGATE

© Georgina Morley 2003

All rights reserved. No part of this publication may be reproduced, stored in a retrieval system, or transmitted in any form or by any means, electronic, mechanical, photocopying, recording or otherwise without the prior permission of the publisher.

The author has asserted her moral right under the Copyright, Designs and Patents Act, 1988, to be identified as the author of this work.

Published by
Ashgate Publishing Limited
Gower House
Croft Road
Aldershot
Hants GU11 3HR
England

Ashgate Publishing Company
Suite 420
101 Cherry Street
Burlington, VT 05401-4405

Ashgate website: http//www.ashgate.com

British Library Cataloguing in Publication Data
Morley, Georgina
  John Macquarrie's natural theology : the grace of being
  1. Macquarrie, John, 1919- 2. Natural theology
  I. Title
  230'.092

Library of Congress Cataloging-in-Publication Data
Morley, Georgina.
  John Macquarrie's natural theology : the grace of being / Georgina Morley.
    p. cm.
  Includes bibliographical references (p.).
  ISBN 0-7546-3040-4 (alk. paper) -- ISBN 0-7546-3039-0 (pbk. : alk. paper)
  1. Macquarrie, John. I. Title.

BX4827.M25 M67 2003
230'.044'092--dc21

2002027804

ISBN 0 7546 3039 0 (Hbk)
     0 7546 3040 4 (Pbk)

Typeset by Manton Typesetters, Louth, Lincolnshire, UK.
Printed and bound in Great Britain by MPG Books Ltd, Bodmin, Cornwall.

Contents

Foreword		vii
Acknowledgements		ix
Introduction		1
Chapter 1	Heidegger on Being Human	7
Chapter 2	Beyond Existentialism	43
Chapter 3	Into the Public Domain	79
Chapter 4	New-Style Natural Theology	97
Chapter 5	The Grace of Being	121
Chapter 6	A Christology of Self-Giving	143
Concluding Remarks		171
Bibliography		175
Index		197

Foreword

It was a great pleasure indeed when Georgina Morley asked me to write a foreword to her book. I am honoured to do this. One of our younger British theologians, she gives hope for the future of the subject in this country, not least by writing clearly and by concentrating on the great central themes of Christian theology.

When I heard that she had written a critical exposition of my own work, my feelings were somewhat mixed. On the one hand, I could not help feeling pleased that someone had found sufficient interest in my writings to write about them at length. On the other hand, the pleasure was tinged with a touch of anxiety – I don't mean the anxiety that the work might turn out to be strongly critical, for in theology, as presumably in other subjects, it is mainly through criticism of existing work that progress has been made, and I have learned a great deal from the criticisms of reviewers, students and others. The anxiety was rather that my intentions might have been misunderstood, for no matter how clearly a writer tries to express himself or herself, the possibilities of misinterpretation seem to be almost infinite. However, on reading Dr Morley's book, I was soon aware that she had accurately and sympathetically interpreted my thoughts, and indeed in some instances improved upon them! In particular, I was pleased that she had positioned me as a theologian who believes that what we inaccurately call 'natural theology' and what we even more inaccurately call 'revealed theology' are parts of a single enterprise and each needs the other. Her criticisms too were of a constructive kind, inviting the reader to look further into the problems.

I am fortunate indeed to have had Dr Morley as an interpreter, and I have no doubt that in future years we shall be hearing more and learning more from this gifted theological writer.

John Macquarrie
Lady Margaret Professor of Divinity (Emeritus)
Oxford University

Acknowledgements

Many people have disproved the notion that research is a lonely business, and my hearty thanks go to them. Among them, Anthony Thiselton, a splendid supervisor for the doctoral research prior to this book, has been as generous with encouragement and wit as he has been with expertise and perceptive criticism, and I am very grateful to him indeed. John Morgan of the Graduate Theological Foundation, Indiana, has offered immeasurable enthusiasm, and provided a community of interest at a key point in the research. Not least, he introduced me to John Macquarrie himself, who has been as gracious in person as in print. I am grateful to them both for sharing a cherished project with a newcomer. My kind colleagues at the North East Oecumenical Course have been patient with my distraction, and have allowed me time to complete my writing doubtless at some cost to their own diaries. Most of all, my thanks to Leslie Morley who has endured the long-term domestic upheaval of Macquarrie-fever with love and equanimity.

I am grateful to the publishers for permission to quote extensively from the following:

John Macquarrie, *The Scope of Demythologizing* (London: SCM 1960)
John Macquarrie, *Studies in Christian Existentialism* (London: SCM 1966)
John Macquarrie, *Principles of Christian Theology* (London: SCM 1977)
John Macquarrie, *Jesus Christ in Modern Thought* (London: SCM 1990; Harrisburg: Trinity Press International 1991)
Martin Heidegger, *Being and Time* (Oxford: Blackwell 1962)

Introduction

During the course of this research, conversations with friends and colleagues about the topic have elicited a common response: a warm appreciation of Macquarrie's role as an expositor of the theological scene, and an account of the personal significance of some pivotal work such as *Principles of Christian Theology* or *Jesus Christ in Modern Thought*,[1] together with a hesitation over how to distinguish exactly what it is that most distinctively characterises Macquarrie's own contribution to the theological world. It would seem that, unlike (say) Barth or Bultmann, Macquarrie is not to be subjected to the distortingly easy popularisation of 'the one who ... '.

No doubt, this owes much to the breadth of Macquarrie's interest: systematics and philosophy, ethics, ecclesiology and comparative religions all come under his gaze. It also owes something to his range of appeal, from his highly technical work on Heidegger or on the neo-Platonic tradition, to the popular accessibility of, for example, *Invitation to Faith*.[2] It is certainly an indication of the dynamic method of his thought as it develops during the more than forty years from its earliest published form at Glasgow to its mature expression in Oxford. Far from defining and persistently defending his own precise thesis, Macquarrie constantly scrutinises the materials to hand and wields them in his own fashion for the context in which Christian theology must make sense.

It is precisely this dynamic quality, however, which raises the question not simply of how to *characterise* Macquarrie's contribution but, more importantly, of how to *assess* this contribution. Is it the case, for example, that Macquarrie makes a number of distinct contributions during the different stages of his thought – as might be claimed for Don Cupitt, for instance, who himself supplies the phrase 'right at the time' to support his changing (and incompatible) positions?[3] Or is it rather that, as with a sympathetic reading of Dietrich Bonhoeffer, an internal consistency in Macquarrie's thought resists fragmentation when understood against the chronological background of its development?[4]

In this book, I shall argue the latter position, and suggest that the developments in Macquarrie's thought emerge in response to a particular context. Certainly, this context does not have the terrifying ultimacy of that which sculpted Bonhoeffer's thought, but I shall seek to show in the chapters which follow that Macquarrie's career, and the influence of colleagues and institutions during his career, provide the temporal narrative which accounts for the particular directions his work takes. As Ernst Käsemann comments, 'An authentic theology certainly never comes into existence as an intellectual construction in a vacuum.'[5] Macquarrie's essay 'Pilgrimage in Theology' gives a first clue to the impact of his career on the development of his thought, and Macquarrie has given a much fuller account at the 1998 *Macquarrie on Macquarrie* Ireland conference of the Graduate Theological Foundation, Indiana, now published as *On Being a Theologian*.[6]

However, this is not merely a biographical exercise. What I shall argue during the course of this book is that it is in precisely this development that the roots of Macquarrie's most distinctive theological contribution lie. I shall suggest that it is in the very alchemy of subjecting the best characteristics of existentialist theology to the socio-political concerns and process interests of colleagues at Union Theological Seminary, New York, and then to the ecclesiastical and philosophical traditions of Oxford, that Macquarrie's mature theology offers a mediating position between gift and being.

Accordingly, in Chapters 1 to 4 I shall trace the development of Macquarrie's thought from a 'narrow existentialism' (his own phrase) to a broader existential-ontological perspective. I shall indicate the increasing concentric circles of relationality (personal, ecclesial, cosmic) by which his thought moves away from the anthropocentric and individualistic tendencies of existentialism to give an account of the human task as the transcendent dimension of the created realm. I shall suggest that a key to understanding the changes in Macquarrie's theology is to recognise that it is, in its very style, reminiscent of the existentialist philosophy which undergirds it. That is to say, it starts 'where Macquarrie is' and reflects the changing 'world' with which he is concerned; it 'becomes' in time. In this sense, his theology emerges as both *biographical* and *responsive*. I shall show, for example, that what he describes as his 'early religiosity' and his tendency to pantheism, as well as his initial preference for philosophy over theology and especially his interest in Bradley, draw him to the later Heidegger and to the balancing of existential concerns with ontology. It will be important to demonstrate, therefore, why existentialism has the demerits it does have for him, and, secondly, where he looks to locate the correctives to these demerits in such a way that the merits are not lost and the theology remains intelligibly grounded and appropriately articulated. This will help to explain his use of extremely varied sources and the degree to which his thought shows the influence of his colleagues at every stage. For this reason, in tracing the development of Macquarrie's thought, I shall engage in dialogue with those thinkers he draws on and those from whom he distinguishes his own position.

By means of the hermeneutical phrase *the grace of being*, I shall argue that the coherence of Macquarrie's evolving thought lies not simply in the commitment to show that theology is intelligibly grounded so as to articulate the Christian faith in the present situation. More significantly, it lies in his insistence that human existence points beyond itself to the ontological reality of God and the nature of the cosmos. I shall trace three interrelated meanings of the grace of being in Macquarrie's thought. First, *human being is the locus of grace* because it is in the very constitution of human existence that the quest for God begins and is answered. Secondly, *God as holy Being is gracious to human being* as its source, sustainer and telos. Thirdly, the reason for this is that *being (existence) is precisely a divine act of self-giving*. I shall argue that it is in these interrelated meanings that the unifying heart of Macquarrie's thought lies. By transposing the strengths of existentialist theology into a natural theology framework, he transforms both in a new synthesis which mediates between gift and being. In this way, he unifies the wholly other divine summons from beyond human being with an account of the kinship and continuity of being, divine and created. Vitally, then, Macquarrie offers a concept of God which is both gracious to and demanding of the human condition.

In Chapters 5 and 6 I shall locate the systematic heart of Macquarrie's work in the trilogy *In Search of Humanity* (1982), *In Search of Deity* (1984) and *Jesus Christ in Modern Thought* (1990). These books are fundamental to understanding the total shape of Macquarrie's thought, and in particular what constitutes the personal in divine and human being. In them, the notion of transcendence comes to the fore as the capacity and resolution to go beyond the self in giving. The personal movements of divine self-giving in creation and human self-giving in the letting-be which, in participation with God, brings the cosmos to new self-expression, meet in Christ. As well as being an ontological account which reclaims the intention of the classical two natures formula, I shall indicate how this grounds the grace of being in that public, embodied sphere in which it must prove meaningful. By means of this doctrinal cluster, I shall raise some preliminary critical questions about Macquarrie's work. Notably, I shall ask whether it is overly optimistic, too dependent on an optimistic anthropology; and whether it is so insistent on a continuity of being that it fails to give an account of divine power.

I have long been interested in the way in which the content of Christian believing issues in a shape of living which varies according to which doctrinal motif is given dominance. This research arose originally from the pressing pastoral question of how to conceive of God in such a way both that God is 'other' enough to invite allegiance and summon into self-transcendent generosity, and yet that human capacities are honoured and celebrated. In previous piecemeal readings of Macquarrie I suspected that he was engaged in a similar task: 'What must God be, if he is to be both the focus of human worship and aspiration, and at the same time to be seen as the source, sustainer and goal of all that is?'[7] This has been the controlling question in my exploration and evaluation of Macquarrie's thought.

Finally, a matter of 'housekeeping': the vexed question of inclusive language: the several difficulties this presents have doubtless resulted in a somewhat uneven approach, not helped by Macquarrie's own changing preferences and the impossibility in the circumstance of using the grammatically offensive but politically innocuous 'they'. *Das Man* lurks in the wings both here and also with 'one'. The strategy I have adopted is as follows. When quoting, I have left the text unchanged; thus the surprising appearance of 'she' along with Gareth Jones. Otherwise, I have (*mea culpa*) used the masculine form. This has the advantage of cohering with the majority of Macquarrie's own use, as well as avoiding the pietistic undertone of 'we' or the confessional, if existential, 'I'.

NOTES

1 John Macquarrie, *Principles of Christian Theology* (London: SCM 1966, 1977[2]); *Jesus Christ in Modern Thought* (London: SCM 1990).
2 John Macquarrie, *Invitation to Faith* (London: SCM 1995).
3 Don Cupitt, *The Time Being* (London: SCM 1992), 44.
4 In contrast with interpreters such as W. Hamilton, T. Altizer and H. Cox, who use Bonhoeffer's *Letters and Papers from Prison* (London: SCM 1953, 1971, 1981[5]) to advocate a form of religionless Christianity quite at variance with his earlier commitments, I am in sympathy with commentators like H. Ott, G. Ebeling and J. Godsey who perceive an inner unity in Bonhoeffer's thought and interpret his later work in the light of his early thought. Godsey's reading of Bonhoeffer particularly is inviting because attentive to the chronology of Bonhoeffer's developing Christological concerns; see, for example, J.D. Godsey, *The Theology of Dietrich Bonhoeffer* (London: SCM 1960).
5 Ernst Käsemann, *New Testament Questions of Today* (London: SCM 1969), 127.

6 John Macquarrie, *On Being a Theologian*, ed. John H. Morgan (London: SCM 1999). This volume contains a complete list of Macquarrie's published works to 1999 and a synopsis of his major works.
7 John Macquarrie, *In Search of Deity* (London: SCM 1984), 55.

Chapter 1
Heidegger on Being Human

INTRODUCTION: HEIDEGGER'S *BEING AND TIME* AND THE EARLY MACQUARRIE

In his article 'Pilgrimage in Theology', John Macquarrie characterises his work in the period from 1953 to the mid-1960s as 'my "existentialist" phase'.[1] In the works of the period, specifically *An Existentialist Theology* (1955), *The Scope of Demythologizing* (1960) and *Studies in Christian Existentialism* (first published in 1965 but consisting largely of earlier articles), Macquarrie explores the use of existentialist philosophy for Christian theology. He has a twofold concern. First, he is concerned that theology should be seen to be intelligibly grounded; therefore he explores the value of existentialism for clarifying the underlying ontological assumptions of theology. Second, he is concerned that the Christian faith should be appropriately articulated in the modern situation, and so he explores the use of existentialist terms to 'revivify' theological language.

In particular, Macquarrie draws on the thought of Martin Heidegger. Arguably, at least in his aim, Heidegger might more accurately be deemed an ontologist than an existentialist, since even his early work, which is undoubtedly existentialist in method and content, constitutes an attempt to approach the ontological question of Being through a preliminary study of human being. Heidegger subsequently abandoned this particular quest for Being, and in Chapter 2 I shall note Macquarrie's attention to Heidegger's later approaches to Being for the way in which it modifies his use of existentialist thought. In this chapter, however, I shall be concerned with Heidegger's programme in *Being and Time* (originally published 1927), and its positive expression in Macquarrie's early work.

In his conclusion to *An Existentialist Theology*, Macquarrie agrees with Tillich that 'a theological system is supposed to satisfy two basic needs: the statement of the truth of the Christian message and the interpretation of this truth to every new generation.'[2] Macquarrie's assessment of the dominant theologies of the first half of the twentieth century in this respect remains pessimistic. Liberal modernism satisfies neither need, sacrificing elements of truth to harmonise theology with contemporary world-views, and failing to address the radical finitude of the human situation because of its prevailing secular optimism. Barthian kerygmatic theology may at least satisfy the former need, but has tended (particularly in Barth's disciples) to be weak with regard to the latter, and runs the danger of 'lapsing into a complacent orthodoxy which is curiously irrelevant to the modern mind'.[3] Macquarrie suggests that it may be the case that existentialist theology can adequately hold together a balance between the two needs, between *kerygma* and *situation*. Although he recognises certain weaknesses and limitations, particularly with regard to kerygma (see below, Chapter 2), it is to this end that he sees benefits in pressing Heidegger's philosophy into the service of theology.

Throughout his writings, Macquarrie points to the way in which theology invariably draws on philosophical concepts, and emphasises that theology must use an appropriate base, 'that it needs a sound and contemporary philosophical basis on which to rear its theological superstructure.'[4] He recognises the need to scrutinise the underlying assumptions of a theological system, since the presuppositions of an enquiry determine the questions asked and the conclusions drawn. Western theology has drawn heavily on substance-oriented philosophy, from Plato through to Descartes, for example in the doctrine of the self as substance which finds full expression in the modern period in Descartes' dualistic *res extensa* and *res cogitans*. But Macquarrie's contention is that substantialist philosophy has not served theology adequately. By taking 'thinghood' as its dominant model, it has tended to a model of knowing appropriate to the study of entities in the empirical sciences which has not been appropriate to the study of human (or divine) being, and which has allowed theology to attempt to explain itself as one empirical science among others. It has also failed to explicate the nature of human (or divine) being in a way consistent with the findings of contemporary Biblical scholarship.

However, attacks by modern critics of the substance model of the self, such as Ryle and Macmurray, together with changes in the scientific community's own understanding of the scope of empirical, non-participative knowledge and a general collapse in liberal confidence in scientific humanism, have opened the way to new expressions of the nature of human being which theology may more successfully appropriate. In this new climate, Macquarrie makes use of existentialist philosophy in three ways: (a) to indicate the type of knowing appropriate to theology; (b) to indicate the common ground upon which a purely formal expression of theological terms can be made in a theologically non-articulate age, and (c) to revivify specific content, in particular theological terms which have become 'worn thin' or have been mis-served by the language of substance.

In this chapter, I shall outline Heidegger's *Being and Time* as the fundamental source of existentialist philosophy used by Macquarrie in his early writings. I shall show how Macquarrie uses key themes from *Being and Time* for his own contribution to the task of stating the Christian message in terms accessible to the contemporary world, and begin to indicate how they shape his subsequent work. I will also indicate how Macquarrie fares in relation to particular criticisms levelled against Heidegger and the use of his philosophy for theology.

HEIDEGGER'S *BEING AND TIME*

The task and the method

In *Being and Time*, Heidegger aims 'to work out the question of the meaning of *Being* and to do so concretely' by means of an exploration of time as the horizon for understanding Being.[5] That is to say, he intends to investigate the meaning of Being by an exploration of what it means to exist in the world of time and space. In his introductions, he defends his task against the tradition of ontology in Western philosophy which deems the question superfluous because Being is universal or indefinable or self-evident.[6] Heidegger suggests rather that the question is demanded precisely because man already has a familiarity (albeit indistinct) with the meaning of Being – a *'vague average understanding of Being'* which guides what is sought and is clarified in the seeking.[7] Heidegger deems his enquiry *ontological*, that is, concerned with Being, rather than *ontical* (concerned with beings, entities, and the facts concerning them). Although it takes an ontical starting point, in so far as it is concerned with the concrete life of *Dasein*, this is not the aim of the study. Rather, it is ontological not only in the sense of an enquiry into the Being of entities, but in the primordial sense of an enquiry into the meaning of Being in general – the ground of all subsequent enquiry into Being and beings:

> the question of Being aims therefore at ascertaining the *a priori* conditions not only for the possibility of the sciences which examine entities as entities of such and such a type, and, in so doing, already operate with an understanding of Being, but also for the possibility of those ontologies themselves which are prior to the ontical sciences and which provide their foundations.[8]

Dasein: possibility, mineness, and my relation to my self

In *Being and Time*, then, this fundamental ontology is sought by Heidegger '*in the existential analytic of Dasein*'.[9] Man is denoted by the term *Dasein* (Being-there) by Heidegger to identify his distinctive way of being: man is not just one entity occurring amongst others, but understands that he exists and is therefore named in a term which is an expression of his way of being.[10] Man knows that he 'is', so Being is already an issue for him, and is disclosed to him in his very existence: 'Understanding of Being is itself a definite characteristic of *Dasein*'s Being', and thus man's *ontical* distinctiveness is that he *is* ontological (or *is* ontologically).[11] Heidegger subsequently characterises *Dasein*'s existence as *Existenz* to earmark its distinctiveness, and notes that *Dasein*'s understanding of himself in terms of his existence means also that he understands himself in terms of possibility.[12] By this he means the possibility to be himself or not himself, true to what is disclosed in his existence or not, a possibility which is decided for only in and through existing itself. Thus the question of existence is an ontical matter for *Dasein*, dealt with by concrete, *existentiell* living, which provides the ground for the existential analysis. Heidegger's preliminary task, then, is to exhibit *Dasein* in his average everydayness,[13] to reveal the fundamental ontological structure of his being as temporality, corresponding to man's possibility which must be entered into through time, but always in the concrete present circumstances of his life.

Heidegger's designation of *Dasein* as *Existenz* distinguishes his existence from the mere presence-at-hand (*Vorhandenheit*) of entities: 'whereas mountains, stars, tables and so on all are and participate in Being or manifest Being, man not only is but has his being disclosed to himself. He *exists*, he can as it were stand out from the world of entities and become aware of his being and of his responsibility for his being.'[14]

This means that the characteristics proper to *Dasein* 'are not "properties" present-at-hand of some entity which "looks" so and so and is itself present-at-hand; they are in each case possible ways for it to be, and no more than that.'[15] These characteristics Heidegger designates 'existentialia' to distinguish them from 'categories' which, though appropriate to the being of entities, are not applicable to *Dasein*.[16] Entities 'have' properties, but the sense in which *Dasein* 'has' possible ways of being is very much stronger: he always has them as some specific entity, not as a type, and in this sense his existence is always characterised by *mineness* (*Jemeinigkeit*). This has two corollaries. First, *Dasein* can be said to *have a relation to himself* in the way he exists: his being is disclosed to him, he enquires about his being, he is both subject and object, and is fundamentally concerned with his own particular personal being.[17] Secondly, *Dasein* must exercise this relation to himself in terms of his *possibility*: he must 'choose' himself and win himself by embracing the possibilities which are truly his, or fail to win himself by ignoring his possibilities and losing himself in the world of entities. That is, he can be authentic (*eigentlich*, related to *eigen*, own) or inauthentic (*uneigentlich*).[18]

Heidegger's point here is to distinguish his own approach from that of other human sciences in the Western tradition which have sought man's 'essence' by dealing with the human person in a depersonalised way as a type of 'thing', a substance or object, similar to entities in nature but with added dimensions (for example, reason in the Greek tradition, or transcendence derived from the image of God in theology). The question of man's being 'is not something we can simply compute by adding together those kinds of Being which body, soul, and spirit respectively possess'.[19]

Being-in-the-world: *Dasein's* workshop

For Heidegger, *Dasein* is not a bare subject, after the Cartesian model, but always occurs in a 'world', in which his being takes on the definite character given within its possible ways of being. This world is *a priori*, given along with being itself. It is not an objectified world in which man exists spatially (like water 'in' a glass), but is a way of being, an *existentiale*, with the connotation of 'dwelling' and 'familiarity' rather than location. 'World', for Heidegger, is an ontological concept: '"world" is not a way of characterising those entities which *Dasein* essentially is *not*; it is rather a characteristic of *Dasein* itself.'[20] Man's knowledge of the world is not that of the knowing subject inspecting an other external sphere,[21] but is a relationship of practical *concern* (*Besorgen*),[22] of *a priori* involvement with and participation in an environment (*Umwelt*).

Entities encountered in the world are not encountered spatially but instrumentally, in terms of their practical use, 'with that kind of concern which manipulates things and puts them to use'.[23] Heidegger designates such entities 'equipment', noting that the Greek πράγματα explicitly reveals the link with πρᾶξις (concernful dealing) so that the Greek ontological tradition should not have separated out 'mere things' from their pragmatic character. If an entity is constituted by *Dasein*'s use, that is, by its 'in-order-to' (for example, a hammer is 'in-order-to bang in a nail'), the kind of being that entity possesses, then, is 'readiness-to-hand' (*Zuhandenheit*), or involvement, known only in the using: 'the less we just stare at the hammer-Thing, and the more we seize hold of it and use it, the more primordial does our relationship to it become, and the more unveiledly is it encountered as that which it is – as equipment.'[24] Even the natural world is to be understood as equipment, 'in the environment certain entities become accessible which are always ready-to-hand, but which, in themselves, do not need to be produced. Hammer, tongs, and needle, refer in themselves to steel, iron, metal, mineral, wood, in that they consist of these. In equipment that is used, "Nature" is discovered along with it by that use',[25] and not only the 'Nature' in natural products (timber, for example), but the forces of nature, such as the river flowing as power.

Because the world as a whole is neither an objective thing in itself, nor the sum total of entities within the world, but a smoothly functioning 'workshop' aimed at various tasks, it is the task which is noticed, and the world usually goes unnoticed. It is not disclosed by analysis, but it becomes apparent when 'equipment' is found to be broken or missing. Broken equipment is not simply an alteration of properties in something present-at-hand, as in traditional substantial philosophy (for Locke, for example, a broken hammer is of the same order of being as a fully functional hammer), but is a disturbance of the 'in-order-to' reference of what is normally ready-to-hand.[26] The reference is not usually noticed, but when disturbed the reference is 'lit up', and with it the whole 'workshop' – the whole context of the equipment and its purpose, that is, its involvement.

It is the totality of these 'involvements' (rather than a totality of entities) which constitutes the world and they all lead ultimately to a purpose for *Dasein*:

> with this thing, for instance, which is ready-to-hand, and which we accordingly call a 'hammer', there is an involvement in hammering; with hammering, there is an involvement in making something fast; with making something fast, there is an involvement in protection against bad weather; and this protection 'is' for the sake of providing shelter for *Dasein*; that is to say, for the sake of a possibility of *Dasein*'s Being.[27]

This totality of involvement which constitutes the world, Heidegger designates *significance*, that is to say, the world is not characterised by various properties, but by its significance for man's practical concerns.[28] In a later section, Heidegger discusses the spatiality of *Dasein* as fundamentally characterised by involvement. *Dasein* does not simply 'take up space' in the world as *res extensa*, but makes room for itself – a *Spielraum* of involvement.[29] By extending his practical concern in the world, *Dasein* develops and fulfils his possibilities – that is, he enlarges the world.

Being-with: us and They

Within the world, *Dasein* encounters others, though again not in the usual sense of the not-Self; not others as 'everyone else but me – those over against whom the "I" stands out. They are rather those from whom, for the most part one does *not* distinguish oneself – those among whom one is too.'[30] They are neither present-at-hand nor ready-to-hand, but are also 'in-the-world' with the *Dasein* which encounters them, and on the same basis as this *Dasein*: 'By reason of this *with-like (mithaften)* Being-in-the-world, the world is always the one that I share with Others. The world of *Dasein* is a with-world (*Mitwelt*). Being-in is *Being-with* Others. Their Being-in-themselves within-the-world is *Dasein-with* (*Mitdasein*).'[31] That is, others are encountered not as separate subjects, but 'environmentally', as mutually concerned with the world. Because they are not entities towards which *Dasein* has practical concern, but are also *Dasein*, his relation to them is designated 'solicitude' (*Fürsorge*). This 'Being with Others belongs to the Being of *Dasein*, which is an issue for *Dasein* in its very Being. Thus as Being-with, *Dasein* "is" essentially for the sake of Others.' That is to say, Being-with is an ontological matter, whether or not *Dasein* ontically is with others: 'Even if the particular factical *Dasein* does *not* turn to Others, and supposes that it has no need of them or manages to get along without them, it *is* in the way of Being-with.'[32] This is a point I shall return to in due course, because the corporate nature of human being becomes increasingly significant for Macquarrie, and even in his earliest and most existentialist writings he is suspicious of the individualism of existentialist philosophy. This is a significant point of difference between even the early Macquarrie and Rudolf Bultmann, in their respective uses of Heidegger's thought.

Heidegger notes that although Being-with is an ontological characteristic of *Dasein*, and may be lived authentically or inauthentically, in the actual encounter with others *Dasein* tends to be constantly aware of his difference from them, so that his Being-with-others has the character of *distantiality* (*Abständigkeit*), which acknowledged or not (and especially if not) 'stubbornly and primordially' works itself out as subjection to others. In a striking passage Heidegger traces out the constitution of *Dasein*'s inauthentic being with others, designated *Das Man* by Heidegger (or, by Kierkegaard for example, the public or the crowd, or the mass by Jaspers); *Dasein*

> itself *is* not; its being has been taken away by the Others. *Dasein*'s everyday possibilities of being are for the Others to dispose of as they please. These Others, moreover, are not *definite* Others. On the contrary, any Other can represent them. What is decisive is just that inconspicuous domination by Others which has already been taken over unawares from *Dasein* as Being-with. One belongs to the Others oneself and enhances their power. 'The Others' whom one thus designates in order to cover up the fact of one's belonging to them essentially oneself, are those who proximally and for the most part '*are there*' in everyday Being-with-one-another. The 'who' is not this one, not that one, not oneself (*man selbst*), not some people (*einige*), and not the sum of them all. The 'who' is the neuter, the '*they*' *(Das Man)*.³³

The distinctiveness, the mineness, of *Dasein* becomes lost in 'inconspicuousness and unascertainability', as 'they' determine behaviour, standards, attitudes.

'They' has its own existential characteristics – averageness and 'levelling down', the ubiquitous and controlling 'publicness', which

> is always right – not because there is some distinctive and primary relationship-of-Being in which it is related to 'Things', or because it avails itself of some transparency on the part of *Dasein* which it has explicitly appropriated, but because it is insensitive to every difference of level and genuineness and thus never gets to the 'heart of the matter'. By publicness everything gets obscured, and what has thus been covered up gets passed off as something familiar and accessible to everyone.³⁴

Dasein is 'disburdened' by *Das Man* and accommodated in his tendency towards the bland and comfortable. *Das Man* is an *existentiale* – it is part of *Dasein*'s basic constitution, and becomes ontic in particular ways. It is distinguished from the authentic self, 'that is, from the Self which has been taken hold of in its own way', which must be recovered from its dispersal into *Das Man* and into the characteristic absorption of *Das Man* in the immediate concerns of the world. The authentic self is therefore an 'existentiell modification' of the basic existential 'they-self'.³⁵ In Macquarrie's work, this emerges as a recurring theme not only in terms of the ethical conscience (as for Heidegger, and also Kierkegaard) but most especially, as I shall show, in terms of the appropriation of classical doctrinal and liturgical formulae within the church community.

Knowing the 'thereness': mood and projection

In his characterisation of man as Being-in-the-world, Heidegger moves on from his investigation of the world (concern, solicitude, being-one's-self), and turns to 'Being-in' as such, that is, the 'thereness' of *Dasein*, and the way in which it is disclosed to him. *Dasein*'s knowledge of his 'thereness' is not a theoretical, cognitive perception (as appropriate to a purely spatial 'there' of location) but is rooted in man's way of being as practically concerned with his world. Although the way of knowing proper to science is recognised as valid, it is considered secondary and derivative from the knowledge that arises from existence 'in' the world in a specific existentialist sense. Heidegger investigates two forms of disclosure – states-of-mind (*Befindlichkeit*, 'the state in which one may be found') and understanding.

State-of-mind or *mood* is an ontological phenomenon which emerges ontically in familiar everyday 'attunement' – for example, in ill-humour and equanimity.[36] Mood is man's way of knowing as 'there'. It is not mere feeling but has a 'disclosive character',[37] that is, it contains its own understanding or reference to the world. What is disclosed is not a mere object, but a structure or pattern which embraces the self and the world, and which is therefore prior to the analytic knowledge of object and subject:[38] 'A mood makes manifest "how one is and how one is faring". In this "how one is", having a mood brings Being into its "there".'[39] Mood always discloses man as 'delivered over' in his being to his 'thereness'. Thus the particular character of this 'thereness' disclosed by mood is 'thrownness', that is, the *facticity* of being thrown into a specific existence which has not been chosen or constructed by and for oneself.[40] In mood, *Dasein* knows that his existence is not wholly open, that his possibility is not unlimited, but is circumscribed by his own particular situation.[41]

Understanding is related to mood. Just as mood is not merely feeling but contains its own understanding, so understanding carries its own mood. Understanding, in Heidegger's existential sense, is prior to cognition, and is related to *Dasein*'s possibility. In understanding, *Dasein* '"knows" *what* it is capable of – that is, what its potentiality-for-Being is capable of'.[42] This does not mean the kind of possibility that lies purely ahead in a series of not-yets which are not at any time necessary (the sort of possibility proper to entities present-at-hand); it means rather a competence for being in the world rooted in an understanding of the possible significance of entities and persons encountered there. Understanding therefore involves *projection* (*Entwurf*), that is, designing a project which is to be carried through. This does not involve a cognitive grasping: 'Projecting has nothing to do with comporting itself towards a plan that has been thought out, and in accordance with which *Dasein* arranges its Being.'[43] Rather, *Dasein* projects *himself* upon his world and the instrumental character it has for him.

Inauthenticity: falling into lostness

Having investigated the ways in which *Dasein*'s 'thereness' is disclosed to him, Heidegger considers some of the features of 'thereness' in inauthentic existence when *Dasein* is immersed in *Das Man* and absorbed in the immediate concerns of the world. Rather than the openness to possibilities which characterises *Dasein*'s being ontologically, inauthentic existence is characterised ontically by what Heidegger designates idle talk, curiosity and ambiguity. These have a value-neutral connotation, but point to the way in which *Das Man* releases *Dasein* from his own responsible existence into the comfort and lack of demand of second-hand opinions and superficial knowledge: 'Idle talk is something which anyone can rake up' – it has a general intelligibility and releases man from the task of genuinely understanding; curiosity does not observe and marvel 'but rather seeks restlessness and the excitement of continual novelty and changing encounters', and is controlled by idle talk which says what one 'must' have seen and read; ambiguity is confusion about what is disclosed in understanding: 'everything looks as if it were genuinely understood, genuinely taken hold of, genuinely spoken, though at bottom it is not.'[44]

Idle talk, curiosity, and ambiguity reveal the character of *Dasein*'s 'everydayness' as *falling* (*Verfallen*), falling from itself into lostness in *Das Man* and fascination with the world, falling into inauthenticity: '*Dasein* has, in the first instance, fallen away from itself as an authentic potentiality for being itself, and has fallen into the "world".'[45] This is not a fall into thing-hood in the world. *Dasein* does not become present-at-hand. Inauthenticity is still a mode of being *Dasein*, but is a continuous plunge of 'temptation, tranquillising, alienation and self-entangling (entanglement)' which draws *Dasein* away from understanding his genuine possibilities.[46]

Care: the unifying stance

Heidegger's analysis to this point has shown *Dasein* as Being-in-the-world to have the ontological characteristics of *possibility, facticity,* and *fallenness*. These are not parts which together form a whole, but are themselves a unity which Heidegger designates *care (Sorge)*. *Sorge* unifies *Besorgen* (concern) and *Fürsorge* (solicitude), and also the fulfilment of *Dasein*'s possibilities, which is 'accomplished' by care: 'in the "double meaning" of "care", what we have in view is a *single* basic state in its essentially twofold structure of thrown projection.'[47] Care, then, is Heidegger's conception of the kind of being proper to man, contrary to the philosophical tradition of 'Reality' and substantiality: his thesis is 'the substance of man is existence.'[48] The model of truth that corresponds to this conception differs likewise:

> Representations do not get compared, either among themselves or in *relation* to the Real Thing. What is to be demonstrated is not an agreement of knowing with its object, still less of the psychical with the physical; but neither is it an agreement between 'contents of consciousness' among themselves. What is to be demonstrated is solely the Being-uncovered (*Entdeckt-sein*) of the entity itself – that entity in the 'how' of its uncoveredness.[49]

This, then, is a rejection of the 'correspondence' theory of truth, in favour of a unitary and transforming *stance* approach.

One of the key disclosures of *Dasein* as care comes in the mood of anxiety, which Heidegger considers to be fundamental because it reveals man's total situation in the world:

> That in the face of which one has anxiety is not an entity within-the-world. Thus it is essentially incapable of having an involvement. This threatening does not have the character of a definite detrimentality which reaches what is threatened, and which reaches it with definite regard to a special factical potentiality-for-being. That in the face of which one is anxious is completely indefinite.[50]

It is not an entity within the world which causes anxiety (as it is with fear, for example); what causes anxiety is 'nowhere': 'it is already "there", and yet nowhere; it is so close that it is oppressive and stifles one's breath, and yet it is nowhere.'[51] It is the world as such that causes anxiety, the fact of being in the world. Anxiety makes *Dasein* feel 'uncanny', not at home – the feeling he seeks to avoid in his falling. This means that anxiety discloses to *Dasein* his possibilities for being, and removes from him the comfort of understanding himself in terms of the world and the fashions of *Das Man*: 'Anxiety individualises *Dasein* for its ownmost Being-in-the-world, which as something that understands, projects itself essentially upon possibilities', and brings *Dasein* face to face with its possibility for authentic existence.[52] Anxiety brings man back from his falling by individualising him – he is in the world, but isolated from it because it has become 'nothing' to him, and now he must grasp his own possibilities for existence.

Authenticity: death's disclosure and the call of conscience

Once Heidegger moves on to discuss *Dasein* in his authenticity, he points to the need to conceive the totality of *Dasein*'s existence if his authentic possibilities are to be understood. Contrary to the tradition of, for example, a unifying soul-substance, or Locke's consciousness, he suggests that an existential interpretation of death provides an appropriate unifying concept. By this he means not the objective, biological or organic 'ending' of death, but death as 'something that stands before us – something impending', the ultimate and certain possibility with which *Dasein* is faced and which he must appropriate as his own: 'the possibility of no-longer being-able-to-be-there'.[53] Contrary to the 'public' opinion of death as something to be covered up and avoided in conversation, *Dasein* must 'anticipate' death.[54] This does not mean bringing it closer as an actual occurrence, but penetrating more deeply into understanding the 'possibility of the impossibility of any existence at all'.[55] This does not give *Dasein* something to do or achieve, but it 'individualises *Dasein* down to itself' and makes plain that the things and persons to which he clings for support are ultimately of no consequence.[56] In this state of anticipation of death, *Dasein* is brought back from his lostness in *Das Man* and face to face with the threat of his own 'nothing' which no one else can experience or live for him, and this is the ontological basis for *Dasein*'s openness to the call of conscience to an *existentiell* decision for authentic existence.

Conscience calls *Dasein* to his 'ownmost potentiality-for-Being-its-Self'.[57] It gives no information but summons *Dasein* to 'that which has been currently individualised and which belongs to that particular *Dasein*'.[58] Both the caller and the called are *Dasein*, but the call is experienced as an alien voice from beyond the self, which addresses *Dasein* as 'guilty'. Heidegger's meaning of guilty transcends the usual moral meaning of owing a debt or being responsible (punishable), which he relates to an existence of concern, and deems derivative from a more primordial guiltiness.[59] 'Guilt' consists rather in *Dasein*'s absence of control over the facticity into which he is thrown, and the absence, nullity, of other possibilities which that facticity imposes; and in the possibility of authentic existence in embracing the possibilities that *are* delineated by its facticity: freedom '*is* only in the choice of one possibility – that is, in tolerating one's not having chosen the others and one's not being able to choose them'.[60] Conscience calls *Dasein* to his guilt, then, by calling him to embrace his facticity, to want to have a conscience, and to appropriate his own possibilities.[61] It does not call *Dasein* away from his facticity, but away from his lostness and irresoluteness and into his facticity to find and face his 'ownmost' possibilities. That is, it calls *Dasein* to his authentic existence, which is characterised by *resoluteness* in the face of both facticity and possibility.

Resoluteness does not remove *Dasein* from the world, but repeatedly 'brings the Self right into its current concernful Being-alongside what is ready-to-hand, and pushes it into solicitous Being with Others'.[62] This means that the significance of the world is disclosed in its full character and *Dasein* is authentically engaged with his context, which Heidegger now designates the *Situation*.[63] Resoluteness will emerge as an important aspect in Macquarrie's mature anthropology. The more concerned he becomes with human transcendence, the more significant this dimension of directedness and commitment becomes in order to show that transcendence is orderly rather than chanced or chaotic.

Heidegger's analysis of authentic existence as characterised by *anticipation* (Being-towards-death) and by *resoluteness*, finds unity in 'anticipatory resoluteness', in which resoluteness 'projects itself not upon any random possibilities which just lie closest, but upon that uttermost possibility which lies ahead of every factical potentiality-for-Being of *Dasein*, and, as such, enters more or less undisguisedly into every potentiality-for-Being of which *Dasein* factically takes hold'.[64] It is this anticipatory resoluteness that is Heidegger's starting point for an investigation into temporality as the horizon from which being is to be understood.[65]

Temporality and historicality

Anticipatory resoluteness, the self as being-towards-death, is futural. It does not refer to a 'not yet' point in time, but is a constant bearing of the future in the present. In the same way, facticity or thrownness refers to the past, to what has been, not in the sense of a finished past, but of 'I-*am*-as-having-been'.[66] Falling refers to the making-present. Macquarrie notes, 'it arises from our natural tendency to shrink on the one hand from responsibility to the future and on the other from acceptance of what has been, and so to become merged and absorbed in the concerns of the present.'[67] These three 'ecstases' of temporality constitute the unity of *Dasein*. Unity is not unity of succession; the ecstases are contemporaneous in *Dasein*: 'The future is *not later* than having been, and having been is *not earlier* than the Present. Temporality temporalises itself as a future which makes present in the process of having been.'[68] Heidegger continues by reviewing his whole analysis of *Dasein* with a temporal interpretation. So, for example, understanding as projection is considered as futural (though inauthentic understanding 'makes present'); mood is considered as 'past' because it discloses what has already come to be the case; curiosity (as an example of falling), while it appears to be futural because related to understanding, is in fact considered as present, because it craves possibility as something that is actual.[69]

Heidegger's interpretation of temporality leads to his distinctively existential interpretation of history:

> *Dasein* does not exist as the sum of momentary actualities of Experiences which come along successively and disappear. Nor is there a sort of framework which this succession gradually fills up ... 'The between' which relates to birth and death already lies *in the Being* of *Dasein* ... Understood existentially, birth is not and never is something past in the sense of something no longer present-at-hand; and death is just as far from having the kind of being of something still outstanding, not yet present-at-hand but coming along. Factical *Dasein* exists as born; and, as born, it is already dying, in the sense of Being-towards-death. As long as *Dasein* factically exists, both the 'ends' and their 'between' *are*.[70]

This means that *Dasein* is not primarily 'in time', 'in history', but is temporal and historical in the very basis of its being and only then is 'in' time and history. Heidegger notes that the usual meanings of history and 'historical' relate to man as the subject of events, but man does not exist 'first' and then become involved in events which place him in history. Man himself is what is '*primarily* historical', and events and things encountered in the world are secondarily historical, that is, historical because of their significance to and involvement with man.[71] Heidegger terms these entities in the world 'world-historical' to emphasise that their historicality is derived from their relation to *Dasein*.[72]

Dasein's being of anticipatory resoluteness is expressed in terms of the historical thus:

> The resoluteness in which *Dasein* comes back to itself, discloses current factical possibilities of authentic existing, and discloses them *in terms of the heritage* which that resoluteness, as thrown, *takes over*. In one's coming back resolutely to one's thrownness, there is hidden a *handing down* to oneself of the possibilities that have come down to one, but not necessarily *as* having thus come down [that is, the possibilities may be in fact *given* by man's facticity, but are *taken up* as also *chosen*].[73]

Heidegger designates this historical expression of man's being, *fate* (*Schicksal*).

The historical expression of the being of a community (which *Dasein* both influences and is determined by) is termed *destiny* (*Geschick*); destiny is not the adding together of various fates, but is a 'co-historising' by Being-in-the-world. Each *Dasein*'s possibilities are thus shaped by being with others in the world, and man must be resolute in both 'fate' and 'destiny'. This resoluteness effects the *repetition* of a possibility of existence:

> *Repeating is handing down explicitly* – that is to say, going back into the possibilities of the *Dasein* that has-been-there. The authentic repetition of a possibility of existence that has been – the possibility that *Dasein* may choose its hero – is grounded existentially in anticipatory resoluteness; for it is in resoluteness that one first chooses the choice which makes one free for the struggle of loyally following in the footsteps of that which can be repeated.[74]

Repetition is not merely repeating the past, but 'makes a reciprocative rejoinder' which Macquarrie and Robinson suggest implies a conversation with the past in which the past proposes certain possibilities for adoption, to which one reciprocates with other proposals.[75]

Authentic historicality, then, is not concerned with information about a 'past', but with the disclosure of possibilities of authentic existence, and therefore 'understands history as the "recurrence" of the possible, and knows that a possibility will recur only if existence is open for it fatefully, in a moment of vision, in resolute repetition'.[76] These themes of repetition and recurrence will prove to be of fundamental significance for Macquarrie, not only with regard to the appropriation of tradition, but more importantly with regard to the question of the historical Jesus.

MACQUARRIE'S USE OF HEIDEGGER

I have already offered a few clues as to the ways in which distinctively Heideggerian themes will emerge in Macquarrie's thought. In the remainder of this chapter, I shall highlight three specific ways in which Macquarrie makes use of the existentialist approach to philosophy as it appears in *Being and Time*: (a) to indicate the type of knowing appropriate to theology, (b) to indicate the common ground upon which a purely formal expression of theological terms can be made in a theologically non-articulate age, and (c) to revivify specific content, in particular theological terms which have become 'worn thin' or have been mis-served by the language of substance.

Knowing in theology

Heidegger's philosophy (and, indeed, existentialist philosophy more widely) provides a way of indicating the nature of 'knowing' appropriate to theology, which both distinguishes it from objective, empirical scientific knowledge and yet reduces it neither to a purely esoteric body of knowledge discontinuous with other knowledge we may have nor to a wholly subjective, emotive account. The participative knowledge or practical understanding which existentialism emphasises has not been absent from theology. Schleiermacher, for example, insists that 'feeling' is not subjective emotion but includes relational awareness and therefore includes a cognitive function.[77] Macquarrie argues strongly that the existentialist way of knowing which is prior to theoretical understanding and which 'touches on the whole constitution of man as being-in-the-world' is the way of knowing which is appropriate to theology as the explication of the content of faith.[78] Theological language 'does not deal with intellectual abstractions but always relates to the concrete situations in which men live and act and choose'.[79] The knowing proper to these situations is not simply that of empirical description, nor is it merely emotion, but is the practical understanding and attunement to the environment which discloses its own content, 'a kind of implicit theory even if it cannot be formulated, which belongs to everyday activities', and which issues in a pattern of action rather than simply a statement – that is, in faith as a committed pattern of obedience rather than agreement with a set of propositional statements.[80]

Gilbert Ryle levels a number of criticisms against Heidegger's phenomenological method. Although this is not the place to enter into an assessment of the philosophies of mind with which he engages in his article, nor to attempt to mediate between Heidegger's position and his criticisms of it, it is important to consider at this stage whether his criticisms have a direct bearing on Macquarrie's appropriation of Heidegger's thought for the theological task. This will also help to clarify more precisely Macquarrie's purpose in utilising Heidegger's phenomenology.

To anticipate for a moment, the heart of Ryle's argument is that whilst it is the case that every act of consciousness has an intentional object, and also the case that every object or event in time and space may be the proper subject matter of the study of intentionality since it may be an intentional object (because 'I may know it or wonder about it or entertain it or be angry with it and so on'), it is not thereby true to say that by studying my experience of something as an intentional object of my act of consciousness towards it, I can know the heart of it, a heart which lies beyond the kind of derivative knowledge gleaned from 'scientific' study.[81] In other words, the fact that a 'real' object may be the subject matter in the study of intentionality does not mean that the study of intentionality is the best way to 'know' that object. Even if it is *a way of knowing*, it is not clear that it is pure of other knowledge read back into the intuition.

Ryle briefly traces a development of ideas in phenomenology which he regards as crucial for the emergence of this error in *Being and Time*. He notes first Brentano's shift from understanding judgement as an association of two ideas to seeing it as a threefold activity involving an idea, an element of acceptance or rejection (affirmation or negation), and a feeling of liking or disliking (wanting or aversion). The three elements are irreducible to one another, and judgement itself is declared by Brentano to be an irreducible and indefinable psychological fact. Already for Ryle this points in a disturbing direction: 'to judge is to have an idea and to do something with it; to feel is to have an idea and to take up an attitude towards it. We, made wise by the event, may already wonder whether such premises will not in due course lead to a subjectivist or agnostic theory of knowledge.'[82]

Brentano is not a solipsist, however, and retains a distinction between an intentional object (to which all acts of consciousness refer) and a real object in time and space (to which some acts of consciousness refer). But he maintains by the theory of Self-Evidence that it is the inner perception of intentional objects which is a source of positive knowledge – which is, indeed, *the* source of positive knowledge. In Brentano, then, phenomenology has its true beginnings; phenomenology emerges as the descriptive science of these psychic phenomena –

the intentional objects – known intuitively in the act of consciousness. Further, the direct inspection of these individual exemplary types is assumed to yield knowledge of the universal which they represent.

Ryle turns next to Husserl and his further analysis of these phenomena of consciousness. Husserl terms the intentional object the 'meaning' of an act of consciousness. Since everything may be an intentional object, everything belongs to the science of phenomenology, and everything can be seen as a tissue of 'meanings' constituted by acts of consciousness; all objects in time and space are correlates of consciousness and consciousness (after Brentano) is the only self-subsistent reality. This, for Ryle, *is* a worrying step towards solipsism.

Developing the work of Husserl in his own directions, Heidegger agrees that phenomenology must be free from pre-suppositions if 'the things themselves' are to be seen, but argues that the history of phenomenological method has not yet achieved this. Rather, it carries the baggage of the Cartesian mind-matter dualism and substance-oriented metaphysics, which must be shed if Being is to be approached phenomenologically. Under the Cartesian view, 'Consciousness and Being are *vis-à-vis* to one another in such a way that in studying Consciousness we are studying something on the outside of which and transcending which lies a region of absolute Reality.'[83] In contrast, Heidegger intends to show that a description of the most primitive level of experience does in fact disclose Being. For *Dasein*, the most primitive level of experience is the experience of being-in-a-world, which is a world of intentionality, 'simply the sum of what I am *about*'.[84] The knowledge of this world is an understanding that comes about by mood and attunement – an intuition which, for Brentano, is self-ratifying.

Here, then, in the alliance of phenomenological method and the rejection of Cartesian dualism, is the fundamental shift to which Ryle objects. He writes, 'while it is a dangerous metaphor to speak of acts having "meanings" or of things as being the "meanings of acts", it is a fatal error to speak of a thing known as a correlate of a knowing-act as if that implied that we could get to the heart of the thing by analysing our experience of knowing it.'[85] For Ryle, two flaws are contained here. The first, with an alarming anticipation (in 1929) of postmodernism, is the general conclusion that 'this theory has in the end to say that the world of things and events *as I apprehend it* must be just a tissue of Meanings, which Meanings must be the contribution of acts of consciousness.'[86] The second flaw, however, is the more basic claim made by Heidegger that it is without pre-suppositions that the world is intuited by mood and attunement. Ryle doubts that this is so, and suggests that Heidegger confuses the anthropologically primitive with the logically primitive.[87] It may indeed be the case that we perceive things initially in their meaning for us, but Ryle suggests that this already involves some context of knowledge which opens up certain avenues of meaning, and closes others. Even the basic awareness of being-in-the-world implies some underlying knowledge: 'We "have" or are "in-the-world" only if we know that at least one "something" exists. Similarly the attempt to derive our knowledge of "things" from our practical attitude towards things breaks down; for to use a tool involves knowledge of what it is, what can be done with it, and what wants doing.'[88]

How, then, should Ryle's criticisms of the phenomenological method as it reaches expression in *Being and Time* be applied to Macquarrie's work?

With regard to the first flaw noted by Ryle, that ultimately this method constructs the world solely on the basis of my own acts of consciousness, three things may be noted. First, although Macquarrie uses the phenomenological method to indicate the place in human consciousness of a purely formal religious expression, 'the possibility of grace – a power from beyond man which can heal his estrangement and enable him to live as the being which he is, the being in whom are conjoined the polarities of finitude and responsibility', this is only his preliminary enquiry.[89] He is consistently and increasingly concerned with the *corporate* dimension of human life and faith, which guards against the tendencies to individualism and subjectivism. Secondly, during the course of his work, Macquarrie becomes increasingly committed to the role of *tradition*, and its reappropriation by the Christian community in a way that corresponds to Heidegger's notion of the repetition of authentic possibility in history. Again, this points beyond the self, and invites the self into a corporate understanding. Finally, Macquarrie follows the later Heidegger's insistence that being must reveal itself: human consciousness *receives* as well as constructs.

With regard to Ryle's second flaw, that knowledge is in practice imported into the supposedly primordial intuition, Macquarrie is entirely in agreement. He acknowledges that enquiry will never be without pre-understandings and prejudices, and argues the benefits of the phenomenological method both to disclose and to cut through these in so far as is possible. No value-free observation is possible, but phenomenology can be used at least as an attempt at 'letting us see that which shows itself (the phenomenon) by removing, as far as possible, concealments, distortions, and whatever else might prevent us from seeing the phenomenon as it actually gives itself'.[90]

Further, the recognition that there is a context of knowledge which breaks into our primordial intuitions is fundamental to Macquarrie's thought. This is so not only in so far as the community and the tradition establish a context of knowledge, but is evidenced in two other persistent features of his work. The first of these can be illustrated from his differences with Bultmann over the meaning of the resurrection. For Bultmann the resurrection, as a 'salvation-occurrence', 'takes place in the word, which accosts the hearer and compels him to decide for or against it'.[91] The meaning of the resurrection lies in the believer's participation in the experience of dying and rising, a fundamentally individual experience. Although Macquarrie is in agreement with Bultmann on the importance of *participating* in the resurrection, he also asks 'does it ... make sense to talk of "dying and rising with Christ" without an assurance that, in some sense, Christ actually died and rose?'[92] I shall return to this later in the context of the question of the historicity of the Christ-event, but it is a valuable insight into Macquarrie's insistence that some objective situation *calls forth* even the most self-involving awareness.

The second feature of Macquarrie's work to note in relation to the question of the primacy of my own acts of consciousness versus a primordial context of knowledge is his insistence that the initiative always lies with God. In his early work this is fundamentally the initiative of address (in contrast, for example, to the address of the conscience as Heidegger conceives it), and in due course becomes increasingly the initiative of the gift of existence itself. It is central to Macquarrie's thought that even in the quest which we make for God, a prior initiative has already been taken by God.

These points are an anticipation of the subject of Chapter 2, the limitations which Macquarrie places on his use of existentialist thought. In spite of these cautions, his utilisation of Heidegger's work to indicate the type of knowing appropriate to theology is fundamentally positive, and centres on its capacity to overcome a false polarity in the objective/subjective distinction.[93] That is to say, on the one hand, it is not a solipsistic form of knowing; not only does it have an intentional object but, for Heidegger, this is a *Gestalt*, a shape of a situation in the world rather than a simple object.[94] Macquarrie notes, 'the feeling does not *create* the character which is asserted of the situation, but *discloses* it.'[95] On the other hand, this is not a purely objective kind of knowing which reduces human (and divine) being to the categories of empirical science. The kind of knowing which phenomenology yields is, by definition, fundamentally participative.

A ground for God-talk in a non-theological age

The second significant use to which Macquarrie puts existentialist philosophy is to establish a common ground upon which at least a formal expression of theological terms can be made, appropriate to an age which is no longer theologically articulate. Macquarrie's choice of existentialist philosophy for this ground will prove to be a key factor in shaping the particular approach of his new-style natural theology.

In his inaugural lecture at Union Theological Seminary, published in *Studies in Christian Existentialism* as 'How is theology possible?' (1963), Macquarrie points out that 'in a secular age one may not assume that language about God affords a universally intelligible starting point for an interpretation of the Christian faith', and suggests rather that the common ground from which an interpretation might begin is humanity.[96] Since the doctrines of God and human being are closely entwined, either can proceed to the other and, therefore, 'if we can start from the humanity which we all share, and if we find that this humanity points beyond itself for its completion, then we have, so to speak, indicated the place of the word "God" on the map of meaningful discourse.'[97]

Macquarrie traces out the way in which the answer to the fundamental question concerning human existence, 'Who am I?', raises a formal expression of God, albeit with a minimum of content. Although the question 'Who am I?' is in an important sense unanswerable because we cannot view ourselves and our context as if by external observation, it is in an equally important sense constantly being answered: 'in every policy that we adopt and in every unrepeatable action that we perform, we are giving an answer and taking upon ourselves an identity. Always and already, we have decided to understand ourselves in one way or another, though such self-understanding may not be explicit in every case.'[98] This polarity (the unanswerable and the answerable) represents our facticity and our possibility: we are thrown into an existence we can never fully grasp or get the measure of and yet we are responsible for it, choosing for it in all the decisions we make. And in this precarious balance between finitude and responsibility there is 'a radical alienation deep within our existence' which pushes us into imbalance, to immerse ourselves in freedom or in finitude: 'man becomes untrue to the being that is his. He refuses to accept himself as *at once* free and finite ... man is estranged from himself by his refusal to take upon himself an identity which on the other hand he cannot completely discard, an identity which includes both the poles of his freedom and his finitude.'[99]

Man's alienation from himself means that there can be no human solution to the problem of human existence, and this gives rise to two possibilities. Either man truly *is* confined to his own resources, in which case the logical outcome is the heroic despair in the face of absurdity (of Sartre, for example), or there is a possibility of *grace*, that is, 'a power from beyond man which can heal his estrangement and enable him to live as the being which he is, the being in whom are conjoined the polarities of finitude and responsibility'.[100] Since man has found the source of grace in neither the world of things nor in other persons (though either might be a vehicle of grace) he is directed to a transcendent source, and to the question of God.

Although this is only a formal expression of the term 'God', and a placing 'on the map of meaningful discourse' of such notions as creatureliness (as finitude) and sin (as alienation and estrangement), the importance for Macquarrie is that it can be said *that the quest for God arises from the very constitution of man's being*. This in turn means that the question about God 'is not a theoretical or speculative question, raised by the intellect alone and asked in a general, disinterested way, but a practical question posed by the whole being of man, who has to exist in the world and decide about his existence'.[101]

If the practical, *religious* question of God is raised in this existential manner, the question proper to entities and substances, 'does it *exist*?' is no longer appropriate. Rather than 'Does God exist?', the question must be formulated as 'Does Being have such a character as would fulfil man's quest for grace?'[102] If the question of God arises from the polarity in man's being and his inability to reconcile the two poles out of their perpetual conflict, then it follows that 'the condition to be satisfied is that the being out of which man arises coincides with the end of his freedom, thus bringing into unity the polarities of his existence and healing his estrangement.'[103] Ontically, this means that man's past (factical) must be reconcilable with his *telos*. Only if the wider context of being in which man has his existence is not indifferent to man's existential predicament, but is responsive to it, can being be equated with God.

An existentialist analysis of human existence, then, is not tangential to the question of God in Christian theology, neither is it an anthropologising of what is properly a theological question, but reveals that the possibility of God is raised by man's own distinctive being. This is a key point for the development of Macquarrie's 'new-style' natural theology, which emerges explicitly in *Principles of Christian Theology*, and will be addressed in Chapter 4. Macquarrie rejects the old styles of natural theology based on deductive argument directed principally to the natural world, and instead bases a new approach on this description of what it means to be human, and the way in which this implies God. In this respect, then, his use of Heidegger to indicate a common ground for the expression of theological terms lays an all-important foundation for his own natural theology and the distinguishing characteristics which differentiate it from traditional (chiefly Thomistic) approaches.

In 'How is theology possible?', Macquarrie admits that his argument so far only allows that theology is 'a possible study of the possible', and that to show that it is possible as 'a study of the most concrete reality' requires the particular disclosure of revelation, the gift-like character of Being which discloses itself to attentive waiting. This is the language of Heidegger's later work, the submission to Being, which I shall consider in Chapter 2. First, I shall note how he finds Heidegger's early material useful in yielding interpretations in specific content in theological language, beyond simply expressing the general quest for grace.

Reclaiming the content of Christian faith

The third use to which Macquarrie puts existentialist philosophy is to reclaim theological terms which, due to their long interpretation under the language of substance, have come to be misleading, or which have become thinned into technical, esoteric words which have lost both their force and freshness in the Christian community and their relation to ordinary language outside of it. Two examples must suffice to illustrate Macquarrie's use of Heidegger's thought in this respect. Accordingly, I shall note his account of *sin* under existentialist interpretation to illustrate the way in which a technical, theological term may be revivified for contemporary use when it has become 'worn thin'. Then I shall note his account of *the body* under existentialist interpretation to illustrate the way in which a term may be reclaimed from misleading interpretations according to a substance-oriented philosophical tradition.

Sin

In his essay 'Existentialism and Christian Vocabulary' (1961), Macquarrie points to the way in which the meaning of basic Christian terms has been 'so worn down that they get understood in a superficial, harmless kind of way, if indeed they are still understood at all'.[104] He traces the example of the word 'sin', and its reduction from the theologically poignant implication of a state of 'separation',[105] to a weaker sense of 'misdemeanour', often in contrast to the more robust 'crime', and with the added implication of the private versus public realm: '"sin" is taken to be an offence against private (usually sexual) morality, while "crime" is a violation of public security and therefore punishable by the state.'[106]

Even if theological terms have become virtually meaningless, Macquarrie doubts that they can simply be replaced by secular words in common usage, since they represent a distinct meaning which is basic to the Christian faith. Rather, a source of illumination is needed to restore some of the original depth of meaning and life to the traditional Christian vocabulary, a set of terms which currently refer to the structures and situations once indicated by traditional Christian terms. Macquarrie suggests that the language of existentialist philosophy has enough affinity with the content of Christian faith for its terms to be used to revivify traditional theological language by restoring lost connotations.[107]

How, then, does existentialism revitalise the weakened notion of sin? It must be noted that Heidegger's 'fallenness' is not itself a reference to sin. It does not refer to 'falling short of the mark' as it does in the Christian understanding of ἁμαρτία, and therefore does not have the implication of failing to attain pre-established ideals or standards. Rather, for Heidegger, 'falling' refers to the temporality of *Dasein* in its *present* aspect, in which, in inauthenticity, *Dasein* tries to escape from the polarity of possibility and facticity. Macquarrie explains that fallenness 'arises from our natural tendency to shrink on the one hand from responsibility towards the future and on the other from acceptance of what has been, and so to become merged and absorbed in the concerns of the present'.[108] Nevertheless, despite this difference, two aspects of Heidegger's concept of fallenness do provide an insight into the traditional meaning of the word 'sin'.

Alienation Alienation occurs as an aspect of *Dasein*'s 'falling' in this way: 'in his concern with and absorption in the world of things, man falls away from the possibilities of a genuine personal being. He becomes alienated or estranged from his true self.'[109] This is, however, not merely an anthropological alienation. In *An Existentialist Theology*, Macquarrie makes the connection to separation from God: 'so far as man is fallen away from his true self, he is fallen away from the being which the creator has given him. He is, therefore, denying God and rebelling against God, whose command is life – that is, the authentic existence for which man was created.'[110] Thus, although Heidegger's concept is decidedly not equivalent to separation from God, by including separation from being, and also from other persons, it points the way towards the meaning of separation from God. Although it cannot be used as a simple substitute for the concept of sin, 'alienation' can help to recapture and restore some of the traditional meaning, and to relocate the word in contemporary understandings.

Das Man   The second aspect of Heidegger's concept of fallenness which Macquarrie draws on to restore traditional connotations to the word 'sin' is the notion of *Das Man*, and *Dasein*'s flight into collectivism. In its inauthentic expression, being-with-others regards the other as an object in the world, in which case 'it makes possible dominance and the corresponding dependence, and it depersonalises, destroying rather than liberating the true being of man.'[111] In the inauthentic way of being-with-others, this domination itself is depersonalised – it is 'no-one in particular' but the uniform mass, *Das Man*, characterised by 'everydayness' (*Alltäglichkeit*): 'the depersonalised and dehumanised collective body, responsible to no one, that dictates the standards of the lowest common denominator to every individual existence', 'a way of being dominated by unthinking habit, a mechanical following of the ways laid down for us in an established order'.[112] The irony of *Das Man* is that man gives himself up to its averageness and unaccountability willingly 'in his stampede from the ultimate issues of his existence into the illusory security of an inauthentic collectivism'.[113] Thus although *Das Man* exercises power over him, he has himself given it that power.

Macquarrie, following Bultmann, uses the concept *Das Man* to interpret the New Testament term κόσμος, the sphere of human relations, men in their totality, which dominates and rules the individuals which constitute it. Thus for example the 'spirit of the world' (John 12:31) expressed in modern speech 'is the atmosphere to whose compelling influence every man contributes but to which he is also always subject'.[114] Macquarrie notes, however, that the New Testament κόσμος is a more terrifying concept than *Das Man*, because *Das Man* is a formal, existential-ontological concept whereas 'the world is a concrete ontical phenomenon met in actual moral and religious experience.'[115] Macquarrie describes this as a 'whirlpool' into which everyone is sucked, and suggests that perhaps this may be called 'original sin' since 'only in and against and out of this milieu can there be any aspiration toward the stature of true selfhood.'[116]

The body

To illustrate the way in which Macquarrie uses Heidegger's philosophy to reclaim a term which has been mis-served by the language of substance, I shall indicate the way in which he interprets Paul's use of σῶμα. Following Bultmann, Macquarrie agrees that Heidegger's understanding of human existence as being-in-a-world helps to interpret Paul's use of σῶμα, when that is not specifically applied to 'the body of Christ' or 'the body of sin' (for which Paul commonly uses the term σάρξ).[117] Bultmann rejects the 'naive popular usage' of σῶμα which opposes it, in 'a naive anthropological view', as body in contrast to the soul or the spirit.[118] Referring to texts such as Romans 12:1, 'Present your bodies as a living sacrifice' (παραστῆσαι τὰ σώματα ὑμῶν), or the interplay in Romans 6:12, 13 between 'your mortal body' (τῷ θνητῷ ὑμῶν σώματι), 'your members' (τὰ μέλη) and 'yourselves' (ἑαυτούς), Bultmann suggests that 'it is clear that the *soma* is not something that outwardly clings to a man's real *self* (to his soul, for instance) but belongs to its very essence, so that we can say man does not *have* a *soma*; he *is soma*, for in not a few cases *soma* can be translated simply "I" (or whatever personal pronoun fits the context).'[119]

'Body', then, refers to the whole person. Furthermore, in the light of the texts referred to, it appears that σῶμα refers to man '*in respect to his being able to make himself the object of his own action or to experience himself as the subject to whom something happens*'.[120] Thus, we may *present ourselves*, or *not allow ourselves to be reigned over*. It follows from this self-relationship that a double possibility presents *itself*, 'to be at one with himself or at odds (estranged from himself)': estranged from himself, not in control of himself, man finds himself at the mercy of a power not his own, which may be 'experienced as an enemy power which estranges man from himself or the opposite, a friendly power that brings the man estranged from himself back to himself'.[121]

Macquarrie shows how Bultmann's interpretation of σῶμα as a way of being corresponds to Heidegger's teaching that man is always being-in-a-world, that he exists in the sense of being related to himself, and that his existence can be authentic or inauthentic.[122] Conceding that there is insufficient exegetical evidence to decide conclusively for or against Bultmann's interpretation, Macquarrie tests its validity by applying it to a notoriously difficult σῶμα passage to see whether it sheds adequate light.

The primary case study he selects is 1 Corinthians 15:44, 'it is sown a natural body (σῶμα ψυχικόν), it is raised a spiritual body (σῶμα πνευματικόν). If there is a natural body, there is also a spiritual body.' In traditional Western philosophy, the 'natural body' causes no difficulty: it is a material substance of flesh and blood. The problem lies with the 'spiritual body', since spirit is also a substance, but an immaterial substance, entirely different from the substance of the body. How, then, can there be a spiritual body? Macquarrie suggests that this apparent contradiction is typically resolved by the unsatisfactory proposal of 'some kind of ethereal stuff, midway between spirit and body … a kind of ghostly replica of the natural body'.[123] Such a resolution is by no means straightforward: it is highly speculative, and materialistic in tendency. More importantly, it is hard to see how it safeguards the continuity of personality which is implied in the doctrine of the resurrection of the body.

An existentialist approach to the natural body and the spiritual body understands both as ways of being: 'the first describes man's way of being upon earth, the second the Christian believer's way of being in the world to come.'[124] σῶμα, ontologically, corresponds to man's being-in-a-world where possibilities confront him; it is this which safeguards the continuity: on earth or in the world to come, man is being-in-a-world and does not exist as 'a bare discarnate ego'.[125] Ontically, however, there is a difference. On earth, man is always more or less estranged from himself, living κατὰ σάρκα; in the life to come he is at one with himself, living κατὰ πνεῦμα.[126]

As well as providing access to the difficulties of 1 Corinthians 15:44, this existentialist interpretation has two other immediate benefits. First, it defends Paul against a suspicion of a tendency to Gnostic dualism when using Gnostic ideas to communicate to that particular audience. When he speaks, for example, of rescue from the 'body of death' (Romans 7:24) he means not deliverance from the body as such, as if it were an alien encumbrance, but from the sinful, inauthentic possibilities of somatic existence. Secondly, this existential interpretation helps to explain the distinction between ἐν σαρκί and κατὰ σάρκα. ἐν σαρκί (Galatians 2:20) recognises man's facticity, his existence in a specific world, 'in which he is not at home and in which his possibilities are circumscribed'.[127] κατὰ σάρκα (Romans 8:5) indicates that man has *chosen* for the world – his *existentiell* decision has been for the creature rather than for the Creator, and where Paul portrays the flesh as personified, it is because man has given it the power to have domination over him.[128]

Confronted by the apparent simplicity of this approach compared to the complex metaphysical speculation involved in a substantival approach, Macquarrie notes:

> Saint Paul wrote to answer concrete questions of human existence, not to satisfy the curiosity of philosophers ... Saint Paul is not concerned to solve intellectual problems but to set before men *existentiell* possibilities. The risen life in Christ is not a philosophical conception but a possibility for which men are asked to decide.[129]

It is his view that Bultmann's use of Heidegger rescues Paul's anthropology from a stagnancy in substance-oriented philosophy, and 'brings it from the realms of speculation to the actual problems of human existence'.[130]

The practical benefits of the existentialist interpretation cannot allow the question of exegetical accuracy to go unmarked, however, particularly in view of Robert Gundry's insistence that there is 'ample exegetical and lexicographical evidence for a consistently physical meaning of soma in Pauline literature (and elsewhere)'.[131] Neither Jewett in his *Paul's Anthropological Terms* nor Schweizer in *The Theological Dictionary of the New Testament* have any disagreement with Bultmann's move from a traditional substantival interpretation. Both acknowledge that some uses of σῶμα in Paul refer to the obvious meaning of the observable human body (1 Corinthians 5:3 or 9:7, for example), and that the common, non-technical usage of the time to denote a corpse or slave (both objectified bodies) appears elsewhere in the New Testament (for example, Mark 15:43, Rev. 18:13) but nowhere in Paul.[132] Both trace the technical meaning (apart from 'the Body of Christ') and insist that it is not a reference purely to substance as complementary to soul, but is theologically emphatic that in both ages life is somatic.[133] It is in the body that 'man has his true life and proves himself and will one day come to heaven or hell', and as it is this body which God will raise up and transform, 'this body must already be seen here and now as a body which is being raised up. This is what makes all life in the body so responsible.'[134] Further, Schweizer agrees that the reflexive pronoun in Romans 6:13, 16 'shows that σῶμα describes man as a whole, not a part which may be detached from the true I'.[135]

However, Schweizer pinpoints the weakness of Bultmann's interpretation in the Heideggerian phrase 'man has a relation to himself', which is inadequate because it implies a self-enclosed individual. Schweizer credits the move to translate σῶμα as 'person' as

> justifiable to the degree that the word always denotes the whole man and not just a part. Yet it does not quite catch Paul's own understanding, since the accent is on the self-enclosed nature of man. In fact, σῶμα means man

in his confrontation with God or sin or fellow-man. σῶμα is the place where faith lives and where man surrenders to God's lordship. It is thus the sphere in which man serves. Paul has no interest whatsoever in appearances, abilities, or character, but only in the work of the body, in what takes place with it ... the totality of the σῶμα in which feeling, thought, experience and action can no longer be sundered.[136]

Viewed sympathetically, and apart from Bultmann's unfortunate adoption of the phrase 'man in relation to himself', this accords comfortably with the existentialist analysis of human existence as being-in-the-world, and gives sufficient ground for exegetical confidence in Bultmann's general approach.

Gundry, however, makes an important connection between Bultmann's interpretation of σῶμα, his individualism and his weakness with regard to 'objective history'. This will be of significance for Macquarrie's own criticisms of Bultmann. In spite of his insistence that σῶμα should be used consistently to denote the physical body, Gundry is not seeking a return to traditional substance interpretation, and does acknowledge that σῶμα refers to what man is, not simply what he has, that is, as 'essential to man's true and full being'.[137] What he is not prepared to concede, however, is that σῶμα thereby refers to man in his totality, lest this should obscure the fact that man *is* physical. So on Romans 8:13 he notes that τὰς πράξεις τοῦ σώματος 'cannot be other than the deeds of the person himself, we must agree. But the proper conclusion is that the physical body belongs to the man as an integral part of him, not that it comprises the whole man.'[138]

This is not, for Gundry, a return to dualism, but an insistence that physicality is intrinsic to the meaning of σῶμα: the σῶμα is not merely an outer shell, but is nevertheless that aspect of man by which he effects concrete actions. Commenting on the Heideggerian understanding of being-in-the-world as fundamentally instrumental, Gundry objects: 'the objectivity of *soma* is not purely functional. It *is* functional in that it denotes a way of being in the world. But it is more than functional in that it denotes a substantival entity which exists in the concrete world. And without the substantival nature of man's *soma*, man's way of being in the world ceases.'[139]

So far, then, Gundry's interpretation of σῶμα as physical denotation appears to be merely an additional nuance to the emphasis safeguarded by Jewett and Schweizer, that being-in-the-world really does entail responsibility in bodily living, precisely because man *is* substance in an objective world (whatever else he may equally or even primordially be).

However, the heart of Gundry's criticism emerges in the claim that Bultmann himself is perpetuating a dualism by devaluing the physical. He argues that whilst emphasising the responsibility of man for his decisions and his future, Bultmann is hardening a dualism between substance and decision which devalues the sphere in which these decisions can be concretely carried out:

> Ironically, what begins as an existentialist stress on human responsibility to decide the future ends in withdrawal from the only arena where we can exercise that responsibility – viz., the material world where objective events take place – because of a prior devaluation of the only means by which we can carry out that responsibility – viz., the physical body.[140]

Although Gundry acknowledges that Bultmann certainly does not intend this result, he defends his criticism by pointing to two widely criticised aspects of Bultmann's thought: (1) his major stress on the self, and its resultant tendency to individualism and, perhaps, subjectivism, and (2) his 'well-recognised flight ... from the meaningfulness of objective history', which again is an unsurprising outcome of the inward-looking tendency of existentialist anthropology.[141] For Gundry, then, Bultmann's 'desubstantialization of man' and 'deobjectivization of history' are directly related, and only when $\sigma\tilde{\omega}\mu\alpha$ is understood explicitly to mean substance can history be 'more than the study of the possible [but] also a study of the factual, the objective'.[142]

As I shall show in Chapter 2, Macquarrie is himself critical of Bultmann's evasion of historical objectivity, retaining a minimal 'that' but rejecting the 'what' and 'how'. Gundry claims that Macquarrie's acceptance of Bultmann's existentialism undermines his criticism, because he has no anthropological or historical base from which to launch his critique. Whilst this is a valid criticism if derived solely from *An Existentialist Theology*, it is precisely my intention to show that Macquarrie's theology develops rapidly to establish the ground for his critique.

CONCLUSION

In this chapter I have been concerned with the fundamental groundwork of Macquarrie's theology. Drawing on Heidegger's early work, particularly *Being and Time*, Macquarrie establishes the philosophical basis upon which a reasonable theology might elucidate Christian faith 'in terms that are understandable to the modern world and designed to make contact with its ways of thinking'.[143] Against the traditional Western orientation to substance, he emphasises *temporality*, showing how theology must give account of the responsibility of human being in the face of possibility. Further, the horizon of temporality understands being in the world as instrumentality rather than the location of *res extensa*, which opens the way to Macquarrie's later work on the microcosmic character of human being. Against the tendency to abstract into objectified universals, Macquarrie emphasises the *mineness* of existence, and the unavoidability both of taking a stance and of knowing participatively.

Finally, of key significance in this first stage of Macquarrie's work, his use of Heidegger's existentialist thought allows him to indicate the way in which the question of God arises from the very constitution of human existence. The first layer of meaning of the *grace of being* begins to emerge: it is grace-full to be human because it is here that the possibility of grace arises. The account of the translation of possibility into concrete reality develops with Macquarrie's openness to broader philosophical and theological horizons.

NOTES

1. 'Pilgrimage in Theology' in *Being and Truth*, eds A. Kee and E. Long (London: SCM 1986), xi–xviii, xiv.
2. Paul Tillich, *Systematic Theology* vol. 1 (Chicago: University of Chicago Press 1951), 3; quoted in *An Existentialist Theology* (London: SCM 1955), hereafter *ET*, 233.
3. *ET* 234
4. John Macquarrie, *Studies in Christian Existentialism* (London: SCM 1965), hereafter *SCE*, 57. Compare his essay 'Philosophy and Theology in Bultmann's Thought' in *The Theology of Rudolf Bultmann*, ed. Charles W. Kegley (London: SCM 1966), 127–52.
5. *Being and Time* (Oxford: Blackwell 1962), hereafter *BT*, 21.
6. *BT* 23
7. *BT* 25. Here, as in all references, the italics are Heidegger's.
8. *BT* 31
9. *BT* 34. This was intended to prepare the way for a study of 'Being' per se, but Heidegger subsequently acknowledged that an ontology could not be reached directly from a study of *Dasein*; such a study could only prepare the way for a glimpse of being. From the mid-1930s his writing about Being becomes more poetic than philosophical.
10. *BT* 33. Stephen Mulhall renders this term as 'there-Being', *Heidegger and Being and Time* (London: Routledge 1996).
11. *BT* 33 n3
12. That is, $\H{\varepsilon}\kappa\sigma\tau\alpha\sigma\iota\varsigma$ in the precise sense of 'standing out' to enquire about his own existence.

13 *BT* 38
14 *SCE* 89
15 *BT* 67
16 *BT* 70
17 *BT* 68
18 Magda King translates *eigentlich* as 'owned' and *uneigentlich* as 'disowned' to emphasise this link, *Heidegger's Philosophy* (Oxford: Blackwell 1964), 6.
19 *BT* 74
20 *BT* 92
21 *BT* 87, and see Macquarrie, *SCE* 49, where he notes the traditional Western view that we are 'primarily thinking subjects, before whom there is spread out for our inspection a world, and this world is to be understood in a genuine way only along the lines of detached theoretical enquiry'.
22 *BT* 88. Compare John Richardson, *Existential Epistemology* (Oxford: Clarendon 1991), 17: 'things matter to us'.
23 *BT* 95; this has its own kind of knowledge, though not that of bare perceptual cognition.
24 *BT* 97, 98
25 *BT* 100
26 *BT* 105
27 *BT* 116
28 *BT* 120
29 *BT* 419
30 *BT* 154
31 *BT* 155
32 *BT* 160
33 *BT* 164
34 *BT* 165
35 *BT* 167, 168
36 *BT* 173, compare the immediacy of God-consciousness for Schleiermacher and Otto.
37 *SCE* 41
38 *SCE* 36. Compare Heidegger, *Vom Wesen der Wahrheit* (Frankfurt am Main: Vittorio Klostermann 1954), 11: *ein Bezugsbereich*, a domain of relatedness.
39 *BT* 173; and see 172 n2. Macquarrie and Robinson note the relation between *Befindlichkeit* and the greeting '*Wie befinden Sie sich?*', 'How are you, how are you feeling?'. Mulhall notes that 'state-of-mind' is a misleading translation in so far as it implies that the relevant phenomena are subjective states. He hazards 'passion' to safeguard the sense of an externally influenced response.
40 *BT* 174
41 The example beloved of Mulhall is the impossibility of being a Samurai warrior in twentieth-century London, 128, 16, 169.
42 *BT* 184
43 *BT* 185
44 *BT* 213, 216, 217
45 *BT* 219, 220
46 *BT* 223
47 *BT* 237, 243
48 *BT* 255
49 *BT* 261

50 *BT* 231
51 *BT* 231
52 *BT* 232
53 *BT* 294
54 *BT* 306
55 *BT* 307
56 Compare Karl Jaspers' notion of the 'boundary-' or 'limit-situation' – death, suffering and struggle which riddle human life with their 'dreadful insecurity and irremediality', *Philosophy* (Chicago: University of Chicago Press 1970), Chapter 7 'Boundary Situations', especially 193ff.
57 *BT* 314
58 *BT* 326
59 *BT* 329
60 *BT* 331
61 *BT* 334. Although Heidegger characterises the voice of conscience as if it came from a third party, *BT* 206, 320, this remains a problematic aspect of his thought. Mulhall comments thus: 'Heidegger claims that the transition is brought about by the very aspect of the self that benefits from it – by its eclipsed capacity for authenticity … But this amounts to claiming that a capacity in eclipse can bring about its own emergence from eclipse', 131.
62 *BT* 344
63 *BT* 346
64 *BT* 349–50
65 Temporality here is understood as the ground for the *possibility* of time, the condition of successiveness which makes time possible. Time in its various forms (solar, clock, human, tempo, allotted, *kairos*) is derivative of its transcendental, temporality.
66 *BT* 376
67 *SCE* 65
68 *BT* 401
69 *BT* 397
70 *BT* 426
71 *BT* 433, compare Carl Michalson in *The Later Heidegger and Theology* eds James M. Robinson and John B. Cobb (New York: Harper & Row 1963), 'History in contemporary thinking is man existing in his acts, not simply describing them', 146.
72 *BT* 440
73 *BT* 435
74 *BT* 37
75 The German makes this meaning clearer: Heidegger puns *wider* (against) with *wieder* (again). *BT* 438, n1
76 *BT* 444. Compare Richardson, involvement in the present 'has the character of repetition when we explicitly come to it from being who we have been', 200.
77 This lies at the heart of Schleiermacher's *The Christian Faith* (Edinburgh: T&T Clark 1989), and is articulated in the second speech of the *On Religion: speeches to its cultured despisers* (New York: Harper and Row 1958).
78 *ET* 55
79 *SCE* 24
80 *ET* 56

81 Gilbert Ryle, 'Critical Notice: Sein und Zeit', *Mind* XXXVIII (1929), 355–70, 361
82 Ryle, 357
83 Ryle, 363
84 Ryle, 365, italics are Ryle's.
85 Ryle, 369
86 Ryle, 370
87 Note the subtle shift: Heidegger uses 'primordial', Ryle 'primitive'.
88 Ryle, 369. Compare John R. Searle's work on 'background', for example in understanding the requirement to cut the grass or cut the sand, 'The background of meaning' in *Speech-Act Theory and Pragmatics* (London: D. Reidel Publ. Co. 1980), 221–32.
89 *SCE* 8
90 John Macquarrie, *Principles of Christian Theology* (London: SCM 1966, 1977²; unless otherwise indicated all references are to the second edition), hereafter *PCT*, 35.
91 Rudolf Bultmann, *Theology of the New Testament* vol. I (London: SCM 1952), hereafter *TNT*, 302.
92 John Macquarrie, 'Philosophy and Theology in Bultmann's Thought', in *The Theology of Rudolf Bultmann*, ed. Charles W. Kegley (London: SCM 1966), 127–43, 141.
93 Especially between fact and value in theology.
94 For example, *BT* 174. In using this understanding, Macquarrie is not dependent on Heidegger's theory alone, but is drawing on an insight which has already found a place in theology through the work of Friedrich Schleiermacher. Although perennially accused of reducing religion to mere emotion by his expression 'the feeling of absolute dependence', *The Christian Faith* 12, Schleiermacher is more correctly understood as drawing attention to the way in which feeling (in this case of creatureliness) conceals within itself an implicit assertion, a trustworthy cognitive content (in this case, that there is a Creator on whom all depends). Compare Rudolf Otto, *The Idea of the Holy* (London: OUP 1923), 8–11.
95 *SCE* 39, italics are mine.
96 *SCE* 4
97 *SCE* 5
98 *SCE* 6
99 *SCE* 8
100 *SCE* 8
101 *SCE* 10
102 *SCE* 12
103 *SCE* 12
104 *SCE* 127
105 There are, of course, other theological connotations to the word 'sin' more explicitly derived from the Greek in relation to Old Testament roots, notably the 'missing the mark' of ἁμαρτία with its double implications derived from *hatta't* (carelessness) and *'awon* (wilfulness). So, for example the Johannine ἀνομία (1 John 3:4) and ἀδικία (1 John 5:17). But Walter Grundmann, in Kittel's *Theological Dictionary of the New Testament* vol. 1 (Grand Rapids: Eerdmans 1964), agrees that the thrust of Paul's theology is not individual acts

but a state of separation which embraces all humanity, perpetuated by a human act of self-assertion in opposition to God; see 309–10.
106 *SCE* 128
107 *SCE* 130
108 *SCE* 65, a condition which Bultmann deems the choice of living κατὰ σάρκα, *TNT* vol. 1, 237.
109 *SCE* 132
110 *ET* 109
111 *ET* 90
112 *SCE* 133, *ET* 91
113 *ET* 93
114 *TNT* vol. 1, 257
115 *ET* 99
116 *SCE* 133. Wolfhart Pannenberg traces the history of the understanding of sin in his *Systematic Theology* vol. 2 (Edinburgh: T&T Clark 1991), and likewise suggests that the root of sin must be located in the seductive, deceptive quality of our aspirations for true selfhood: 'all of us sin because we think we can attain a full and true life thereby.' It is thus that we give consent to our alienation. See 262–63.
117 σῶμα is an ontological term, σάρξ an ontical term. Hans Conzelmann suggests 'σῶμα is man as the one who can fall, and in fact has fallen, victim to sin and death. σάρξ is man as the one who has fallen', *An Outline of the Theology of the New Testament* (London: SCM 1969), 178. For the history of the research, see further R. Jewett, *Paul's Anthropological Terms* (Leiden: Brill 1971), 201–50.
118 *TNT* vol. 1, 193
119 *TNT* vol. 1, 194, italics are Bultmann's. See Johannes Weiss, *Der Erste Korintherbrief* (Göttingen: Vandenhoeck & Ruprecht 1910), 161, '*bedeut ihm σῶμα nicht die Körperlichkeit*'.
120 *TNT* vol 1, 195, italics are Bultmann's.
121 *TNT* vol 1, 196
122 *ET* 41
123 *ET* 44
124 *ET* 45
125 *ET* 41
126 Contrary to Macquarrie on this point, πνευματικός is now taken more usually to denote 'of the Holy Spirit', characterised by God's spirit.
127 *ET* 105
128 For example, we are debtors, Romans 8:12.
129 *ET* 46
130 *ET* 46
131 Robert H. Gundry, *SOMA in Biblical Theology* (Cambridge: CUP 1976), 195.
132 See for example, R. Jewett, *Paul's Anthropological Terms* 456; E. Schweizer, 'σῶμα' in *Theological Dictionary of the New Testament* vol. VII, ed. Gerhard Friedrich (Grand Rapids: Eerdmans 1971), 1057–8.
133 Except in the traditional Jewish greeting at 1 Thessalonians 5:23, Schweizer 1060.
134 Schweizer 1058, 1062; Jewett does note, however, that in *TNT* Bultmann's interpretation of σῶμα has lost all meaningful association with *physicality*, and

where it appears with that meaning is attributed no theological significance, see 209–10.
135 Schweizer 1064
136 Schweizer 1065–6; I shall return to this view in noting Käsemann's understanding of the body as 'the sphere of service' below.
137 Gundry 53; compare Bultmann's 'belonging to the self's very essence' *TNT* vol. 1, 194.
138 Gundry 50
139 Gundry 187, the italics are Gundry's.
140 Gundry 190
141 Gundry 191
142 Gundry 193
143 John Macquarrie, *Theology, Church and Ministry* (London: SCM 1986), 179.

Chapter 2

Beyond Existentialism

INTRODUCTION: TENSIONS AND LIMITATIONS

Even in Chapter 1, some tensions have begun to emerge between Macquarrie's thought and the narrower existentialism of the earlier Heidegger and Bultmann. Thus I noted Macquarrie's concerns with the corporate dimension of human life and faith, with tradition, and with the way in which Being gives itself to be known. I also noted his turn to grace as a power beyond human existence which enables man 'to live as the being which he is', uniting his possibility and facticity, in contrast to Sartre's absurdity and heroic despair. And I noted, both in regard to κόσμος as 'a concrete ontical phenomenon' and in regard to σῶμα as requiring a 'what and how' of historical objectivity, that Macquarrie's commitment to a functional understanding of being-in-the-world does not preclude attention to the objective physicality and historicality which that entails.

Already in *An Existentialist Theology*, Macquarrie writes of the difficulties of retaining a *Christian* theology if attempting to undertake a 'purely existential theology'.[1] In this chapter, I shall identify the three fundamental concerns by which Macquarrie limits his own use of existentialist thought, even during this early period. These are: (1) a concern with kerygma, by which Macquarrie establishes that the existential summons is both *from beyond human existence* and also is *to a genuine possibility* which has already been exhibited in the *existentiell* conditions of human living; (2) a concern with ontology, by which Macquarrie establishes that the existential summons and the responding decision disclose something of 'how things are', with regard both to the one who calls, and to the character of the world which forms the context of the summons and response, and (3) a concern with the corporate character of human life and faith, by which Macquarrie establishes a more secure ground for the practical expression of fellowship and love. I shall illustrate Macquarrie's position with reference to those ideas and thinkers against which he distinguishes his own thought. Then I shall give some indication of the source of these concerns, in Macquarrie's attention to Heidegger's later work, his early interest in F.H. Bradley, and his own Celtic roots.

KERYGMA

For Macquarrie, theology has the task 'of exploring and elucidating the Christian faith, and of seeking to arrive at a fuller understanding of it',[2] and therefore has as its primary source the content and experience of the Christian community and its tradition. Whilst this may (and, indeed, must) be subjected to scrutiny and fresh articulation, it does involve recognition of the experience of a transcendent God active in history. Such a recognition, 'even if it is expressed in language drawn from human existence, carries a reference which points to a reality beyond the confines of any existentialist analysis'.[3] Theology, in other words, is not exhausted in anthropology or existential interpretation, but must also give attention to the distinctive matter of the kerygma. This is not, for Macquarrie, a matter of contradiction but, in a disciplined sense, a paradox, the polarity of two opposites within a whole.

Bultmann's 'sudden swerve'

It is this issue of kerygma within an existentialist interpretation of the Christian faith that Macquarrie explores with regard to Bultmann's work in *The Scope of Demythologizing* (1960). In this work, Macquarrie moves beyond the expository approach of *An Existentialist Theology* to evaluate Bultmann's use of existentialist thought in the context of the controversy it raised. He notes a central problem in Bultmann's demythologising programme which has provoked controversy from both 'left-wing' and 'right-wing' corners. This is the problem of the *limit* Bultmann imposes on his own demythologising, and the apparently arbitrary imposition of this limit. For whilst Bultmann translates mythological language in the New Testament into language about human existence, he denies that the Christian faith can be entirely dissolved into a philosophy of existence, and insists that the task of demythologising is precisely to free the kerygma, 'the proclamation of the decisive act of God in Christ' to address us.[4] This means that Bultmann is subject to criticisms from the 'right' for the use he makes of existentialist analysis in fear that it endangers the kerygma (especially if no clear account can be given of the point at which the New Testament teaching is no longer to be reinterpreted into the language of human existence), and from the 'left' for not pressing that use sufficiently far to 'de-kerygmatise' as well as demythologise the New Testament.

So, for example, Helmut Thielicke is critical that Bultmann's hermeneutical principle of a pre-understanding by which the text is approached *determines* what will count as kerygma. Thielicke does not disagree that the pre-understanding is a self-understanding which the kerygma will challenge and transvalue. However, he suggests that in Bultmann's work 'the natural self-understanding is ready to allow itself to be transvalued only in a way that is completely *conditioned*, namely, it inquires of the *kerygma* in conformity with *that which is already contained in itself in its urge towards transvaluation*.'[5] Instead of allowing that 'the Biblical text examines *me*, ... that it throws all my orderly formulations of the question on to the dust heap, and teaches me the right question', Thielicke suggests that Bultmann uses pre-understanding like a sieve to filter the kerygma: 'Through the sieve there passes only that which has a valid claim to truth, namely, that which can become the content of a self-understanding.'[6]

On the other hand, however, H.P. Owen expresses a very different view. His criticism is that Bultmann ignores rather than exaggerates the continuities between natural self-understanding and the summons of grace. Thus he writes:

> Bultmann's analysis of *Dasein* involves what may be called an existentialist version of the *via negativa*. God comes to man in a wholly negative way; he comes to contradict nature, but not to fulfil it; he appears always as the Stranger and never as the Guest. Yet it is the teaching of the New Testament that there are positive elements in man's nature to which God appeals and upon which he builds.[7]

Macquarrie's task in *The Scope of Demythologizing* is to evaluate both aspects of Bultmann's thought, and his conclusion is that both sides of Bultmann's theology have stood up remarkably well to the criticisms directed against them. On the one hand, he notes the value of demythologising and existentialist interpretation for pressing the point that 'if there is anything like a *kerygma*, it must be a proclamation to man as existing, and it must be unfolded in its existential significance' if it is to be capable of appropriation.[8] On the other hand, human existence demands an account of grace and revelation if the possibilities of existence are to be realised, and not merely recognised: 'only an act from beyond man, such as Bultmann finds proclaimed in the *kerygma*, will be adequate to effect salvation for those who are fallen and unable to lift themselves.'[9]

If both aspects of Bultmann's thought have their validity in human existence and in Christian faith, a further question arises about the paradox: why does it appear so acute and so aggravating of controversy? Macquarrie's answer is to seek an 'extra element' in Bultmann's work, linked to existentialist interpretation but not demanded by it. He suggests that:

> the alarm and despondency which the orthodox feel as they visualise Bultmann sliding towards the dissolution of the Christian faith, and the acute disappointment which the philosophers feel when Bultmann brings the *kerygma* onto the scene, are evidences of something that is highly misleading in Bultmann himself. Why should his appeal to the *kerygma* seem so arbitrary as to be almost an afterthought, and the limit he sets to demythologizing so abrupt and incongruous?[10]

The 'extra element' Macquarrie identifies is a confused acceptance of secularised self-understanding as the norm to which Christian faith must address itself. Certainly Macquarrie agrees that there is a *modern world-view*, significantly informed by the sciences, and differing from the world-view(s) of the New Testament, which faith and theology must address, and commends Bultmann for his attempts to do so. However, related, but distinct, there is a *modern self-understanding*, which Macquarrie rightly identifies in this description of Niebuhr's: 'There is a power of pride in which the human ego assumes its self-sufficiency and self-mastery and imagines itself secure against all vicissitudes. It does not recognise the contingent and dependent character of its life and believes itself to be the author of its own existence, the judge of its own values, and the master of its own destiny.'[11]

Bultmann agrees: 'the New Testament addresses man as one who is through and through a self-assertive rebel.'[12] Macquarrie is adamant that if the New Testament is to be interpreted *with regard to* this self-understanding, rather than be allowed to speak in challenge to it, there can be no place for the kerygma:

> If it can be re-interpreted for such a self-understanding at all, then it can be presented only as a human possibility – a turning from the world and from the preoccupation with the mastery of things. This is indeed the teaching of some secular existentialist philosophers, but to represent it as the teaching of the New Testament is so to impoverish the New Testament as positively to falsify it.[13]

Macquarrie's assessment is that Bultmann recognises this (hence the frustration of his left-wing critics) *and yet* in some degree confuses it with the need to speak to the modern world-view. Therefore, he moves further towards a humanistic philosophy with a greater reliance on willing and resolve than Macquarrie allows, and can only introduce the kerygma by a *tour de force*. The opening paragraph of *The Scope of Demythologizing* provides a graphic image: a car proceeds briskly downhill until, almost at the last moment, it swerves violently to avoid plunging into a blind dip in the road – a dip in which there *might* be an abyss of some sort.

Significantly, this illustrates that even in his 'existentialist phase', Macquarrie's allegiance is less to Bultmann than to Heidegger himself, and that he is more able than Bultmann wholeheartedly and consistently to affirm the kerygma because he is less concerned to eliminate myth from the New Testament for the sake of modern self-understanding.

In his own insistence on the kerygma, Macquarrie emphasises two aspects which distinguish his approach from narrower existentialist interpretations and, especially, from Bultmann's demythologising programme: (1) that it comes from beyond human existence in order to address human existence, and (2) that it contains at least a minimal core of factuality because it refers explicitly to the event of Jesus Christ.

The gift from beyond

Macquarrie insists that man needs God's act of grace in order to move from inauthentic to authentic existence, and not simply the action of his own authentic self calling to his fallen self (that is, conscience), for though the existential possibility of authentic existence remains, the *existentiell* possibility is lost to him.[14] I shall consider this point further with reference to Macquarrie's treatment of Fritz Buri's notion of 'indwelling grace' in *The Scope of Demythologizing*. For Macquarrie, it is Buri's failure (following Jaspers) to distinguish between 'existential' and '*existentiell*' that leads him to both an inadequate concept of grace, and the view that any 'saving act of God' will inevitably be 'something utterly foreign to man and unrelated to his experience'.[15]

Macquarrie agrees with Karl Barth that Buri's work is an 'ultra-radicalisation of Bultmann's radicalism'.[16] Buri accepts Bultmann's demythologising programme, but rejects his insistence on retaining the kerygma. For Buri, the kerygma is a residue of myth which should be dealt with as other myths, so that the New Testament is de-kerygmatised as well as demythologised. Buri's own approach is to reinterpret the kerygma into the language of authentic existence, to produce a 'theology of existence' which goes deeper in its translation of the New Testament, so that the New Testament record as a whole has the status of myth, and so that there is no difference in principle between a *theology* of existence and a (secular) *philosophy* of existence, other than that theology speaks out of a particular symbolic tradition.[17]

Macquarrie assesses Buri's approach to grace. Buri claims to attempt a middle course between Heidegger, whom he understands as saying that man can attain an authentic existence without the aid of grace, and Bultmann, who insists that grace is an act of God in Christ.[18] Following Jaspers, Buri accepts that authentic existence has a gift-like character, but maintains that this gift is immanent in existence itself: 'There is a grace in existence itself – existence includes grace ... It is not something from beyond me, but something which already belongs to me. Certainly it has nothing to do with a saving act, such as the kerygma proclaims. It is already given with my existence itself.'[19] Macquarrie argues that this is not, then, a gift, not *grace* in the 'clear and proper sense', but *nature*, albeit in the non-absolute sense that 'nature' can never be fully divorced from 'grace' if God is regarded as Creator and therefore the giver of the very being of man.

Macquarrie rejects a sharp distinction between grace and nature. I have already noted how Macquarrie identifies the character of grace in relation to the unifying polarities of facticity and possibility in human existence, and this becomes an increasingly significant theme in *Principles of Christian Theology* as his existential-ontological natural theology reaches deeper expression. In *The Scope of Demythologizing*, he rejects the distinction between grace and nature which depends on 'nature' being understood as 'the ordered universe and its processes' and 'grace' as a wholly irruptive act. He agrees with Bultmann that if 'nature' is understood as 'the constitution proper to anything, in virtue of which it behaves as it does', then the Christian life is the 'natural' human existence.[20] Nevertheless, Macquarrie insists that grace must mean something which is given to man in addition to his natural existence – *donum superadditum*. He notes the experience of being enabled to do something which it is not 'in our nature' to do as an experience of grace: 'Grace is therefore conceived as something which comes to the recipient from beyond himself – it is something which he experiences not as his own but given to him. Yet it does not come to him as something utterly foreign. The recipient can and must make it his own.'[21]

Against Buri, Macquarrie maintains that in order to realise his possibility for authentic existence, inauthentic man, alienated not only from God but also from his own authentic self, is dependent upon 'a gracious act from beyond himself to make the possibility one for which he can choose in his situation'.[22] And he affirms that although this act is from beyond man, it is not foreign to man and unrelated to his existence; it is not imposed but received, precisely because the existential possibility is already present in the constitution of human existence.

This is of great significance to my theme, the characterisation of Macquarrie's theology by the phrase 'the grace of being'. I have already indicated in Chapter 1 that a preliminary meaning of this phrase is that *it is grace-full to be human* because it is in the very constitution of human being that the quest for grace arises and is met. A second meaning will become explicit in due course: that being is graced in the sense that *existence itself is a gift*. However, an important pointer emerges here in Macquarrie's response to Buri to indicate that, for Macquarrie, to establish that existence is a gift is insufficient to secure the move to authentic existence. Certainly, the existential possibility which characterises human being *is* a gift (as is the very fact that there is 'something rather than nothing'), but even more the *realising* of that possibility as *existentiell* is a gift. However, precisely because the *existentiell* possibility is already potential as existential, the act of grace from beyond which makes it possible to lay hold of it is not foreign to us or unrelated to our existence, but its fulfilment.

The 'what' and 'how' of history

Having established Macquarrie's insistence that a truly kerygmatic dimension be retained in the interpretation of the New Testament for contemporary hearers, a further question arises. To what extent does Macquarrie agree with the existentialist tendency to ignore the question of the objective historical content of the events to which the kerygma refers? I noted above that he draws a distinction between the active historical scepticism introduced by Bultmann's demythologising programme, and the simple failure to address the question: an existentialist interpretation (of a gospel account, for example) simply 'makes no pronouncement whatever concerning the factual content of the story which it professes to interpret ... The objective reference has somehow become irrelevant. Whether we affirm it or whether we deny it or whether we suspend judgement about it, the existential significance appears to remain quite unaffected'; Macquarrie's retort is, 'Just how irrelevant can the factual content of the gospel become without its ceasing to be a gospel?'[23]

Macquarrie's concern here is not to devalue the contribution of an existentialist understanding of history to theology, since, for example, it enables us 'to understand how the cross of Christ can have the character of an atonement for men who live nineteen centuries after the event'.[24] Indeed, the group of principles which characterise an existentialist interpretation of history provide a more appropriate approach to 'sacred history' than a purely scientific historical approach which attempts to identify 'facts' in isolation from their interpretation, or a metaphysical approach which attempts to pronounce on history from some extra-historical standpoint in order to assess its relation to the total scheme of cosmic reality.[25] By means of the existentialist interpretation, 'the sacred history can be exhibited in terms of a way of life, a possibility of human existence.'[26]

Macquarrie is adamant, however, that the 'inside' of an event cannot be separated from its 'outside'. The Church has consistently opposed Gnosticism and the tendency to suppose that once the gnosis (in this case, the existential significance) is grasped, the story which embodies it is irrelevant. The ground for Macquarrie's insistence here derives explicitly from Heidegger's analysis of human existence and the corresponding meaning of history. In the context of the facticity and possibility of human being-in-the-world, Heidegger maintains that history is concerned primarily with the possible, and as such is oriented to the future. Since, for Heidegger, 'possibility' is always a possible way of existing *for which an existent can decide*, it does not mean just any free-floating possibility. Macquarrie is right to identify it rather as meaning 'the possibilities which are open in a situation that is "factical" in the sense that it has arisen out of what has been'.[27] History therefore discloses factical possibilities of authentic existing which may be authentically 'repeated' if taken up and appropriated. As Macquarrie notes in *An Existentialist Theology*, 'History is concerned with repeatable possibility, and for a possibility to be repeated, it is necessary that it must once have been actual. To say that history is concerned with the possible does not release it from the course of real happenings, that is to say, from the facts.'[28]

This is highly significant for the kerygma, especially as understood as the summons to a way of life, in order to establish that the possibility to which it summons is a genuine one within the factical conditions of human existence. As Macquarrie notes, 'how can we know that it is a *genuine* possibility that is being set before us, unless it can be pointed out in history? How can we know what can be done except on the basis of what has been done?'[29] If a given event or pattern of life is to be of relevance to our existence, it must be the case that it can be genuinely realised in our *existentiell* situation – because it has already been realised under *existentiell* conditions:

> Just as it would be senseless to urge an athlete to aim at the physiological impossibility of running a mile in a minute, so it might be senseless to urge a man to love his enemies, unless one could point to an actual historical instance of someone who had done this and thereby shown that this is not an existential or psychological impossibility.[30]

This is not demanding a *guarantee* for faith from its historical roots, but acknowledging that a faith-commitment 'must be realistic and have regard to the factical human condition' if it is to be taken seriously.[31]

So far, Macquarrie is demanding little in terms of a core of historical factuality. Certainly, this is not a call for a biographical portrait or even for 'a short list of supposedly essential incidents or sayings'.[32] Were such a thing possible, even that limited degree of objective-historical information could render faith dependent on historical research. A minimal assertion, for Macquarrie, is that 'the Word became flesh and dwelt among us', or at greater length 'simply the assertion that at the source of the Christian religion there was an actual historical instance of the pattern of life proclaimed in the *kerygma* under the notions of dying and rising.'[33] It is this 'actual historical instance' which provides the empirical check that the connection between Jesus of Nazareth and the Christ of the kerygma is not merely accidental, and that the life to which the kerygma calls man is neither utopian nor, in fact, alien to 'a world which seems so inhospitable to it'.[34]

How, then, does this differ from Bultmann's position, from which Macquarrie seeks to distinguish himself? In *Studies in Christian Existentialism* he notes:

> Bultmann himself seems content to hold *that* there was a Jesus who was crucified, and he sees no compelling reasons to go beyond this simple fact that there was a Jesus to *what* Jesus was or did ... But I do not think that this minimal core is simply *that* there was a Jesus who was crucified, for this in itself would seem to be a matter of no consequence whatever, unless we had some idea of *what* he was.[35]

So, for example, where Bultmann insists that to follow Christ is to make the cross one's own, Macquarrie goes further: 'Does it ... make sense to talk of "dying and rising with Christ" without an assurance that, in some sense, Christ actually died and rose? Can men be summoned to a possibility without the assurance that it has been verified in actual happening?'[36]

Bultmann's position on the 'that' and 'what' of Jesus is laid out in his essay 'The Primitive Christian Kerygma and the Historical Jesus', an address given to scholars of the 'new quest for the historical Jesus' school.[37] Bultmann recognises that the old Life-of-Jesus research intended to free the historical Jesus from the 'dogmatic overlay' of the Church's teaching in the kerygma, but that the new emphasis is on establishing the unity of the historical Jesus with the kerygma. In the context of his own emphasis on the wholly other character of the kerygmatic summons, and his rejection of modern self-sufficiency, Bultmann is still suspicious that the attempt to establish unity is in practice a move to legitimise the kerygma by means of its historical reference. It is his insistence that 'it is the Christ of the kerygma and not the person of the historical Jesus who is the object of faith, that the man whom the kerygma addresses may not enquire behind the kerygma for a legitimation offered by historical research'.[38]

He argues that the material unity of the historical Jesus with the kerygma is confused in current discussion with the historical continuity, so that it is assumed that certainty of historical continuity establishes the material unity (or, conversely and in the case of his critics, that inattention to historical continuity is tantamount to a denial of material unity). Bultmann willingly admits that there is a continuity between the historical Jesus and the kerygma; indeed, how could there not be, when 'the kerygma presupposes the historical Jesus, however much it may have mythologised him. Without him there would be no kerygma. To this extent the continuity is obvious.'[39] This, then, is the 'that' of the historical Jesus. But, beyond this, Bultmann claims to demonstrate that Paul and John both indicate that there is no need to go further than the 'that' by the absence in their writings of any kind of biographical portrait of the human Jesus.

Bultmann notes that there are two types of attempt to press beyond the 'that' to include a 'what' and 'how' of the historical Jesus within the continuity of the kerygma. Some attempts seek to show that the picture of Jesus' person and activity is implicit in the kerygma, by appeal to the combination of the description of the historical Jesus and of the Christ of the kerygma in the synoptic gospels; other attempts seek to show that Jesus' preaching already has a 'kerygmatic character' in its eschatological urgency and its christological call for a decision with regard to the person of Christ as the bearer of the word of God.[40] This second approach, viewed not as an objective-historical continuity but as an existential-historical relation, provides the ground for

Bultmann's own account of continuity. According to his account, 'the "now" of yesterday [becomes] the "now" of today' – so that the self-understanding of faith is a continually recurring event, and not a historically mediated return to the historical Jesus.

It is, however, the first approach which is of particular interest for the way in which Macquarrie distinguishes himself from Bultmann's approach. Bultmann is dismissive of the claim that the synoptics offer a biographical picture of Jesus, and notes the widespread agreement that the earlier Life-of-Jesus research failed. He does, however, agree to 'meet such attempts part way' and is prepared to concede that although 'the Synoptic Gospels do not suffice as sources for a reconstruction of the life of Jesus, and although they are not sufficient to give a portrait in the real sense, since they say nothing of Jesus' inner development, nevertheless they do indicate something of Jesus' activity from which a few of his personal characteristics may be inferred.'[41]

But crucially Bultmann asks, even if this much is gleaned:

> what is to be gained by it? Would the result really be a legitimation of the kerygma which proclaims the historical Jesus as the Christ who died for us? ... The combination of historical report and kerygmatic christology in the Synoptic Gospels is not for the purpose of giving historical legitimacy to the Christ-kerygma, but quite the reverse, of giving legitimacy to the history of Jesus as messianic history, as it were, by viewing it in the light of the kerygmatic Christology.[42]

But this all-important phrase 'giving legitimacy to the history of Jesus as messianic history' is precisely Macquarrie's point: something must justify the human life of Jesus as constituting the summons of God to authentic existence. This justification can only be that Jesus' own life was itself an authentic existence lived in the *existentiell* situation. The kerygma only arises in response to this human life which discloses something *more* than human life.

Macquarrie, then, is quite in agreement with Bultmann that critical historical research acts in vain if it seeks to establish faith on the objective historicality of the person of Jesus. But Bultmann is so concerned to safeguard the kerygma against any sign of a return to theological liberalism, or any more general encroachment of modern self-sufficiency, that he moves too swiftly away from the need of the early Church to articulate the way in which the human life of Jesus itself invited, even demanded, the kerygma. In contrast, it appears to Macquarrie that 'as soon as the historian admits the objective-historical reality of the figure of Jesus, he must also admit that he was a big enough figure to found the Christian religion – or to put the same thing in another way, he must recognise an objective-historical which can support the existential-historical.'[43]

Enough has been said at this point to indicate Macquarrie's insistence that the existential-historical cannot be wholly divorced from the objective-historical, if it is to be shown that the existence to which the kerygma summons is a genuine possibility in the concrete conditions of human living.

ONTOLOGY

A second distinction from a narrow concern with existentialism can be noted even in this early 'existentialist phase'. This is Macquarrie's concern with ontology, which after this early period comes to characterise his 'existential-ontological' approach in *Principles of Christian Theology*. By 'ontological' Macquarrie does quite clearly mean ultimate questions about 'how things are' in a metaphysical sense, but he is anxious to distinguish his interest from the objectifying method of traditional metaphysics. Thus he refers in *Studies in Christian Existentialism* to 'the ultimate questions of existence – the "metaphysical" questions, if we care to call them such, though it might be better to call them "ontological" questions, since to call them "metaphysical" seems to point not only to their ultimacy but to a particular way of approaching them, that is to say, by rational speculation.'[44]

Two examples will serve to illustrate Macquarrie's interest here. Accordingly, I shall review his rejection of R.B. Braithwaite's notion of religion as purely conative in his essay 'A New Kind of Demythologizing?', and his observations on the dual function of the notion 'God' in his review of Roman Catholic objections to Bultmann's theology in *The Scope of Demythologizing*.[45]

Ultimate truth about the universe

Macquarrie views Braithwaite's *An Empiricist's View of the Nature of Religious Belief* as a type of demythologising comparable to Bultmann's, offering an interpretation of religion which is neither the acceptance of a world-view nor primarily emotion (though it does have an emotional content) but which is conative, characterised by an ultimate decision to accept a way of life. For Braithwaite, this essentially concerns a *moral* way of life. Thus, for example, 'the statement, "God is love", which

Braithwaite takes to epitomise the assertions of the Christian religion, is to be interpreted as the declaration of an intention to follow what he calls an "agapeistic" way of life.'[46] Macquarrie's response to this is important:

> We may have grave doubts as to whether religion can be so far humanised without its ceasing to be religion. It may well be that commitment to a way of life implicitly commits us at the same time to a belief about 'how things are', perhaps a metaphysical belief or at any rate some kind of ontological belief, if we allow the possibility of an ontology which is not reached by way of the traditional methods of metaphysics.[47]

He enquires whether there might not be a transcendental element in Braithwaite's thought, albeit an unacknowledged one.

Braithwaite attempts to rehabilitate the verification of religious statements without recourse to metaphysics, by means of the principle of use: religious statements receive their meaning from the way they are used. Braithwaite contends that 'the primary use of religious assertions is to announce allegiance to a set of moral principles: without such allegiance there is no "true religion".'[48] Although the principle of use has an advantage over the narrow verification principle of logical positivism, in so far as the claim for meaningfulness is upheld, Macquarrie is sceptical about the adequacy of the meaning adduced in relation to the lived experience it claims to represent: 'Who would have thought, that when the Christian says that God is love, he is really evincing an intention to follow an agapastic way of life?'[49] In the same way that Macquarrie has argued that feeling carries understanding (so that to feel 'at one with the universe' discloses an understanding of the universe as 'the kind of thing with which I could be at one – if, for instance, it were the creation of a God of love'), he insists that the commitment to a way of life implies some kind of belief.[50]

Thus whilst religion may be primarily a commitment to a way of life, in so far as it answers a summons to an authentic existence known as a genuine possibility because already lived by Jesus under *existentiell* conditions, such a commitment reveals some underlying beliefs. These are not necessarily prior to and causal of the way of life. That is to say, belief does not *necessarily* entail commitment to a way of life: 'like the demons mentioned by St James, I could believe Christian doctrines to be true without being committed to a Christian way of life' – and, indeed, are only truly understood in the living of them.[51] Nevertheless, even the initial act of commitment to accept a way of life is not a blind leap in the dark (unless it is wholly arbitrary), but is taken in the light of some beliefs, which at the time will seem to be reasonable and worthy of acceptance. These beliefs may well be revised in the course of following a way of life, but Macquarrie's argument is that they must at least be present at the outset.

Having indicated *how* belief is related to the commitment to a way of life, Macquarrie raises the more important question of the *nature* of the belief which accompanies such a commitment. In Braithwaite's terminology, the answer to the question, 'Why do you intend to follow an agapastic way of life?' might (from a Christian) most reasonably be 'because God is love'. However, once this answer is submitted to Braithwaite's interpretation, the result is tautologous: 'I intend to live an agapastic way of life because I declare (evince or show forth) my intention of following an agapastic way of life.'[52] Not only does this render the intention an arbitrary one, and scarcely the ground for a resolute way of life, but it is also 'quite certainly not what the Christian means' by the intention to live an agapastic life.

Rather, for Macquarrie, the Christian intention depends on the belief that 'love is the ultimate power in the universe' and even on an experience of that love which elicits a response of love and empowers the resolve.[53] This is an *ontological* belief. Contrary to Braithwaite's suggestion that a commitment to an agapastic way of life does not disclose a belief about the fundamental truth of the universe, Macquarrie insists that the commitment discloses an 'as if':

> The Christian acts (or intends to act) *as if* love were the most real and important thing of all. His understanding of what love is will become clearer and purer through following in the way of love. But love cannot cease to be a personal quality, so that to act *as if* love were the fundamental truth about the universe is to believe in a God who is *at least* personal – perhaps more.[54]

Ultimate truth about God

Macquarrie pursues this point in relation to a different theme in *The Scope of Demythologizing*, where he discusses the official response to Roman Catholic modernising tendencies. Following B.M.G. Reardon, he notes similarities between Modernists influenced by the activism of Bergson and the pragmatism of James, and Bultmann's existentialist interpretation. Reardon notes that both Bultmann and the turn-of-the-century Modernists operate in circumstances where traditional expressions of faith cling to 'modes of thought inconsistent with the knowledge and outlook of modern man'.[55] And yet both parties are critics not only of orthodoxy but also of liberalism in its attempt to address the problem. On the one hand, both are sceptical of the dependence of faith on the attempted reconstruction of historical events. On the other hand, both reject the total humanising of the gospel and insist 'that the Risen Christ comes to us' – whether in individual faith or the sacramental life. The philosophy to which the Modernists turn for assistance is akin to (or even an anticipation of) existentialism: 'activism' or pragmatism. Reardon notes the point of similarity with Bultmann's use of Heidegger's self-understanding and authentic existence in the following way. Theology proclaims a truth 'to be found within us, in what we are and what we ought to be'.[56]

The similarity between Bultmann and the Modernists which particularly interests Macquarrie is the way in which, for both, 'the dogmas of Christianity are not statements of objective truth but are to be regarded as symbols which function as rules of action ... [which] commend a particular kind of conduct.'[57] Reardon quotes from Edouard Le Roy's *Dogme et Critique* (1907) words which he applies to Bultmann but which are even more strongly resonant of Braithwaite. Le Roy describes dogma as *'une prescription d'ordre pratique, une règle de conduite pratique'*.[58] So Macquarrie suggests that 'there is not much difference, for instance, between saying that the resurrection is a symbol which enjoins a particular kind of conduct, and saying that it is a myth which is to be understood in its existential significance.'[59]

The issue here is not whether there is *some truth* in the pragmatic approach to christology, but whether such an approach is *adequate*. Certainly, to say that Jesus Christ is Lord is to speak of his significance for faith and to make a commitment to the way of life which is involved. But Macquarrie, with Bultmann's Roman Catholic critics, asks 'is the content of dogma exhausted when we have perceived its pragmatic sense? Is christology nothing more than the explication of Christ's significance for human existence?'[60]

Macquarrie himself argues the importance of maintaining both understandings of dogma: that on the one hand it expresses revealed, objective, supernatural truths, and that on the other it expresses a way of life. Once again, this anticipates his (explicitly) dialectical approach to theology. Here he simply suggests that 'like transcendence and immanence, subjectivity and objectivity, and many other pairs of opposites, it may be that these two views imply each other, and that each needs to be supplemented by the other.'[61]

To illustrate how this might be the case, Macquarrie investigates the dual function of the word 'God' in religious language. On the one hand, following Ritschl, Luther, Melanchthon and, indeed, Paul, Macquarrie notes the use of 'God' as a value-word, indicating supreme value and disclosing an attitude, a commitment. This is the source of existential and pragmatic interpretations of religion. On the other hand, since to declare one's own ideals as of supreme value would be idolatrous, the supreme value which demands commitment is recognised as coming from beyond us: 'It is not simply that we set a supreme value on something and call it God ... the true God is the God who is experienced as standing over against us and demanding that we set value on him. He is independent of us in being not just a subjective ideal or an imaginary focus.'[62] This is the ontological interpretation of religion, and is, for Macquarrie, equiprimordial with the axiological interpretation. To lose either aspect is to lose a fundamental aspect of the meaning of the word 'God'.

In this respect Macquarrie draws attention to Tillich's work on God. Generally he draws explicitly on Tillich's work very little, despite the obvious similarity of concern in maintaining the ontological as well as existential aspects of theology.[63] Here, however, he notes Tillich's two characteristic ways of talking about God. The first of these is 'ultimate concern', which corresponds to the existential/axiological aspect; the second is 'ground of being' (that is, ground of *beings*, of entities, of everything that is) or 'being-itself' which corresponds to the ontological aspect.[64] What Macquarrie finds helpful here is that Tillich draws attention to the ontological dimension without implying thereby that God is '*a* being'. Saying that God is the ground of being is to attribute to him 'more' reality than that of any entity or even of the sum of entities. It is in this *ground* of being that the ontological difference between Being and beings lies for Heidegger. In his essay 'The German Discussion of the Later Heidegger', James M. Robinson notes that in his earlier writings Heidegger denotes Being as *das Sein* and beings as *das Seiende*, but in his later writings he tends to replace *Sein* with *Anwesen*, emphasising that being fundamentally *takes place*, to avoid the confusion of the reifying implications of the *Sein/Seiende* parallel.[65]

Tillich is himself critical of Bultmann's inattention to ontology.[66] Although Macquarrie recognises some transcendent reference in Bultmann's work in his insistence on the kerygma, and suggests that as a disciple of Heidegger he is quite aware of the connection between the existential and the ontological, I have already indicated that Macquarrie seeks more rigour than Bultmann actually offers. Indeed, the scope of Bultmann's ontology remains sufficiently ambiguous that Gareth Jones is able to argue that his theology *is* ontological and not purely existential.

A brief consideration of his argument will provide a helpful way of distinguishing Macquarrie's ontology as concerned with continuity and kinship rather than with confrontation and irruption.

The heart of the matter: confrontation of will or kinship of being?

Jones' argument, in *Bultmann: Towards a Critical Theology*, is that Heidegger's influence on Bultmann is not just on the human existential question, but is primarily on the God question. By this he means that Bultmann draws on the later Heidegger as well as on *Being and Time*, in order to establish 'the event of ontological difference' which undergirds 'Bultmann's own understanding of the kerygmatic Christ as the event in which God encounters the individual, and she encounters – in the moment of decision – her possibilities of existence'.[67]

This is in explicit contrast to Macquarrie's reading of Bultmann. Particularly, Jones rejects the 'folklore' which he claims Macquarrie's reading has (wittingly or unwittingly) established: that Bultmann is merely a religious anthropologist. That is to say, Jones suggests that Macquarrie's comparison of Bultmann's thought with Heidegger's *Being and Time* 'has encouraged the view that Bultmann has merely "borrowed" a specific terminology, a transcendental analysis or deduction of the individual's historical predicament, which he then "marries" to his explicitly religious and Christian understanding of the human context *coram deo*'.[68] In contrast, Jones seeks to establish that the 'philosophical deep structure' of Bultmann's theology is also derived from Heidegger's philosophy, in the 'event theory' which does not appear until after *Being and Time*.

Jones' argument succeeds up to a point. Certainly, Bultmann is not to be regarded as an existentialist on the narrow (and pejorative) interpretation which Jones employs. He refers to an existentialist reading of the New Testament as one 'in which its religious message is reduced to an understanding of the individual's historical predicament, expressed in broadly anthropological and psychological terminology', and of the existentialist 'emphasis on the psychological disposition of the individual'.[69] On this interpretation, it is easy to agree that Bultmann has 'ontological' concerns, in so far as he is interested not in the psychology of individuals, but in the meaning 'of human existence as being-towards-God, either accepted or rejected'.[70] However, it is not necessary to argue that these concerns are derived from Heidegger's later work, since his *intention* in *Being and Time* provides sufficient connection between existential enquiry and ontological concern.

It is in attempting to show that Bultmann's understanding of the event of revelation depends on Heidegger's later work on the revelatory event of Being (*Ereignis*), that Jones' argument falters. Indeed, in part he admits that this is so. He notes that for Bultmann

> the ontological difference *is not, as with Heidegger*, one of Being and being, *Sein* and *Dasein*, but one of Will and will; that is, divine Will and human will. When confronted by the divine Will in Christ, the human will can either accept or reject God. This is of course the meaning of the infinite qualitative distinction, that God's Will is separated from the individual's will until God destroys that distinction by breaking the bounds of death and raising up Christ. It is this act of God's will that confronts the individual's will and that in turn determines that being as authentic or inauthentic existence.[71]

The introduction of the notion of will as fundamental to the ontological difference is of the utmost significance. In the first place, it establishes Bultmann's dependence at this point on Kierkegaard rather than Heidegger. Jones secures the ontological difference in Bultmann as fundamentally confrontational and irruptive, centred on a clash of wills only reconciled in the cross. But this is quite at variance with Heidegger's assertion that 'man is the being whose Being as ek-sistence consists in his dwelling in the nearness of Being. Man is the neighbour of Being.'[72] Further, it provides the clue that Bultmann is dependent on Kierkegaard rather than Heidegger for his understanding of time as, most importantly, the 'moment' in which time and eternity intersect. In the course of Jones' own argument, this is a key grounding for his criticism that Bultmann's theology fails to take account of its socio-political context, despite its apparent emphasis on the ethical imperative. More importantly for my concerns with Macquarrie, it is the ground whereby for Bultmann 'the question of revelation is reduced to the question of what is new each moment.'[73]

This 'new each moment' is the crucial phrase for understanding the distinction Macquarrie makes between his own insistence on the need for ontology and whatever 'ontology' might be claimed for Bultmann. For Bultmann, the theological endeavour is to release the kerygma from inappropriate terminology so that it can address human existence. The ontological event, then, is always the single eschatological event of Jesus Christ which breaks into human life 'new each moment'. For Macquarrie, however, the theological endeavour is concerned equally with the kerygma and with giving an intellectually valid account to establish the continuity between faith and the common experience of human being and knowing.

An example from Jones' treatment will illustrate this point. In his discussion of Heidegger's event of revelation and its significance for Bultmann's thought, Jones discusses Heidegger's use of Leibniz' question, 'Why is there something rather than nothing?' in the lecture 'What is metaphysics?' (1929). Jones' interpretation of Heidegger's meaning is that he is interested in Being as 'that which overcomes Non-Being *by giving meaning*'.[74] This emphasis on giving meaning allows a false step back into the phenomenological analysis of *Dasein* in *Being and Time*, but is precisely the ground for the analogy which Jones draws with Bultmann's thought to indicate his 'ontological' emphasis. He says that Bultmann too, 'as a Christian, wishes to assert an ultimate reality, in this case the Creator God, as the being which overcomes Non-Being in the creative act of self-revelation, the eschatological event of grace, Jesus Christ'.[75] For Bultmann, then, as Jones interprets the matter, non-being is the inauthentic existence of the will opposed to the divine Will, not reconciled in the cross. The event of the ontological difference is the 'new each moment' irruptive act of summons, of Word and Will. However, Heidegger himself is concerned (explicitly and directly by this stage) with Being and nothing, rather than with inauthentic and authentic existence. In 'What is Metaphysics?' he speaks of the *recovery* (rather than the meaning) of beings. Nothing discloses the strangeness of (there being) beings, which arouses and evokes wonder in the context of *Dasein*'s experience of nothing. This is less an irruptive act, than a context of existence by which the question of ultimate reality is raised. As Robinson reminds us, the ontological difference in Heidegger 'is not a separation, as if being were some entity alongside the beings. It is rather their being, seen in itself. Being speaks to us through the beings, by unveiling to us what they are. It is because of their being that beings become the theme of thought.'[76]

It is this wonder at being which Macquarrie draws from Heidegger's later work. What is important to note even at this early stage is that, for Macquarrie, *ontology is fundamentally about continuity*, about *das Sein* as the source and ground of *Dasein* so that to have the awareness of *Dasein* is already to have a glimpse of *das Sein* itself. The ontological difference is not fundamentally 'ethical' as it is if discussed in terms of competing wills, but is precisely *ontological*. Being is ontologically different from being in its capacity to bring into being; being is ontologically different from Being in that it is wholly contingent and participative. This is not, therefore, Kierkegaard's 'infinite qualitative difference' which establishes the event of ontological difference as irruptive and confrontational, but is the ground of the *grace of being.* That is to say, it is the ground of experiencing Being as gracious, as the very source, support and goal of everything which is.

THE CORPORATE CHARACTER OF HUMAN EXISTENCE

The third concern by which Macquarrie distinguishes his thought from a narrower existentialist approach is a concern with the corporate character of human existence. There is some ambiguity as to whether or not existentialism *requires* an individualistic stance. Without doubt, Søren Kierkegaard insists on the primacy of the individual over against the mass or the crowd. He emphasises the aloneness of the individual before God, and the importance of becoming an individual in contrast to an escape into sociality. Accordingly, he desires to separate religion from all group practice and to insist that God speaks to each one individually. Kierkegaard, then, is explicitly 'anti-group', and actively promotes an extreme individualism.[77]

Gabriel Marcel, on the other hand, insists on inter-subjectivity, 'the relationship expressed by the preposition *with*'.[78] He insists that existence is not merely participative (in-the-world, or even with-others-in-the-world) but fundamentally concerns communion. To be a person is to be 'with'. Indeed, Clyde Pax suggests that Marcel's 'whole philosophic task is an effort to reinstate a viable bond between men ... what is given is a re-definition of personal individuality in terms of a structural relationship of one person to another, understood in such a way that this relationship defines, better to say establishes, the uniqueness of myself and thou.'[79]

Certainly it is the case for Heidegger that the human person is never an isolated subject, but is always being-with-others (*Mitsein*) in a shared world (*Mitwelt*). This being-with-others gives the other the character of *Mitdasein*, and the relation of *Dasein* to *Mitdasein* is not *Besorgen*, which is appropriate to entities, but *Fürsorge*, solicitude. However, this account retains an ambiguity, and how truly corporate an understanding it provides will emerge in discussion of Bultmann's dependence on it.

In *An Existentialist Theology*, Macquarrie raises two sets of criticisms against Bultmann's individualism. The first concerns Bultmann's discussion of the characteristics of the life of faith, especially love. The second concerns his inattention to the Church.

Bultmann on love as event

Macquarrie remarks, 'Considering the central importance of love in the New Testament teaching, it is surely rather remarkable that Bultmann seems to have relatively little to say about it in his exposition of that teaching? ... Is it not rather strange that freedom figures much more prominently in his account of the life of faith than does love?'[80] Further, this is revealing because Bultmann's account of freedom is fundamentally individualistic, and dominates his account of the characteristics of faith, overshadowing not only love but also hope and joy.

Bultmann understands freedom as 'nothing else than being open for the genuine future', in contrast to captivity in the engulfing causal network where past decisions wholly determine the present, which characterises life 'according to the flesh'.[81] In parallel with Heidegger's understanding of freedom, for Bultmann too it has a threefold structure. First, freedom is freedom 'from the depersonalised collective body, liberation from the tyranny of the fallen mass of mankind'.[82] It is freedom from law through obedience to God. Bultmann says, 'Christian freedom is *freedom from all human conventions and norms of value* ... The Christian, then, is free from all men, and yet there is a proper subjection of himself as "slave to all".' In practice, then, the individual stands alone but, through obedience to God, submits himself to a certain kind of relation to the rest. Secondly, freedom is, for Bultmann, freedom from fallenness into the controlling power of the world of things, which binds to the past.[83] Thirdly, it is freedom from death because 'in the possibility opened to [the Christian believer] in the resurrection of Christ, he has been brought into life, and since that life is founded upon God, it is eternal.'[84] Freedom is fundamentally *the unity of the self* in openness for the future.

In his account of love, too, Bultmann's understanding is characterised by an event of openness. In particular, Bultmann depends on the notion of grace as event. He deals with the love of God as a parallel to the act of grace, which is the sending of Christ. Grace or love is the *deed* of God, or 'the occurrence which is bestowed upon men as a gift'.[85] In Bultmann's thought this is the event by which God restores to man the possibility of attaining his true being. The nuance that Bultmann gives to love over grace is that 'in *agape* the sentiment is emphasised more', but it is still fundamentally a *deed* rather than a feeling or disposition or stance. Thus, for Bultmann, Paul is concerned with '*agape at work, in action*. When he says in Rom 5:8, "God shows his love for us in that while we were yet sinners Christ died for us", *agape* certainly has, as part of its meaning, the sentiment of love, but

Paul speaks of it only as God "shows" it – by letting Christ die for us.'[86] For Macquarrie this is an inadequate account because 'we usually think of God's love as the *motive* of his act, and the act as the *manifestation* of his love, rather than that the two are one and the same.'[87]

Turning from the love of God to our love of our neighbour, there is an equivalent understanding, of love as an act continually in the present moment by which one helps another to his true being.[88] This is consonant with Heidegger. For Heidegger, an authentic being-with-others recalls them to their true selves: in authentic existence *Dasein* is able 'to let the Others who are with it "be" in their ownmost potentiality-for-Being, and to disclose this potentiality in the solicitude which leaps forth and liberates'.[89] Macquarrie agrees that love cannot be purely emotion, since Christ commands love, and an emotion cannot be produced at will in order to fulfil the command. But he finds Bultmann's account too individualistic, an individualism he deems to be derived from the ambivalence towards the corporate character of life in Heidegger's thought.

For Macquarrie, there is no disagreement that this is an appropriate way to be with others. What he doubts is that this is a sufficient understanding of love. He suggests that it is more akin to *witness*, to 'a proclaiming of the Word, recalling the other to himself through love', if it is the counterpart of being the conscience of the other, in Heidegger's terms. Crucially, however, it gives no account of fellowship or communion, 'a quality of love, a sharing of being or a participation in being' which is founded on communion with God in Christ.[90]

Bultmann on the Church and radical isolation

This absence in Bultmann's understanding of love brings Macquarrie to the second part of his criticism of Bultmann's individualism. In turning his attention to the Church, Macquarrie comments, 'It is surely rather remarkable that in a major work devoted to the exposition of New Testament thought and to the analysis of its concepts, the index of nearly one hundred and fifty Greek terms should omit the word κοινωνία, which might have been supposed to have some importance.'[91] The work to which Macquarrie is referring is Bultmann's *Theologie des Neuen Testaments*. To confirm what this might indicate about a bias to individualism, Macquarrie reviews Bultmann's essay 'Forms of Human Community'.

Bultmann distinguishes four types of community formed by different 'forces', but in each the individual self is the pre-supposition of genuine community: 'The will to be oneself is the presupposition of real community – for only men who are "persons", that is, who are each one of them their selves, can be in a real community.'[92] Without this truly personal dimension, depersonalising processes render the community inauthentic: *das Man*, again. Bultmann argues that, if it is the case that 'true community can only exist between men who are individuals, who are themselves', then true community is ultimately rooted in religion. It is only in the life of faith that we are given our true self in the encounter with God. However, this gives rise to a contradiction: 'Community with God ... first of all tears man out of every human community and places him in a radical *loneliness* before God ... The way to God, in fact, means *withdrawal from the world*.'[93]

The 'community of the called', the *ecclesia*, is then the community 'in which are linked together those who have heard the Word with a believing ear and pass it on as they confess it'. It is fundamentally *event*, constantly at risk from its institutional organisation and from its tendency to transmute faith into dogma. The community of the Church reaches out as the 'community of love' 'which embraces all men, in an effort to capture their hearts'.[94] Once again, this is not an emotion or an attitude, but a *deed*. The revelation of God, which 'is simply the love which confronts man, liberating him for himself in saving him from himself', liberates him for his neighbour presumably only by liberating him from his neighbour.

Two anxieties can be expressed, which anticipate Macquarrie's criticism. The first is that Bultmann's view of community is fundamentally individualistic. Individuals join a community as it were one by one, from the context of the event of radical isolation before God, and this isolation provides the essential content of the community and its relation to others beyond its boundaries. The second anxiety is that the content of isolation before God consists in withdrawal from the world, from self-sufficiency and all human attempt at community. As Bultmann recognises, this gives the Christian common cause with those engaged in equivalent nihilism, both humanistic and atheistic. However, as the groundwork for an understanding of the Church, it raises the question of the identification of the distinctiveness of Christian community beyond the 'understanding' of the event of radical isolation.

These anxieties are borne out when Macquarrie considers what Bultmann does say about the Church in *Theology of the New Testament*. Fundamentally, the Church is an eschatological congregation, in existence because its members have been encountered by the eschatological event. Its task is to preach the eschatological kerygma, and organisational structures arise to further this end. From the eschatological congregation as the centre 'there develops a secular faith-determined community of living in which there is mutual obligation and mutual service: "assistances" and "administrations", the functions of "presiding" (προίστασθαι), "laboring" (κοπιᾶν), and "ministering" (διακονεῖν) in various forms.'[95] The corporate character of the Church is, on this understanding, wholly secondary to the summons of individuals in radical isolation before God, and their subsequent inclusion in a congregation.

As well as this understanding of the Church, which Macquarrie deems utilitarian, Bultmann comments on the notion of σῶμα Χριστοῦ. For Bultmann, this is derived from Gnostic origins, and is employed for those of non-Jewish background who would not naturally identify the Church as the new Israel. The Church is, in this sense, *cosmic*. Christ already exists as a cosmic figure prior to and apart from the Church, and the individuals belong to him: 'It is not the members that constitute the body, but Christ. Christ is there, not through and in the members, but before they are there and above them.'[96] Macquarrie notes an inconsistency between Bultmann's use of σῶμα here as unworldly, and his earlier use of σῶμα as *Dasein*'s way of being by virtue of which he is being-in-a-world. Further, this 'cosmic' use of σῶμα removes from it any organic, corporate reference it might otherwise have. Bultmann suggests that the Church as σῶμα means for Paul 'not that several members of the body, being various, constitute the whole and therefore, in their variety, are equally important for the body. His main thought is, rather, that the members are equal because they belong to Christ, and therefore their differences are unimportant.'[97]

Again, Macquarrie raises the question, 'Is it really adequate to say that the unity of the body of Christ arises from the fact that worldly differences have ceased to mean anything for the believers?'[98] He agrees that concern for worldly things and for self-sufficiency creates divisions, and that the surrender of these in faith heals divisions and enables unity. But it is this *negative* definition alone of the body of Christ that Macquarrie finds inadequate, because it fails to distinguish it from any other group who have turned away from worldly concerns and are free for genuine relationship with each other. He notes that, 'as Bultmann defines it, the body of Christ has nothing specifically Christian about it ... Surely we are entitled to ask for a more positive conception of the unity of fellowship and love in the Christian community than we find in Bultmann's theology?'[99]

I shall consider the developments in Macquarrie's own theology with regard to the corporate nature of faith in Chapter 3. For now, I shall simply note the difficulties he raises in achieving a balance between individualism and community in the Christian life, which form a context for his own modifications of the emphasis on the individual in narrower existentialist approaches.

First, Macquarrie notes the danger that the Church tends to usurp what rightly belongs to the individual. So, for example, although the Church is intended to proclaim the Word and bring the individual to the moment of decision, it has at times taken away the possibility of decision by presenting the gospel as a 'tradition to be unthinkingly accepted'. Similarly, the Church may transform the existential aspect of faith into a set of dogmas to which assent must be given, and thereby 'take away from the individual the new understanding of himself in faith'.[100] Secondly, Macquarrie notes that the Church *as an organisation* tends to approximate to the pattern of *das Man*. With the need for government, administration, property ownership and relation to other associations, an element of depersonalisation emerges. With a clear echo of Reinhold Niebuhr, Macquarrie notes that, 'just as the Christian individual is exposed to temptation as long as he is in the flesh, so is the church as long as it is in the world, and it appears that the collective body is always more vulnerable than the individual.'[101]

Despite these dangers, Macquarrie insists that an organic view of the Church must be upheld alongside a utilitarian view, and that community must be upheld alongside individualism. Although Bultmann is right in thinking of the Church as consisting in individuals for whom earthly distinctions have ceased to matter, it is also the case that it is in relation to others that the faith of the individual reaches concrete expression. This relation is not merely that of social contract, but needs to give some account of sharing in being – with one another and with Christ.

AN INTERIM REVIEW AND A GLANCE AT SOME FORMATIVE INFLUENCES

I have sought to show in this chapter that Macquarrie makes three specific limitations in his own use of existentialist theology, and that these are of key significance for the ways in which his work subsequently develops.

First, although Macquarrie insists on the kerygmatic summons and its existential significance, he focuses the way in which the kerygma is to be understood by two markers. The first, contrary to Jaspers and Buri, is that the kerygma *comes from beyond* human existence. However much Macquarrie affirms that being is itself grace-full ('existence as grace' in Buri's terms), he maintains that this gift is an act from beyond human existence, and not a given within existence. This does not mean that it is alien to human existence, however, because it fulfils the existential possibilities of human being. The second focus Macquarrie insists on with regard to the kerygma is that the life to which it summons has been exhibited as a genuine possibility under the *existentiell* conditions of human living. That is to say, his insistence on a *minimal core of historical factuality* is grounded in the need to establish that the summons is relevant precisely because it is possible.

Secondly, Macquarrie introduces a heightened concern with ontology. He argues, contrary to Braithwaite and other pragmatists, that commitment to a way of life discloses a belief about 'how things are'. In relation to his insistence on the kerygma it is important to note, further, that his understanding of ontology points to a *continuity* of being. The ontological difference does not lie in a confrontation of wills but in the capacity to confer being. Whilst still a dynamic, temporal model of ontology, it is not solely dependent on the continually new *moment* of confrontation, but allows for an element of continuity within the temporality of being.

Thirdly, Macquarrie begins to articulate a more participative understanding of being-with than that generally provided by existentialist thought. Rejecting the utilitarian and almost contractual position of the social in Bultmann's thought, Macquarrie already raises questions about an organic understanding of unity in Christ and about a love which is not merely instrumental but which arises out of a shared being.

What is significant about these modifications is that they establish very early in Macquarrie's work a commitment *both to the gift of God* which has the initiative, confers being, summons into possibility, *and to the context of kinship* between God and human being, between human being and human being, and between human being and the nature of the world. From this mediation between kerygmatic act and the affinity of being, Macquarrie's *grace of being* moves in concentric circles from an early (moderated) concern with the individual person to a concern with the corporate and public, to an emphasis on the cosmos.

The question arises, what is the source of this departure in Macquarrie's thought from narrow existentialist concerns, particularly with regard to the emphasis on ontology which grounds the theme of continuity and kinship? It may be that reference to the experience of the community and tradition of the Christian faith is alone enough to account for his desire to maintain an ontological dimension. Just as Bultmann tries to include within his demythologising programme the use of analogical language of God's acts, so Macquarrie seeks to be true to the Christian experience of God: whilst we can only speak of God as he 'speaks' to us in our being, we must nevertheless recognise him as being beyond us, the transcendent God who calls us to our authentic possibilities. This insistence on the integrity between theology and lived Christian experience finds precedent in Schleiermacher's understanding that 'Christian doctrines are accounts of the Christian religious affections set forth in speech.'[102] It is also a significant anticipation of the current emphasis in the resourcing of Western theology from the eastern tradition. Thus Mark McIntosh affirms that 'when theology is divorced from spirituality it is likely to begin talking about a different god, a deity who depends on theological performance for vitality and verisimilitude.' Like Schleiermacher, McIntosh is concerned fundamentally with the *communal* nature of the encounter with God.[103]

However, a network of other influences is suggested. The particular content and shape of Macquarrie's ontology points also to the influence of the later work of Heidegger. In turn, Macquarrie's receptivity to the later Heidegger is suggested by his earlier interest in F.H. Bradley. And, yet further back, his own Celtic roots suggest a receptivity to Bradley which would otherwise be surprising in the context of his own stark Protestant upbringing. All of these themes will emerge in various forms subsequently; I shall note them only in brief now.

The later Heidegger

Opinion is divided as to whether Heidegger's later work represents a fundamental shift away from his early intentions, or whether the 'turning' (*Kehre*) from man's existence to Being itself is simply a 'working out of a dialectic that belongs to the very nature of Heidegger's problematic and of which he has been more or less aware from the beginning'.[104] The latter view is Macquarrie's, and in his article 'Heidegger's Earlier and Later Work Compared' he argues for the unity of Heidegger's thought on existence and Being on three counts.

First, Heidegger is himself explicit that the object of his search in *Being and Time* is Being itself. Thus, although *Being and Time* consists of an analysis of human existence as being-in-the-world and the later writings refer enigmatically to Being, Heidegger is explicit that the former was intended to open the way to a study of the latter. Later writings emphasise the continuity; in 'Letter on Humanism' Heidegger suggests that the final part of *Being and Time*, which was 'held back', is now being approached.[105] Secondly, man is not the 'measure of things' in *Being and Time*, as he is in Sartre's humanism, for example. He is the theme of Heidegger's analytic 'only to the extent that he is the ontological being, the one who, in virtue of the very being that is his, raises the question of Being'. At no point is Heidegger interested in philosophical anthropology for its own sake. Thirdly, Heidegger's thought exhibits a kind of hermeneutic circle: 'In order to open up the question of being, it is proposed to explicate in its being that particular being which inquires about Being.' In the earlier and later works taken together this allows for 'a dialectic that moves from existence toward Being and then from Being toward existence, but that is governed throughout by the single question of Being'.[106]

Macquarrie draws attention to various shifts within this unified project, which distinguish the earlier and later periods. First, a shift occurs from analytic, calculative thinking to 'primordial' or 'essential' thinking. Although the analysis of *Dasein* in *Being and Time* is not objectifying, it is 'scientific' in so far as it provides an ordered, investigative account. Later writings become poetic and mystical. James Robinson identifies the emergence of this turn in the essays 'The Origin of the Work of Art' (1935) and 'Hölderlin and the Essence of Poetry' (1936). Thus, for example, in 'The Origin of the Work of Art' Heidegger writes 'In a world's worlding is gathered that spaciousness out of which the protective grace of the gods is granted or withheld.'[107]

Whereas calculative thinking is active, primordial thinking is *receptive*. Heidegger says, 'thinking is the thinking of Being. The genitive says something twofold. Thinking is of Being inasmuch as thinking, propriated by Being, belongs to Being. At the same time thinking is of being insofar as thinking, belonging to Being, listens to Being.'[108] Being claims man, and unveils itself; man steps back behind the realm of opinions and viewpoints, into the realm where he is *encountered* by thought.

This points to a second related shift, in the meaning of 'world'. In *Being and Time*, *Dasein* is in-a-world and exists by projecting – and thus expanding – that world. In the later writings, *Dasein* exists by 'standing out' into Being. The world is now this openness for Being, or, in Heidegger's lyrical expression, 'the self-opening openness of the broad paths of the simple and essential decisions in the destiny of a historical people'. Later, the 'world' becomes the openness *of* Being, 'the clearing of Being into which man stands out on the basis of his thrown essence'.[109] The world is no longer *Dasein*'s instrumental matrix, but transcends his interests and reveals itself to him.

There are, then, in Macquarrie's work resonances with Heidegger's total project. There is a confidence (subsequently abandoned by Heidegger) that an exploration of human existence will point towards the *transcendens*, but also a recognition that the *transcendens* lies beyond worldly or human categories and must take the initiative in some kind of revelation if it is to be known. This appears in Macquarrie's own dialectic between a God independent of man who nevertheless 'speaks' and is known only in so far as he addresses man in his existence. For Macquarrie, as for Heidegger, the failure of traditional metaphysics indicates that to begin the search for Being only with an objective analysis of particular beings (whether man or nature) is inadequate. Such an attempt must be continually balanced, not only by a phenomenological analysis of human existence, but also by a more primordial receptivity to the gift-like character of the ground of existence itself.

The 'world', in the sense of being-in-a-context, remains an important theme in Macquarrie's work. Throughout his writings, he emphasises the responsibility of human being, from the instrumentality of existentialist understanding to the role as 'microcosm and mediator' which emerges in his later work. It is significant that increasingly Macquarrie overcomes the dualism between human being and nature inherent in existentialism. He moves away from the transcendence of human being *over* the world, to a position in which human being is the transcendence *of* the world. This echoes Heidegger's own shift from *Dasein*'s instrumentality to the world as the clearing in which Being discloses itself to *Dasein* as the guardian of Being.

In 'Heidegger's Earlier and Later Work Compared', Macquarrie suggests that 'the most fruitful theological application of Heidegger's teaching is still the work of Bultmann in his theories about the demythologizing and existential interpretation of the Bible.'[110] Certainly, in his own early writings, Macquarrie is more dependent on *Being and Time* than on Heidegger's later works, and the use of the later Heidegger for hermeneutics never becomes a significant part of Macquarrie's programme. What gives Macquarrie the openness to develop beyond Bultmann's use of *Being and Time*, then, to draw on the more explicitly ontological concerns of the later Heidegger? It may well be that the thought of F.H. Bradley exerts an influence.

F.H. Bradley

In his article 'Pilgrimage in Theology', Macquarrie notes the attraction which Bradley's thought held for him during his undergraduate studies in philosophy. He was 'bowled over' by his *Principles of Logic*, and subsequently *Appearance and Reality* was for several years his 'Bible'.[111] In *An Existentialist Theology*, however, Macquarrie is critical of Bradley, explicitly in contrast to Bultmann:

> [Bradley] is poles apart from Bultmann's position. The idealist identifies the essence of Christianity with a high philosophy of the universe, but for Bultmann Christianity is a religion with saving power. For the idealist the mighty acts become mere optional symbols of supra-rational truth, but for Bultmann they constitute God's unique act of grace. For the idealist the significance of these acts for the individual is a purely intellectual one, but for Bultmann they summon to a decision.[112]

Indeed, he notes in 'Pilgrimage in Theology' that it was his studies of Bultmann that brought him closer to reconciling religious faith with intellectual integrity than had proved possible while he was immersed in Bradley's philosophy. Certainly, he consistently rejects aspects of Bradley's Idealism, for example, the portrayal of Christianity as a universal and timeless truth. Nevertheless, he admits to Bradley's influence on the first edition of *Principles of Christian Theology*: 'perhaps Bradley's suprarational Absolute was still lurking there in the new guise of Heidegger's Being.'[113] It may be, then, that this earlier interest in Bradley fostered his openness to Heidegger's later thought, for although Bradley's ultimate position is not congenial to Heidegger's work, there are a number of points of similarity.

For Bradley, as for Heidegger, the fundamental form of knowledge is not analytic but is based in feeling. He notes that (discursive) thought must be absorbed into a fuller experience, to embrace feeling and will.[114] Analytic thought is valuable for its given purpose, but is derivative from primordial knowledge. For Bradley, primordial knowledge is prior to the awareness of the subject/object distinction, and discloses the understanding that Reality is One. Compare Heidegger's disclosure of being-in-the-world as prior to the contribution of experience. In each case, intuition discloses a whole prior to the analytical distinguishing of parts in themselves.

For both Bradley and Heidegger, though for different reasons, entities only have their meaning from their reference to other things. For Heidegger this means the instrumental system with which *Dasein* orders its world, and for Bradley it means the theory of internal relations by which the independence of things, though they may appear to be diverse and discrete, is denied since 'only the whole is real.' Compare, for example, 'The identity of a thing lies in the view which you take of it' and *Dasein*'s forming of his own world of tools.[115]

For Macquarrie, following Heidegger, the question of whether God 'exists' involves a category mistake, since Being is not an entity, and it is more appropriate to ask 'whether Being has such a character as would fulfil man's quest for grace'.[116] Similarly, on the analogy of authentic human selfhood, Being might be said to gather up all time into a vaster unity.[117] These notions bear a similarity to Bradley's contention that the Absolute is not an entity and does not have properties, but gathers up into a unity and into fulfilment all 'appearances' of reality. Neither Being nor the Absolute 'are' apart from particular beings/appearances, and there are different degrees of existence or reality according to the degree of participation in Being/the Absolute. W.H. Walsh explains:

> To speak of the Absolute is not to draw our attention to a new entity, occupying a region somewhere beyond the range of sense-experience; it is rather to urge on us a certain way of looking at familiar facts. The particular things and events of everyday life, though not illusory, are nonetheless misconceived if taken as fully real; to comprehend them properly we need to see each of them in a different light. We need to take every allegedly separate element in the world as a fragment from a wider context, every apparent reality as part of a wider reality within which it evidently falls.[118]

Celtic roots

One final influence on Macquarrie's early thought can be noted here, which may give account of how it was that a student from a Calvinist background took so readily to the philosophy of F.H. Bradley. In *On Being a Theologian* Macquarrie writes, 'When I reflect on my life and how I have grown from childhood to manhood, I begin by taking full cognizance of my ethnic background. Not just my own family or the people of my hometown but of the Celtic peoples themselves. I am a Scot, and the product of hundreds of years of Scottish pride and Scottish culture.'[119]

Of particular significance in the theological heritage of these Celtic roots is, for Macquarrie 'the profound sense of the immanence of God in the world ... They remained very much aware of a divine presence in all nature, and it is this sense of an all-pervading presence that is characteristic of their Christian piety.'[120] Macquarrie's Celtic roots emerge explicitly in *In Search of Deity*, when he draws on the work of John Scotus Eriugena (810–77), who provides a theological basis for the Celtic immanentist spirituality.[121] But even in this early period of his writings, the sense of the immanent presence of the transcendent, Other God is a clear feature of Macquarrie's theology. Eriugena's inclusive concept of nature, which undergirds his *De Naturae Divisione*, in which nature embraces both God and the creatures, has a resonance in Bradley's Absolute. And the notion that God is in all things and the essence of all things, such that the whole world might be a theophany, is resonant with Heidegger's work on existence and Being.

NOTES

1. *ET* 242–43
2. *SCE* 99
3. John Macquarrie, *The Scope of Demythologizing* (London: SCM 1960), hereafter *SD*, 227.
4. Rudolf Bultmann, 'New Testament and Mythology' in ed. Hans-Werner Bartsch *Kerygma and Myth* vols. 1 & 2 combined (London: SPCK 1972), 1–44, 13.
5. H. Thielicke, 'Reflections on Bultmann's Hermeneutic I', *Expository Times* 67 (1956), 154–56, 156; italics are Thielicke's.
6. Thielicke, 156.
7. H.P. Owen, *Revelation and Existence* (Cardiff: University of Wales Press 1957), 105.
8. *SD* 227
9. *SD* 225
10. *SD* 228–29
11. Reinhold Niebuhr, *The Nature and Destiny of Man* vol. 1 (London: Nisbet 1941), 201.
12. 'New Testament and Mythology' 30.
13. *SD* 235. Compare Helmut Thielicke's 'Reflections on Bultmann's Hermeneutic', *Expository Times* 67 (1956), 154–57 and 175–77.
14. In *In Search of Humanity* (London: SCM 1982), hereafter *ISH*, Macquarrie returns to the role of conscience in summoning to authentic possibility. Even then, his use does not oppose the call of conscience to the kerygmatic summons, and is not inconsistent with Pauline use. Paul appears to draw the term from slogans in the Corinthian church about food sacrificed to idols, and turns the word to his own use; 1 Corinthians 8:7–13; 10:25–30. Paul's use does not mirror the prevailing Greek notion of evaluative self-reflection, or the Old Testament emphasis on obedient listening to God, but refers to the unity of an act and the awareness of it grounded in the inner law of Christ.
15. *SD* 150
16. Karl Barth, 'Bultmann – an attempt to understand him' in ed. Hans-Werner Bartsch *Kerygma and Myth* (London: SPCK 1972), 83–132, 130.

17 See, for example, Fritz Buri, *Theology of Existence* (Greenwood: The Attic Press 1965), 21.
18 'New Testament and Mythology' 22, 27. This is a fine example of Bultmann's vulnerability to double criticisms: Buri is critical that Bultmann retains an *act* of grace, but more conservative theologians question whether this act amounts to more than a new self-understanding.
19 *SD* 145
20 *SD* 143–44, and see 'New Testament and Mythology' 26.
21 *SD* 144–45
22 *SD* 149–50; Macquarrie designates this the recognition of 'Christ for us' as well as 'Christ in us'.
23 *SD* 19, 20
24 *SD* 224
25 These principles are that: (i) historical reflection has for its subject-matter human existence in the world, (ii) in historical reflection, the reflecting subject participates in a particular way in the object of his reflection, (iii) the function of historical reflection is to provide a self-understanding, and (iv) historical reflection is concerned primarily with possibility. See *SD* 81–89.
26 *SD* 89–90
27 *SD* 89, and see *BT* 436, 437.
28 *ET* 178
29 *SD* 90, italics are Macquarrie's.
30 *SCE* 146. In *Christ without Myth* (New York: Harper and Row 1961), Schubert Ogden wilfully narrows Macquarrie's principle into inappropriate specifics. Thus he suggests that a research team searching for a cure for cancer cannot be driven by the assurance that they are repeating a possibility; or that the fact that poems of the stature of Homer's have in fact been written does not mean that *I* can be assured of repeating the possibility, 179. However, Macquarrie's point is that a historical instance points to a repeatable *possibility* within different factical particulars, not that the instance itself is to be *replicated*.
31 *SCE* 147. As James Robinson recognises, the 'emphasis in the kerygma upon the historicity of Jesus is existentially indispensable, precisely because the kerygma, while freeing us from a life "according to the flesh", proclaims the meaningfulness of life "in the flesh".' *A New Quest of the Historical Jesus* (London: SCM 1959), hereafter *A New Quest*, 88.
32 *SCE* 149
33 *SD* 93, *SCE* 149
34 *SD* 101
35 *SCE* 148
36 John Macquarrie, 'Philosophy and Theology in Bultmann's Thought' in ed. Charles W. Kegley *The Theology of Rudolf Bultmann* (London: SCM 1966), 141.
37 Rudolf Bultmann, 'The Primitive Christian Kerygma and the Historical Jesus' in eds Carl E. Braaten and Roy A. Harrisville *The Historical Jesus and the Kerygmatic Christ* (New York: Abingdon Press 1964), 15–42; hereafter, 'Primitive Christian Kerygma'. This is a valuable point of reference because it is a late essay, delivered when the 'post-Bultmannian' new quest is under way.
38 'Primitive Christian Kerygma' 17
39 'Primitive Christian Kerygma' 18
40 'Primitive Christian Kerygma' 21, 28

41 'Primitive Christian Kerygma' 22. A certain amount emerges in Bultmann's account: 'Characteristic for him are exorcisms, the breach of the Sabbath commandment, the abandonment of ritual purifications, polemic against Jewish legalism, fellowship with outcasts such as publicans and harlots, sympathy for women and children; it can also be seen that Jesus was not an ascetic like John the Baptist, but gladly ate and drank a glass of wine. Perhaps we may add that he called disciples and assembled about himself a small company of followers – men and women', 22–23. Additionally, Bultmann is prepared to ascribe to Jesus a 'prophetic consciousness'.
42 'Primitive Christian Kerygma' 24–25. The particular implications of the adjective 'messianic' need not delay us here; at stake is the general issue of Jesus' ministry constituting a divine summons.
43 *ET* 180. Compare Robinson, *A New Quest*, 'the *kerygma* is decidedly an evaluation of the historical person', 90.
44 *SCE* 175
45 *SCE* 170–80; *SD* 102–28, especially 119ff.
46 R.B. Braithwaite, *An Empiricist's View of the Nature of Religious Belief* (Cambridge: Cambridge University Press 1955), 34. In *SCE* 'agapeistic' is rendered by Macquarrie 'agapastic', a use I shall follow for simplicity in quoting Macquarrie.
47 *SCE* 173
48 Braithwaite, 19
49 *SCE* 174. The significance here is that Braithwaite's interpretation is simply inadequate to the described religious experience.
50 *SCE* 175, 176
51 *SCE* 176, and see James 2:19.
52 *SCE* 177
53 *SCE* 177–78
54 *SCE* 178, italics are Macquarrie's.
55 B.M.G. Reardon, 'Demythologizing and Catholic Modernism', *Theology* 59 (1956), 448
56 Reardon, 449. Macquarrie points to a history of pragmatism in the Protestant tradition as well. So, for example, Ritschl regards a christological statement to be a value-judgement, and Melanchthon teaches that 'to know Christ is to know his benefits, not ... to contemplate his natures.'
57 *SD* 116
58 Reardon, 449
59 *SD* 116. It is interesting to note, however, that Gareth Jones, in *Bultmann: Towards a Critical Theology* (Cambridge: Polity Press 1991) is critical of the failure of Bultmann's theology to issue in socio-political engagement. Jones argues that although it may commend a certain conduct, it fails to ground such conduct in concrete reality because of its over-emphasis on event and novelty, 203–4.
60 *SD* 118. L. Malevez is one of the Roman Catholic critics of Bultmann cited by Macquarrie. He deems Bultmann's theology so reduced 'that the first charge the Christian will bring against Bultmann is that he has taken away his Lord', *The Christian Message and Myth* (London: SCM 1958), 123–24, 117.
61 *SD* 120
62 *SD* 125
63 Largely this is because he deems Tillich to have drawn significantly on Heidegger, and Macquarrie turns directly to this source himself.

64 See, for example, Paul Tillich, *Systematic Theology* vol. 1 (Chicago: University of Chicago Press 1951), 10–14, 155ff, 164, 172–73 *et passim*.
65 James M. Robinson, 'The German Discussion of the Later Heidegger' in eds James M. Robinson and John B. Cobb *New Frontiers in Theology vol. 1: The Later Heidegger and Theology* (New York: Harper & Row 1963), 22. For Macquarrie, increasingly the distinction between Being and beings is expressed as Being *lets-be* being, pouring itself out to confer being; see, for example, *PCT* 114.
66 See, for example, Paul Tillich, *Systematic Theology* vol. 2 (Chicago: University of Chicago Press 1957), 106.
67 Gareth Jones, *Bultmann: Towards a Critical Theology* (Cambridge: Polity Press 1991), 8.
68 Jones, 4
69 Jones, 1, 78; clearly, he is not taking account of being-in-the-world and the cognitive content of reference to the *Gestalt* which feeling contains.
70 Jones, 64
71 Jones, 70, italics are mine.
72 Martin Heidegger, 'Letter on Humanism' in *Basic Writings: Martin Heidegger* ed. David Farrell Krell (London: Routledge 1993), 245.
73 Jones, 202
74 Jones, 108, italics are mine.
75 Jones, 109
76 James M. Robinson, 'The German Discussion' in *The Later Heidegger and Theology* eds James M. Robinson and John B. Cobb (New York: Harper & Row 1963), 25.
77 'Anti-group' is Frederick Sontag's expression, *A Kierkegaard Reader* (Atlanta: John Knox Press 1979), 55.
78 Gabriel Marcel, *Mystery of Being* vol. 1 (London: The Harvill Press 1950), 177.
79 Clyde Pax, *An Existential Approach to God* (The Hague: Martinus Nijhoff 1972), 38–39. This is very much more in sympathy with current approaches than is Kierkegaard's. Compare, for example, Paul Ricoeur, *Oneself as Another* (London: University of Chicago Press 1992); Wolfhart Pannenberg, *Systematic Theology* vol. 2 (Edinburgh: T&T Clark 1994).
80 *ET* 211
81 Rudolf Bultmann, *TNT* vol. 1, 335. Compare the exodus paradigm of *freedom for*, see for example J. Severino Croatto, *Exodus: A Hermeneutics of Freedom* (Maryland: Orbis 1981).
82 *ET* 207; in *Being and Time* this collective body is *das Man*.
83 *TNT* 343, 334, italics are Bultmann's.
84 *ET* 209. For Heidegger, freedom is freedom *for* death as the unifying factor in human existence. For Bultmann, this unifying factor is the eschatological decision for Christ, and death operates as part of 'fallenness'.
85 *TNT* 290
86 *TNT* 292; italics are Bultmann's.
87 *ET* 211; italics are mine.
88 Rudolf Bultmann, 'To Love Your Neighbour', *Scottish Periodical* (1947), 42–56.
89 *BT* 344
90 *ET* 213, 214

91 *ET* 215
92 Rudolf Bultmann, 'Forms of Human Community' in *Essays: Philosophical and Theological* (London: SCM 1955), 291–304, 293.
93 'Forms of Human Community' 301, italics are Bultmann's. Bultmann quotes Luke 14:26 in support of his argument: 'Whoever comes to me and does not hate his mother and father ... cannot be my disciple.'
94 'Forms of Human Community' 303
95 *TNT* 309
96 *TNT* 310
97 *TNT* 310. Thus, for example, he understands 1 Cor 1:12.
98 *ET* 220
99 *ET* 220
100 *ET* 221, 222
101 *ET* 223. Compare Reinhold Niebuhr, *Moral Man, Immoral Society* (London: Scribner's Sons 1942), 107.
102 Friedrich Schleiermacher, *The Christian Faith* (Edinburgh: T&T Clark 1989), 76.
103 Mark McIntosh, *Mystical Theology: The Integrity of Spirituality and Theology* (Oxford: Blackwell 1998).
104 'Heidegger's Earlier and Later Work Compared', *Anglican Theological Review* 49 (1967), 3–16, 6. This is Heidegger's own view, see 'Letter on Humanism' in *Basic Writings*, 217–65, 231–32.
105 'Letter on Humanism', 231
106 'Heidegger's Earlier and Later Work Compared' 10, 11
107 Martin Heidegger, 'The Origin of the Work of Art' in *Basic Writings*, 143–212, 170.
108 'The Origin of the Work of Art' 220
109 'The Origin of the Work of Art' 174; 'Letter on Humanism' 252
110 'Heidegger's Earlier and Later Work Compared' 6–7
111 John Macquarrie, 'Pilgrimage in Theology' in eds Alistair Kee and Eugene Thomas Long *Being and Truth* (London: SCM 1986), xi–xviii, xii. Indeed, *Principles of Christian Theology* was titled in reference to Bradley's *Principles of Logic*.
112 *ET* 191
113 'Pilgrimage in Theology' xv
114 F.H. Bradley, *Appearance and Reality* (Oxford: Clarendon Press 1930), 151.
115 *Appearance and Reality*, 63
116 *SCE* 12
117 *SCE* 76
118 W.H. Walsh, 'F.H. Bradley' in *A Critical History of Western Philosophy* ed. D.J. O'Connor (New York: Free Press of Glencoe 1964), 426–36, 430.
119 *On Being a Theologian* ed. John Morgan (London: SCM 1999), 11. This is not laying claim to the current romanticised fashion for the Celtic; Macquarrie's grandparents were native Gaelic speakers from Islay.
120 John Macquarrie, 'Celtic Spirituality' in ed. Gordon Wakefield, *A Dictionary of Christian Spirituality* (London: SCM 1983), 83–84, 83.
121 A variant spelling is Eriguena. Macquarrie admits, 'Although I would like to claim him for Scotland, he was probably Irish!' *Macquarrie on Macquarrie* conference, 1998.

Chapter 3

Into the Public Domain

INTRODUCTION: INTO THE PUBLIC DOMAIN

In Chapters 1 and 2, I have explored Macquarrie's 'existentialist phase' while at Glasgow (1953–62), in terms of his use of Heidegger's *Being and Time* and Bultmann's existentialist theology, and in terms of the modifications and limitations which Macquarrie imposes to broaden his own work beyond narrow existentialism. I have shown that Macquarrie finds aspects of existentialist thought useful for his theological task. I have also shown that he imposes certain limits on the appropriateness of existentialist thought for theology. In particular, he is concerned to safeguard (1) the kerygma against exaggerated humanising and subjectivising tendencies; (2) the ontological reference of religious language against one-sided conative interpretations, and its meaning as fundamentally concerned with the kinship of being rather than the confrontation of will, and (3) the corporate character of human being and faith against exaggerated individualising tendencies. These three themes (kerygma, ontology and the corporate character of human being) are developed under particular influences during Macquarrie's years in America (1962–70) and become key elements of Macquarrie's distinctive theology.

In Chapters 3 and 4 I shall be concerned with these developments. I shall seek to show that Macquarrie's work in his American period is not only an explicit consolidation of concerns which were emerging during his 'existentialist phase', but is also of great significance for the mature thought of the Oxford period (1970–86) which will be the subject of later chapters. In particular, I shall seek to show how the American period provides a link between the typically individualistic and anthropocentric character of existentialism (albeit resisted by Macquarrie even in his self-identified 'existentialist phase'), and the corporate, cosmic emphases of Macquarrie's Oxford period. What account can be given of this move to increasing personal, ecclesial and cosmic relationality? In Chapter 4 I shall examine the way in which Macquarrie's ontological concerns emerge in the existential-ontological method of *Principles of Christian Theology*. First, however, in this chapter I shall examine some of the ways in which concerns with the kerygma and the corporate character of human being take particular shape in the context of dialogue with John Knox.

I shall begin by revisiting the criticisms made by Robert Gundry about Bultmann's understanding of σῶμα (which I discussed in Chapter 1), and Gareth Jones' criticism that Bultmann's theology fails to issue in socio-political engagement (to which I referred in Chapter 2). I shall seek to show that developments in Macquarrie's theology in America safeguard his theology from the heart of these criticisms, and, by moving to a more corporate and relational model of faith and being, lay the foundations for his mature thought with its concerns not only with intelligibility, nor indeed with ethics and religious studies, but more significantly with the nature of *human being as the transcendence of the cosmos*.

I noted in Chapter 1 that Gundry's criticisms of Bultmann's interpretation of σῶμα become particularly trenchant when he draws attention to the dualism between substance and decision which it supports. By diminishing the physical reference of σῶμα, Bultmann devalues precisely that realm where existential decision and responsibility can be exercised, the sensory environment. And, correspondingly, he devalues precisely the means by which that responsibility is carried out, the physical body.[1] Although his argument arises from different concerns to Gundry's, Jones makes a similar criticism of Bultmann's work. For Jones, it is Bultmann's insistence on the 'eternal nature of the moment of decision', and the release from all worldly conditions in order to be open in the moment which results in his inability to articulate the meaning of faith in specified socio-political practice in the public domain.[2] Jones' ultimate assessment of Bultmann's theology is that it 'simply floats away' from the everyday world, that is to say, from the social, economic and material realm. Even the corporate life of the Church cannot be of help; encounter and decision do not accumulate into patterns of behaviour, and the individual 'cannot ascertain any concrete form of behaviour from her predecessors in the historical churches of the Christian religion'.[3]

What these criticisms have in common is that although existentialism calls the individual to responsibility as being-in-a-world, it fails in Bultmann's theology to ground this in practical responsibility in the shared public domain. As Gundry insists, 'From the Biblical perspective, the material world, including the physical part of ourselves, does not so much limit our freedom to decide for the future as provide an opportunity to carry out our decisions in concrete fashion.'[4] Jones correctly points out that Bultmann's fundamentally Lutheran stance with regard to the gospel holds him captive in the 'iron grip' of the *sola fide*. Thus, although Bultmann would not deny the importance of good works, 'they nevertheless have no significance for his understanding of grace.'[5]

This reminder of Bultmann's Lutheranism points to the fundamental difference between Bultmann's motivation and that of Macquarrie. Bultmann's theological programme is directed to the end that modern man must *hear* the gospel, that the disjunction between the biblical accounts and the modern world should not deafen man to the summons which the gospel directs to him. Macquarrie's theological task, however, is concerned that the life of faith to which the gospel summons is seen to be *intelligible*; that is, that it is *possible* in the conditions of human existence and that it *coheres with* other understandings and assumptions about the world. Thus, it is important for Macquarrie, in a way that it is not for Bultmann, to be able to exhibit (and to speak about) the place of faith in the public, commonly observable realm. It is to *this* that Macquarrie's use of existentialist theology is directed. It is for this reason that he insists on a minimal core of factuality with regard to the historical Jesus.[6]

By the time of publication of *Principles of Christian Theology* in 1966, Macquarrie's preliminary insistence on the genuine possibility of Christian self-giving based on a minimal core of factuality has been joined by an insistence on the role of the community of faith in preserving and mediating the Christian faith. Likewise, his preliminary indications that Bultmann's account of corporate life is inadequate have been complemented by a robust account of the community of faith. Although the American period does not constitute a 'turning' in the sense of a conversion from one mode of thought to another, this shift of emphasis, or, better, the integration of a new emphasis, is significant enough to warrant attention. By reference to the example of the work of John Knox, I shall seek to show that the Anglo-American attention to the public, observable realm allows Macquarrie to develop his concerns in outward directions. Although not losing the self-involving character of existentialism, Macquarrie establishes firmer grounds to address empiricism, and turns to more corporate understandings which give the *grace of being* an increasingly broad sphere: no longer just the experience of the individual existent, but the life of the community and, by the Oxford period, the cosmos itself.

Macquarrie himself notes the impact, personal and professional, which John Knox had on him from the very start of his time at New York, so it is with the influence of Knox that I shall be principally concerned. I shall show that Macquarrie moves beyond Knox, however, because of his attention to ontology, and unites a corporate understanding of faith with an ontological grounding for the Church's task in the world.

JOHN KNOX, THE CHURCH AND THE CHRIST EVENT

Macquarrie took up a post in systematic theology at Union Seminary, New York, in 1962. Five years earlier, having been recommended by John Baillie, he had given a series of lectures and been considered for a post in *philosophical* theology. Before he could be appointed, however, the 'Barthian ascendancy' at Union had seen that post abolished, and Macquarrie was subsequently appointed to one of the seminary's posts in systematic theology, to work alongside Paul Lehmann and Daniel Day Williams.[7] John Knox was also then on the staff of Union.

Almost as soon as he arrived in New York, Macquarrie read Knox's *The Church and the Reality of Christ* (1963), and he attributes to Knox's writings and friendship influence in two overlapping aspects of his life and work at that time: his move to the Episcopal Church, and his development of a more corporate understanding of the Christ event. In the first place, Knox was seeking ordination in the Episcopalian Church and encouraged Macquarrie in his own explorations in that direction. Previously ordained in the Presbyterian Church, Macquarrie was increasingly feeling the attraction of Catholic traditions within the Protestant Churches. Research for *Twentieth-Century Religious Thought* (1963) had introduced him to the work of Hans Urs von Balthasar and, especially, Karl Rahner. Rahner's study of death and particularly his christology provided Macquarrie with 'that synthesis of catholic faith and philosophical thought' for which he had been searching.[8] The move to America allowed Macquarrie to join the Episcopal Church, a change which family loyalties had prevented whilst still in Scotland. He was ordained in 1965, and his writings during this period show an increased familiarity with and commitment to the distinctive character of Anglican theology.

Macquarrie comments of Knox and himself that 'we both felt that it was important to *practice* the kind of religious faith that we were expounding in our teaching, for theology without corresponding practice is surely empty.'[9] In Macquarrie's work this dual commitment to Anglican practice and theology manifests as, for example, an increasingly explicit commitment to the particular forms which faith takes: its communities, institutions, rites and traditions, and a corresponding insistence on the continuity of tradition with Scripture. So, for example, in *Principles of Christian Theology* the introduction establishes that theology, '*through participation in and reflection upon a religious faith*, seeks to express the content *of this faith* in the clearest and most coherent language available', and reiterates that this implies involvement in a *community* of faith, on whose behalf the theologian speaks.[10] Key formative factors in theology (experience, revelation, Scripture) are recounted in relation to the community of faith and not to the individual alone. Thus, the experience of the life of faith is mediated by participation in community (in sharp contrast to Kierkegaard); the primordial revelation founds a community and becomes fruitful and normative in that community, and by Scripture the community keeps open its access to that primordial revelation in conjunction with 'a present experience of the holy in the community of faith', and thereby retains its stability and sense of continuing identity.[11] The tasks of symbolic theology, as well as its sources, are explained in relation to the community; and the whole philosophical and symbolic content of the book is applied to the life of the Church in Part Three. However, it is not simply that the community of faith becomes more important as the locus of theology. It also takes on particular theological significance. Clearly this reflects Macquarrie's Anglican practice, but it also reflects the more specifically theological influence of Knox's understanding of the Christ event, for whom 'Christ and the church comprise together the unity of the Christ-event'.[12]

The fact of the existence of the Church

Knox's book *The Church and the Reality of Christ* (1963) engages with the insistence of New Testament scholarship that the gospels as well as the epistles are the record and reflection *of the early Church* rather than the historical Jesus. He writes, 'What confronts us immediately and directly in the New Testament documents is simply and only the primitive community – what it remembered, what it knew, what it thought, what it felt'; even the gospels in intention and practice 'bring us Jesus *as the early community thought of him*'.[13] Knox's concern, however, is to express how faith in Christ can be essentially *related to* historical fact, and yet not be *dependent on* 'mere probabilities of historical fact'.[14] The quandary Knox addresses is exactly that posed by Bultmann's historical scepticism and the failure of the Life-of-Jesus school. If the fact that Jesus existed, and was the particular man he was, is central to theology and to the Church's devotion, there runs the risk that faith grasps at the supposed security of 'fact'. On the other hand, if this fact is not central, 'have we not cut the objective historical ground out from the Church and its message?'[15]

Although Macquarrie and Knox are in agreement against Bultmann that a certain amount can be reliably known, they differ on the relevance of this knowledge. For Macquarrie, as I have already indicated, it is of fundamental relevance because it indicates to the individual existent that 'the way of life which lies at the heart of the Christian proclamation is not something utopian or belonging to a wish-world, but something that has been realised in history, under the conditions of being-in-the-world.'[16] Knox, however, does not consider these probable historical facts about the life and work of Jesus to be significant of themselves. Turning attention to *the Church*, rather than the individual, he suggests that they are not information that the Church vitally requires, and they are less attestable than the indubitable fact of the coming into existence (or the having come into existence) of the community of faith. For Knox, the minimum core of factuality refers not to what Jesus said or did but to what the early Church knew and remembered him to say and do. It is this memory that contains what the Church really needs to know of Jesus, and it is grounded in the concrete existence of the Church itself.

In *The Church and the Reality of Christ*, then, the Christ-event is identified as

> simply the historical beginning of the Church itself ... The Church traces its origin to an event which only its own existence has made historically significant. Disregarding the remoter beginnings, we may say that this Event began when Jesus first drew disciples around him, that it was in progress during the months or years of his life with them, and that with his death and Resurrection it reached its culmination – the Church, which had been in process of becoming all along, now clearly emerging as the distinctive, self-conscious community it was and is.[17]

If this event is to be symbolised by a specific point, Knox identifies the moment 'when *after Jesus' death* a group of his disciples recognised in a divine Presence wonderfully new and strange, the very one they have known and loved: "It is the Lord" (John 21:7).'[18]

The importance and the accessibility of the factual event lie not in what Jesus said and did *per se*, but in what he was seen and heard to say and do, 'not even in what he simply was as such, but in what he was known to be'. The *historical* factuality is therefore radically grounded in the community of faith. It is the 'solid historical existence of the early church' which is the historical rootedness of the Christian faith. In this way, Knox unites the historical factuality and its existential significance *in the fact of the existence of the early Church* – the community of faith is a past *and present* objective reality:

> Although belonging to the past, [the Church] does not belong to the past only; it is also a present, an existent, fact, and therefore is not subject to the fortunes of historical discovery and the findings of historical research in the way events must needs be when our knowledge of them can be derived only from documents or other 'objective' evidence.[19]

It is this actual indisputable existence of the community in the public, observable realm that manifests the existential significance of the life and work of Jesus. For both Knox and Macquarrie, that which is made present in existential commitment refers to a specific actual historical occurrence, to publicly observable facts or events.[20]

Corporate memory and experience

Exploring how the community participates in this existential significance, and thus how the fact of the Church is not objectified in place of the historical Jesus as a false source of security, Knox offers a discussion of *memory*. It is in the Church's memory that the human Jesus has present reality and significance, and Knox explores the possibility and nature of *communal* memory. He insists that participation in shared memory is a sharing in remembrance: 'it is more than having a lively impression of the character or quality of an event in another's past; one also has a lively impression of its truth, of its having actually occurred.' What is significant is that 'the essential character of the image I have ... consists not simply (or even primarily) in its being a vivid, lively image, but in its being an image of something *remembered* and therefore of something which was indubitably known to have occurred.'[21] The significance of communal memory for Knox, then, lies not in its accuracy of details like names and dates (though these may indeed be accurate) but in its capacity to preserve 'something of the concrete quality, the felt meaning of an event in the past' and thus the certainty of its reality. Remembrance is, in this sense, historically reliable: 'to share in a common memory is to participate in an experience of the meaning of a past event whose actuality can be as little doubted as the meaning itself.'[22]

The memory passed from generation to generation in the Church, that is to say, the corporate memory of tradition, is intrinsically related to the New Testament documents. On the one hand, it is to the existence and nature of the early Church's memory of Jesus that the New Testament bears witness; the New Testament writings are 'more valuable for the testimony they bear to the existence and nature of the early Church's memory of Jesus than for any statement of more "objective" fact they may make about him and his career'.[23] And yet the memory is distinguishable from the New Testament because the Church can be said to remember both less and more than the gospels contain.

It remembers less in the sense that the part of its memory which is wholly independent of the gospels is minimal. It remembers more in the sense that the image the Church carries of Jesus is not *derived from* the gospels, but *gave rise to* them, and gives them life and meaning beyond the text. So, Knox suggests that the Church 'has always known more of Jesus than the gospels tell us – not ... more facts about him or his life, but more of the man himself'.[24] This 'more' is a matter of moral stature and, most particularly, of the love Jesus had for his followers – known not because Jesus' feelings are reported but because the quality of that love was already existing and remembered in the Church. For Knox, the Church's memory of Jesus is part of its existential reality: 'Whatever evaluation may be made of it by others, the Church's picture of Jesus has what seems to it to be the character of a remembrance – that is, it is the picture of someone known to be real. And this remembrance is absolutely vital to its existence.'[25]

Additionally, the Church has from the beginning been a sharing not only in a common memory of Jesus, but also in a common experience of the Spirit. 'Just as the Church actually remembered Jesus, so it actually experienced the Spirit'; and just as the memory of Jesus is of a concrete reality, so the experience of the spirit is of 'an actual entity, an object of concrete knowledge'.[26] The character of the experience is twofold. On the one hand, it is the experience of 'the actual presence in their midst of the transcendent God to whom they looked up in worship'; on the other hand, it is 'the actual presence of the Jesus to whom they looked back in remembrance'.[27] The unity of these two aspects, the experience of the spirit of God *as* the spirit of Jesus, is the experience of Jesus as Lord.

Macquarrie's account of tradition gives the same attention to the existential aspect of the corporate life of the Church as Knox's work. Macquarrie's basic account of revelation in *Principles of Christian Theology* is close to an account of 'religious experience' in general. However, he adds this significant qualifier: 'We do not normally dignify our day-to-day experiences of the holy by the name of "revelation", and no theology properly so called could be founded on private revelations, for, as has been stressed already, theology expresses the faith of a community.'[28] What can most properly be given the name 'revelation' is that classic or primordial revelation, 'a definite disclosive experience of the holy granted to the founder or founders of the community', which is the founding of the community and the normative paradigm for subsequent experiences of the holy within the community. While it is present experiences of the holy which renew the classic revelation, so that it continues to *be* revelation in the community, Macquarrie cautions that if faith 'is to be saved from the dangers of subjectivism, the varieties of experience within the community must be submitted to the *relatively objective content* of the classic revelation on which the community is founded.'[29]

Further, it is this tradition of the classic revelation which maintains the continuing identity of the community. So Macquarrie insists,

> To deny fundamental doctrines, like that of the Trinity; to reject the creeds; to set aside the beliefs of the early councils of the still undivided Church – these may be actions to which individuals are impelled by their own thinking on these matters, but they cannot take place in Christian theology, for they amount to a rejection of the history and therefore of the continuing identity of the community within which Christian theologising takes place.[30]

Macquarrie is not, of course, advocating passive allegiance to a static body of tradition. Two points can be made to clarify his intention. In the first place, he is concerned with the *reappropriation* of the community's tradition: 'Each generation must appropriate the tradition, and in order to do this it has to interpret the ancient formula, or whatever it may be, into its own categories of thought.'[31] This is a clear example of where Heidegger's notion of 'repetition' becomes a *corporate* task, in this period of Macquarrie's work. For Heidegger, repetition is key to authentic historicity, which 'understands history as the "recurrence" of the possible, and knows that a possibility will recur only if existence is open for it fatefully, in a moment of vision, in resolute repetition'.[32] Macquarrie explains, '"repetition" is to be understood as meaning much more than a mere mechanical going over again. It implies rather going into some experience that has been handed down in such a way that it is, so to speak, brought into the present and its insights and possibilities made alive again.'[33] This is the approach Macquarrie himself takes to the Church's doctrinal tradition in *Principles of Christian Theology*, in his work on symbolic theology. The task as he describes it is to 'penetrate behind the possibly quaint and even alien language of the dogma to the existential issues that agitated the Church at the time of the dogma's formulation, and appropriate for our own time and in our own language the essential insight which the dogma sought to express'.[34]

The second confirmation that Macquarrie is not recommending a passive acceptance of a body of tradition is his concern with the dynamic *continuation* of the tradition by each generation. Reappropriation does not merely borrow from a static tradition in order to apply it to a particular present situation, whilst leaving the tradition untouched. Rather, it is itself a part of the dynamic development of the tradition, and will itself demand a new act of interpretation in due course. The givenness of the primordial revelation is continually reformulated and re-expressed, and this makes for doctrinal development. The community of faith has the task of deciding what are legitimate developments of its belief, what has arisen from the 'inner dynamic and creativity of the given revelation'.[35]

THE BODY OF CHRIST: PRESENCE-AND-MANIFESTATION IN THE WORLD

Embodiment: a corporate reality

Already this is a significant shift to the corporate. It represents a considerable advance on Bultmann's utilitarian and event-oriented view, establishing that the corporate character of faith is primary and always a given. To indicate how Macquarrie moves beyond Knox it is necessary to consider further how they conceive of the relation of the Church's organic wholeness to its *task* in the public observable realm. I shall do this by means of the motif of the body of Christ.

In *The Church and the Reality of Christ*, Knox's argument is that 'the whole meaning of Christ *as historical Event* is embodied in the Church', and that, further, 'to say this is to say that the Church is "the body of Christ".'[36] For Knox, the primary meaning of the Church as the body of Christ is precisely this *embodying* of the event. As such, 'the body of Christ' is not a metaphor, nor a mere comparison: 'The Church is not merely *like* a body; it is *in fact* the body of Christ.'[37] By 'body', Knox means 'the spatio-temporal locus of human existence and the medium of its expression ... Without a body one could not belong to this realm of space and time, of nature and history.'[38] It is in this sense that the Church is Christ's body, exactly as the historical locus, the 'embodiment' of God's saving action within the public, temporal order.

This embodiment is, for Knox, the true meaning of the incarnation, and to safeguard this against the criticism that this says 'too much' for the Church in relation to the person of Jesus, he introduces his argument in two stages. The first stage is the recognition of the tradition that the incarnation is the *incarnation of the Word*, that is, of 'the creative, revealing, redeeming *action* of God'.[39] This means that the incarnation is to be thought of not as a static condition, the divine substance becoming visible and tangible ('congealing', as it were) but the 'bodying forth' of God's ongoing action in history. Jesus is incarnate in the sense of being the 'dynamic personal medium of God's saving action', God's action embodied in an authentic human life. The second stage of the argument, however, is to recognise that this incarnation does not antedate the Church, but includes the Church or, better, lies 'within the period and the process of its beginning'. God's action in Jesus is, for Knox, the bringing into being of the Church. This means that 'the "embodying" of God's action in Jesus and the "embodying" of his action in bringing the Church into being is one embodying of one action.'[40]

This connection of the Church with the embodiment of God's saving action gives a particular understanding to the character of atonement in Knox's thought. Salvation is, exactly, *reconciliatory*, it is at-onement. The need for salvation arises from estrangement from one another, from the self, from God: 'Man is estranged from God and therefore divided against himself. This is his "fallenness", his "brokenness", his wretchedness, his hopelessness, his desperate, fatal sickness. The recovery of his health, of his own inner wholeness, depends upon his being brought home again.'[41] For Knox, this is not merely a reconciliation between God and the individual, but a uniting of human beings in a new existence. Knox suggests that even in the simple example of a reconciliation between two people, it is evident that reconciliation implies a new existence: 'reconciliation in such a case is not an abstract relation between two discrete individuals; it is the existence of a third entity, in which both share and by which each is to an extent remade.'[42] If this is so in the case of two people, then Knox insists:

> how much more obviously true it is of the reconciliation of which the gospel speaks: the total and ultimate reconciliation, involving God and man, our neighbours and our hearts, and indeed 'all things in heaven and on earth'! Such reconciliation means the coming into being of a new objective order of relationships, a new 'body' – a 'body' more inclusive, more enduring, more significant than any of the other 'bodies' to which we may belong.[43]

This is the body of Christ: *a new corporate reality embodied in the world.*

Again, there are substantial areas of agreement between Macquarrie's thought and Knox's, as well as sufficient discontinuity to ensure that Knox's influence is not exaggerated. Although Macquarrie understands incarnation as 'the raising of manhood to Godhood', for him too this not only concerns Jesus Christ, but continues in the Church: 'within the church, humanity is being conformed to christhood, a transfiguration, resurrection, ascension is going on as the believers participate in the life of Christ, or in a couple of words, there is a new creation.'[44] This new creation takes place 'in Christ', and here Macquarrie explicitly acknowledges the resonance with Knox: 'To be in Christ is to belong to a new corporate reality … The "new creation" has taken place, and the Church is the historical embodiment of the new humanity.'[45]

Likewise, salvation has the character of reconciliation and inclusion in a new corporate reality. For Macquarrie, this emphasis on reconciliation best explains what the doctrine of justification tries to bring to expression: 'the experience of being accepted by Being, of emerging from lostness and alienation, into a right relation with Being'.[46] Baptism into one body, the body of Christ, expresses this reconciliation with God, with our place in the scheme of things and with one another. Thus Macquarrie notes, 'Through baptism we are accepted, incorporated, delivered from the isolation of meaninglessness and set in the living context of the community of faith, as members that count in it.'[47]

Macquarrie is more emphatic than Knox, however, that Christ is the *head* of the church. Where Knox acknowledges this, it is primarily to insist that the church is *Christ's* body, and not in a more general way 'the "body" of the *Event*, or the "body" of *God's action*'.[48] For Macquarrie, however, Christ's headship has a more active meaning: 'Christ is the head of the body, and therefore the source of its unity. It is he who makes it a body, a unitary co-ordinated organism, rather than a collection of individual entities.'[49] This is not a lapse into mind/matter dualism on Macquarrie's part, with the head ruling the members. Rather, it is an example of his dynamic understanding of transcendence. Christ is the head in that he is the 'first fruits' of the new creation (1 Cor 15:23): 'the incarnation which reached its completion in him is in process in the church', and is the *telos* to which the Church tends.[50] Further, as such the Church represents the destiny of humanity itself: 'if we think of the church as extending from its militant aspect to its triumphant aspect, we may regard it as a kind of bridge between the place where humanity actually is and its destiny as the Kingdom of God.'⁵¹

Macquarrie retains a threefold distinction in the meaning of the body of Christ: Jesus of Nazareth's actual personal being-in-the-world as the incarnate Word, the sacramental host, and the worshipping community. The three are interdependent. Jesus' personal being-in-the-world generates and gives being to the sacrament and the community, yet it is through these derivative forms that we have access by the divine gift of self-expression to the primordial form.⁵² Only through the living unity of the three forms is the fullness of the expression 'the body of Christ' received. Each of these forms is a case of what Macquarrie refers to throughout *Principles of Christian Theology* as the 'presence-and-manifestation' of Being in the beings, and what becomes apparent is the relevance of Macquarrie's move into the corporate public realm not only to the Church in relation to humanity but more importantly to a new understanding of the role of human being in the world.⁵³ A shift begins to emerge, away from the fundamentally individual Heideggerian notion of instrumentality (where human transcendence is *transcendence over* the world of things), opening the way to an ontologically comprehensive notion of human transcendence as the *transcendence of* the cosmos.

Environment: from instrumentality to transfiguration

As I indicated in Chapter 1, in his existentialist period, Macquarrie borrows from Heidegger's *Being and Time* to conceive of the relation between human existence and what is encountered in his environment as 'instrumental'. Entities in the world are encountered with regard to their practical use as equipment, and it is by enlarging his field of practical concern that man develops and fulfils his possibilities: he enlarges his world. The world refers only to that sphere of significance with which *Dasein* is engaged. Furthermore, there is a fundamental dualism between human being (which *exists*) and the natural realm which is simply *Vorhandenheit* (presence-at-hand). It is only when *Dasein* becomes concerned with an aspect of the natural realm and makes it *Zuhandenheit* (readiness-to-hand) that it takes on significance because *Dasein* has incorporated it into his world.

In *Principles of Christian Theology*, this notion of instrumentality is retained, but is recast in an existential-ontological framework as a cooperation with Being. Being is understood in a dynamic sense 'as enabling to be, empowering to be, or bringing into being', that is to say, as *letting-be*.⁵⁴ In a religious dimension, this letting-be is experienced as 'being's self-giving, the grace of being which pours itself out and confers being'. Being does not merely confer being 'at a distance', as it were, but mediates itself through what it lets-be. It is thus that Macquarrie can speak of Being as present-and-manifest in beings which participate in Being.⁵⁵

The *presence* of Being is everywhere, since Being is the condition that anything at all is. But to indicate how Being becomes known, Macquarrie talks of the way Being can be 'present and manifest' in the beings. Being gives itself in and with and through particular beings, but when these are seen in a new way, 'in depth', what is seen is the presence of Being. *Manifestation* refers to Being's own initiative and action in making itself known in the beings. Fundamental to this notion of presence and manifestation is the understanding that beings participate in Being. They are not simply a channel through which Being makes itself known, but participate in varying degrees in Being. So, for example, 'an inanimate object exhibits material being, while an animal exhibits not only material being but also organic being. In man, a material body and an animal organism are united with his distinctively personal being.'⁵⁶ Human being is thus the fullest range of Being we know, and it is in human being that Being has become most fully present-and-manifest in the incarnation. By participation in this presence-and-manifestation, that is to say in this self-giving of Being, the community of believers increasingly becomes a locus of God's presence and manifestation in the world. Macquarrie therefore places much greater emphasis than Knox on the way in which participation in the body of Christ is relational – it is participation in Being's self-giving and not merely observable location in the world.

Human being participates most fully in Being, then, and part of its character as distinctively personal (that is, transcendent) existence is that it cooperates with Being. Principally, this is in its own existence. As *Dasein* goes forward in his possibilities, he cooperates with Being. He is, in this sense, a guardian of Being: he may cooperate with Being and be faithful in letting-be the being that has been committed to him. Equally, however, man 'can forget Being and their guardianship of Being, and can choose to be for themselves, gathering up their being and ceasing to manifest that letting-be which is the essence of the Being of which they were the guardians'.⁵⁷ *Dasein* also cooperates with Being in regard to other beings. In part this is the bringing of things into his world to give them significance. Macquarrie relates this to the creation accounts in Genesis:

the activities of tending the garden and naming the animals in the creation story are only the beginnings of a long process by which man more and more converts mere nature into a humanised world. That world is organised in terms of human needs and activities ... in it, things no longer confront us in their sheer givenness and strangeness; they have been assigned a place and a meaning in an environment that is seen from the human point of view.[58]

However, this cooperation with beings also takes on a new dimension. This is what Macquarrie refers to in *Principles of Christian Theology* as the 'eschatological transfiguration of the world', and refers less to the 'humanising' of the world than to the completion of the creation itself. 'The whole of life and existence is to be penetrated by the grace of Being, and the entire creation is to be transfigured in the direction of that goal when its fullest potentialities for being have been realised.'[59] Macquarrie notes both that the lower levels of creation manifest a kind of *nisus*, a striving towards a goal albeit below the level of conscious thought, *and* that the movement towards this goal is only possible through the action of 'those responsible agents that have been brought forth in creation'.[60]

CONCLUSION

This theme is fully developed in Macquarrie's Oxford period, and will be addressed further in Chapters 5 and 6. My aim in this chapter has been to identify that strand in the development of Macquarrie's thought from individualism to a corporate perspective which contains within it a development from a dualistic instrumentality to an ontologically grounded participative responsibility in the social, economic and material realm.

NOTES

1. Robert Gundry, *SOMA in Biblical Theology* (Cambridge: CUP 1976), 190, 191.
2. Gareth Jones, *Bultmann: Towards a Critical Theology* (Cambridge: Polity Press 1991), 205–6. See, for example, Bultmann's essay 'On Behalf of Christian Freedom' in *Existence and Faith* (London: Hodder & Stoughton 1961), which suggests that freedom for God is 'release from all worldly conditions', 241.
3. Jones, 207
4. Gundry, 189. Compare Ernst Käsemann's insistence that the material and relational world is precisely the arena in which obedience to Christ is to be lived,

see for example his essay 'On the Subject of Primitive Christian Apocalyptic' in *New Testament Questions of Today* (London: SCM 1969).
5. Jones, 204
6. See, for example, *SD* 90, *PCT* 278. The importance of being able to affirm a minimal core of truth about the historical Jesus is that we affirm 'that the way of life which lies at the heart of the Christian proclamation is not something utopian or belonging to a wish-world, but something that has been realised in history, under the conditions of being-in-the-world'.
7. Though as Macquarrie has remarked, 'The way I do systematic theology, it's not really all that different to natural theology, is it!', *Macquarrie on Macquarrie* conference, 1998. The close connection between his systematic theology and his natural or philosophical theology can be seen in *PCT*. A substantial third of this one-volume systematic theology consists of philosophical theology as foundational prior to the systematic theology proper.
8. 'Pilgrimage in Theology' xiv. The essay which had particular impact was 'Current Problems in Christology' now published in *Theological Investigations* I (London: DLT 1965), 149–200.
9. 'Pilgrimage in Theology' xv
10. *PCT* 1, 2, italics are mine.
11. See, for example, *PCT* 5, 8, 9, 10.
12. 'Pilgrimage in Theology' xv. It must be acknowledged that the direct influence of Knox's theological *content* is not obvious. Certainly, Knox's approach cannot simply be read off Macquarrie's developments. It is my own view that Knox's friendship was more influential on Macquarrie than his theology, and that Macquarrie's move to a more ecclesial approach owes more to their shared journey into the Episcopalian Church and ordination.
13. John Knox, *The Church and the Reality of Christ* (London: Collins 1963), hereafter *Reality of Christ*; 9, 15, emphasis is Knox's.
14. *Reality of Christ* 13. Knox is not questioning the element of probability or risk in faith. But he does insist that this is the absolute, *eschatological* risk: 'We are risking the possibility that the God of heaven and earth will in the ultimate and final reckoning fail to justify our trust in him, not that the chance discovery of an ancient document or a new conclusion of historians could conceivably rob us of it', 17.
15. *Reality of Christ* 13
16. *PCT* 278. This highlights a fundamental difference between Macquarrie's christology and Knox's. Macquarrie's christology is driven by his anthropology, which is explicated in terms of his existential and ontological concern for being, and grounded in the individually responsible tones of the European (Heideggerian) tradition. Knox's christology owes more to the demands of Anglo-American empiricism, and indicates that the incarnation can be appropriated because it occurs in the public domain. It is important to be clear on this point: Knox's influence is not being detected in Macquarrie's *christology* per se but in his commitment to faith in the *corporate and public realm*.
17. *Reality of Christ* 26. Knox, like Bultmann, uses the term 'Christ-event'. This is a notion Macquarrie himself favours for its value in holding together 'history and theology, event and interpretation', *JCMT* 19.
18. *Reality of Christ* 79. For Macquarrie, however, the key christological moment is Jesus' own agony in the garden, and his decision for self-giving, *PCT* 322, *JCMT* 402.

19 *Reality of Christ* 31–32
20 *PCT* 274, 278
21 *Reality of Christ* 40, 41, italics are Knox's. He gives the example of his wife sharing in the memory of his father, whom she never met. Although this memory is not the same as a memory of things which have happened directly to her, nevertheless 'his reality as a person is present to her in something like the same sense in which it is present to me. It would be inadequate to say that she is aware of my father's existence only by hearsay. A denial of his existence would seem to her to be a denial of something intimately and surely known, very much as it would seem also to me', 39.
22 *Reality of Christ* 43. Macquarrie agrees with Knox on the importance of the continuity of the Church's memory; see, for example, *JCMT* 348 where he cites *Reality of Christ* 61.
23 *Reality of Christ* 49. This does not reduce the capacity of the New Testament to act as a check on the Church, but rather enhances it: it speaks to the Church from its most authentic age, not from a position outside or alongside it, but as its own authentic memory of Jesus.
24 *Reality of Christ* 53. Compare the shift from 'proclaimer' to 'proclaimed' in Bultmann's essay 'The Primitive Christian Kerygma and the Historical Jesus' in *The Historical Jesus and the Kerygmatic Christ* eds Carl E. Braaten and Roy A. Harrisville (New York: Abingdon Press 1964), 15–42, and especially 27ff.
25 *Reality of Christ* 58
26 *Reality of Christ* 63. Knox's choice of words is unfortunate, though designed to emphasise the objective rather than subjective nature of the experience of the spirit: this is not a psychological attitude which is under discussion.
27 *Reality of Christ* 65
28 *PCT* 8
29 *PCT* 9, emphasis is mine.
30 *PCT* 12
31 *PCT* 13
32 *BT* 444. In his earlier work, Macquarrie uses this notion with regard to the individual reappropriating the life of Jesus, see *SD* 84. He also uses Heidegger's notion of repetitive thinking in *SCE*, 'a thinking that "repeats" the great historical insights of the past ... so that by thinking their thoughts after them and with them, one might get back to the original sources of philosophising before misleading ontologies had made their influence felt', 91.
33 *PCT* 92
34 *PCT* 181, and see 475 on repetition in the eucharist.
35 Macquarrie suggests that whilst it is by no means the case that an uninterrupted progressive deepening of understanding has characterised the church's doctrinal development, at least 'the more bizarre developments' called forth by the pressure of external events (rather than by the character of the revelation itself) 'have tended in time to wither away', *PCT* 20. However, it could also be argued that this is an optimistic view, dependent upon an unduly positive view of tradition. Macquarrie is a little more cautious by *JCMT*, where he is critical of the post-Chalcedonian disputes on the wills of Christ, for example.
36 *Reality of Christ* 84, italics are Knox's.
37 *Reality of Christ* 85, emphasis is Knox's. Knox admits that this use is clearer in Colossians and Ephesians than in Corinthians, but suggests that whether they

were written by Paul or not, they 'set forth in this respect the authentically Pauline view'.
38 *Reality of Christ* 85–86
39 *Reality of Christ* 87, italics are Knox's. Compare Norman Pittenger's *The Word Incarnate* (Welwyn: Nisbet & Co 1959), a work which both Knox and Macquarrie cite with enthusiasm.
40 *Reality of Christ* 87–88. To emphasise the Church in this way is not, in Knox's view, to denigrate Christ, who remains central to the event.
41 *Reality of Christ* 103
42 *Reality of Christ* 104
43 *Reality of Christ* 104
44 *PCT* 388
45 *Reality of Christ* 106, quoted by Macquarrie in *PCT* 389.
46 *PCT* 342
47 *PCT* 460
48 *Reality of Christ* 107; italics are Knox's.
49 *PCT* 402
50 *PCT* 389. Thus, while Knox is wary of referring to the Church as an *extension* of the incarnation because it might imply a two-stage event which demotes the Church, Macquarrie is cautious in case the term puts the Church at the same level as Christ and attributes to it an exaggerated status or authority, *PCT* 389.
51 *PCT* 390
52 *PCT* 477. Macquarrie draws a parallel with Christ the incarnate Word and the derivative yet mediating forms of scripture (the written word) and preaching (the proclaimed word), *PCT* 454.
53 It is interesting to note that Ernst Käsemann also gives an account of the body and the body of Christ which issues in responsibility in the embodied public realm. Fundamental to Käsemann's interpretation is the motif of obedience in Paul. See, for example, his account of baptism and the Church in 'On the Subject of Primitive Christian Apocalyptic' in *New Testament Questions of Today* (London: SCM 1969), 108–37, and the body as man in his 'worldliness' in 'The Theological Problem Presented by the Motif of the Body of Christ' in *Perspectives on Paul* (London: SCM 1971), 102–21. Christ's rule in the world is documented precisely in the 'bodily obedience of the Christian, carried out as the service of God in the world of everyday, … [Christ's] own are already engaged today in delivering over to Christ by their bodily obedience the piece of the world which they themselves are', 'Primitive Christian Apocalyptic', 135.
54 *PCT* 113
55 *PCT* 114, 115
56 *PCT* 143
57 *PCT* 201
58 *PCT* 231
59 *PCT* 512
60 *PCT* 222, 512

Chapter 4

New-Style Natural Theology

INTRODUCTION: A PARALLEL STRAND IN THE AMERICAN PERIOD

In Chapter 3, I have noted Macquarrie's shift to a more corporate approach, in which his early hesitations over Bultmann's individualism are given fuller expression in dialogue with John Knox's theology and in the context of their shared move into the Anglican Church. I have also noted the way in which this shift re-envisions the kerygmatic summons as a summons into a new corporate reality, which correspondingly recasts the notion of instrumentality in such a way as to address the completion of creation rather than simply the 'humanising' of the world. Chapter 4 forms a parallel chapter, not charting further *sequential* developments, but rather investigating the complementary strand of Macquarrie's concern with ontology and its development into his characteristic existential-ontological method. This strand is significant because it marks a new degree of attention to how theology must conduct itself as a discipline, not simply to how it is to communicate Christian faith in contemporary context.[1]

It is at this point that Macquarrie's theology becomes framed as what he terms a 'new-style' natural theology in *Principles of Christian Theology*. Macquarrie's dual concern for the *statement of the truth of the Christian message* and its *interpretation for the present generation* (that is, for kerygma and situation) continues into a more comprehensive theological framework. His dual concern with the character of the *human quest* and the *divine initiative* emerges as a concern with theology as both intellectual discipline and as participation in faith, whilst avoiding that special pleading of which Fritz Buri accuses theology in its typical appeal to revelation. Of particular interest is the way in which Macquarrie's commitment to the benefits of existentialist theology is positioned within the framework of natural rather than revealed theology, and the decisive significance this has for the *grace of being*.

PRINCIPLES OF CHRISTIAN THEOLOGY: SYSTEMATICS IN NATURAL MODE

The importance of *Principles of Christian Theology* in the Macquarrie corpus must not be underestimated, particularly as an identifying marker in Macquarrie's development of his own distinctive dialectical theism. To a certain extent, *Principles of Christian Theology* can be said to straddle all three periods under discussion: it was commissioned while Macquarrie was in Glasgow, completed in New York and revised in Oxford. On the basis of *An Existentialist Theology* and *The Scope of Demythologizing*, Macquarrie was invited to submit for publication a one-volume systematic theology in contemporary mood, which offered a viewpoint of its own and yet was not so tied to that viewpoint that it could not indicate the ecumenical nature of theology.

Titled in honour of F.H. Bradley's *Principles of Logic*, *Principles of Christian Theology* represents a conscious move on Macquarrie's part from existential theology to existential-ontological theology, and it is here that he lays out his theological method and characteristic 'new-style' natural theology. Beginning with the human situation and man's search for grace from beyond himself, and using Heidegger's philosophy of being, *Principles of Christian Theology* traces a path from human existence to the discovery of ultimate being. It explores the nature and function of theology as a whole, and establishes the conditions for natural theology. Then it investigates the symbols by which the faith centred in the particular revelation given in Jesus Christ may be explicated in accordance with this natural theology, and the guidelines for applying Christian faith in the world.

The aim of theology

Space does not allow for a thorough investigation of Macquarrie's approach to theological method, but one salient point must be noted to give a context to the 'new-style' natural theology which follows. Macquarrie begins his preface to *Principles of Christian Theology* with the statement, 'Christian theology seeks to think the Church's faith as a coherent whole.'[2] By this he means that theology aims to show not only the internal coherence of the faith, that is, that various doctrines constitute a unity, but also that the faith coheres with the other beliefs and attitudes held in contemporary thought so that the faith may be 'held intelligibly and be integrated with the whole range of human life'. This means that theology both participates in and reflects critically upon faith, that is, a specific faith and therefore a specific historic community, not just an anonymous 'faith in general'. Theology is therefore both continuous with and distinct from faith: in theology a particular faith is 'bringing itself to a certain kind of expression' and yet is also subject to critical, descriptive or interpretative reflection in which theology has 'stepped back' from the immediate experiences of faith.[3]

In aiming at intelligibility and consistency, theology implicitly lays claim to a place within the intellectual activity of human beings. Macquarrie prefers to speak non-committally of theology as a 'study', rather than as a science, since 'science' is most typically taken to refer to the natural sciences. However, he acknowledges Wilhelm Dilthey's recognition of human sciences (*Geisteswissenschaften*) which are characterised precisely by participation in the subject matter with which they deal. Such a model provides a better framework for theology to claim to be a science, but Macquarrie still distances himself from that conclusion. For all its common aim of striving for intelligibility and coherence, theology is distinguished by its relation to faith 'and because of the remarkable claim, implicit in its very name, to be somehow a "divine" science'.[4]

This illustrates a dual concern which consistently characterises Macquarrie's work. On the one hand, theology participates in faith, and therefore operates with a particular pre-understanding which distinguishes it from all intellectual disciplines which are not explicitly concerned with faith as a *datum*. But on the other hand, as an intellectual enterprise, theology does stand in relation to other disciplines, and these borders may prove fruitful for reciprocal insight. It is already clear that Macquarrie regards the borders between philosophy and theology as particularly valuable, and likewise the understanding of historical existence and the nature of historicity derived from the study of history. He also notes the importance of engagement with both the human and the natural sciences, as the means to address the false claim of the adequacy of a positivistic account of religious phenomena and to clarify precisely the 'extra dimension' which faith perceives in the phenomena and the 'scientific observer' does not.[5]

The problem of natural theology

In introducing his new-style natural theology, which he terms *philosophical theology* to distinguish it from old-style rationalistic natural theologies, Macquarrie indicates that it is 'an inquiry into the possibility of any theology whatsoever. It tries to show us what are the foundations of theological discourse – how this talk arises, how it refers, what are its presuppositions.'[6] Its function is to bring into the open the assumptions that lie behind any theological statement, to express them in a precise philosophical language, and, by means of critical reason, to assess their intelligibility, coherence, and importance for human existence. Its concern, therefore, is with the conditions that make any theology possible, and with the link between secular thought and theology proper. It is, then, concerned with *transcendentals*, with the conditions of possibility.

Traditional natural theology previously attempted to fulfil this function by offering a supposed rational demonstration of the subject matter of theology. Macquarrie wishes both to place his own work in the tradition of natural theology, and to mark some radical differences. In terms of basic function, there is no difference between his new-style philosophical theology and the old-style natural theology:

> It will provide a bridge between our everyday thinking and experience and the matters about which the theologian talks: it will relate religious discourse to all the other areas of discourse. It will do this by setting out from ordinary situations that can be described in secular language, and will seek to move from them into the situations of the life of faith. In the course of these descriptions, distinctively religious words such as 'God', 'sin', 'revelation', 'faith', will be given their meanings.[7]

However, the differences which Macquarrie introduces are very significant, and mark a very real alteration in both the character and aim of natural theology. He notes three differences between his theology and traditional natural theology.

First, Macquarrie aims to make his new-style philosophical theology *more fundamental* than traditional natural theology. He notes that although traditional theistic proofs of the existence of God appear to have the form of logical argument, in fact 'the person offering the proof has already been himself convinced of God's reality on grounds quite other than those mentioned in the proof', and that the proof arises from reflection on the conviction, not vice versa.[8] Whilst it is valuable that the conviction has been exposed to critical reflection, there remains the question of where the conviction is derived from, if not from the logical argument. It is at this point that Macquarrie moves behind traditional natural theology and indicates that the role of new-style natural theology is 'to push back the inquiry into the fundamental ways in which we come to know anything, and [to] try to elucidate the basic structures and patterns of experience that might seem to offer valid credentials for a religious conviction'.[9]

Secondly, then, this new theology *describes rather than deduces*. It does not attempt to prove by logical argument, but it *'lets us see*, for it brings out into the light the basic situation in which faith is rooted, so that we can then see what its claims are'.[10] What is seen is the *existentiell* self-understanding implicit in faith. Although the apologetic function of Macquarrie's theology is secondary, he does note that description is more likely to be effective as an apologetic than rational argument, since it invites a far greater degree of participation by asking others to 'look with us'.

Thirdly, the approach Macquarrie develops is *existential rather than rational*. That is to say, it is based on a broad understanding which arises out of the whole range of human existence in the world, and not on purely rational speculation (or on rational speculation derived from observation of the 'objective' cosmos).[11] He acknowledges that, at the time of their formulation, traditional natural theologies would have used 'reason' and 'rational' in a far wider sense than has been the case since Descartes and the rise of a mathematical model of reasoning which casts reason as individual, abstract and cerebral. But he recognises that the modern mind cannot now reach back to that meaning, and therefore natural theology must be reinterpreted to make explicit that its concern is with the entirety of human existence and experience.[12]

In marking these differences between his own project and traditional natural theology, Macquarrie is acknowledging the collapse of traditional natural theology under the weight of both philosophical and theological objections raised largely in the modern period. He recognises, for example, Kant's criticism of the ontological argument (that is, that existence is not a property), Camus' and Nietzsche's pessimistic rejection of the cosmological argument as well as the logical difficulty in moving from empirical data to a trans-empirical reality, and Hume's rejection of the teleological argument in favour of the immanence of the principle of order.

His treatment of theological objections is generally less sympathetic. He rejects outright the objection 'urged from Calvin to Barth' that man's sinfulness has so corrupted his intellect as well as his will, that his capacity for reasoning is so perverted that any attempt to think of God can only result in distortion and falsehood. For Macquarrie, 'to hold that our intellect is so perverted that we just cannot think straight is to fall into a skepticism so bottomless that further discussion becomes pointless.'[13] He acknowledges that any thinking can be distorted by 'selfish and unworthy desires', but that to know this is already to be struggling against it. He suggests that 'there need not be a skeptical resignation of the possibility of trustworthy thinking (this would be a kind of intellectual suicide); rather, there needs to be an effort to think more strictly and more rationally.'[14]

Macquarrie is more favourably disposed to the objection that man's finitude limits the success of natural theology. To live a human existence is to live in risk and uncertainty, choosing courses of action without full knowledge of the circumstances or consequences. Therefore, to demand 'the guaranteed certitude of rational demonstration ... is to refuse to acknowledge one's own finitude, or to refuse to accept oneself'.[15] It is simply contrary to the conditions of a radically finite existence to expect faith, unlike life, to proceed on the basis of certainty rather than risk. The risk, the faith, may be a reasonable one, but can never be removed by reason.

A third theological objection raised against natural theology is that it is inappropriate to talk about God in the terms available to deductive argument, since it treats God as an object amongst other objects perceivable within the world (or as a hypothesis within the world which it explains). Macquarrie agrees that if the theistic proofs are truly indistinguishable from wholly secular inquiry, then it cannot be denied that God is being treated as an object or hypothesis. If, however, the argument is distinguished by an attitude of reverence then natural theology cannot claim to offer proof in the accepted objective sense, because the inquiry is shaped by an element of subjectivity. Macquarrie himself is not prepared to put aside a degree of something akin to reverence which he regards as a distinguishing characteristic proper to theology's participation in faith, but then, as he has already argued, he does not seek to offer 'proof' from his theology. However, the fact that he derives his understanding of reverence not only from the community of faith but also from the later Heidegger's attitude to being enables him both to maintain that theology is an inquiry with characteristics that distinguish it from purely empirical inquiry, and also to argue its coherence amongst other secular intellectual disciplines.

Underlying these objections to natural theology is a common theme: that in natural theology man attempts to find a way to God, when in all our knowledge of God the initiative actually lies with God: 'he makes himself known to us, so that the movement is from his side to us, not from our side to him.'[16] Leaving aside the exaggerated form of the objection found in some Protestant theology, Macquarrie acknowledges the principle: 'it seems clear that our knowledge of God could never be like our knowledge of some fact in the world. Our knowledge of facts in the world is gained by our own active discovery of them, but since God himself is the supremely active principle, he does not await our discovery but presents and manifests himself in an active manner.'[17] This means that the distinction between 'natural' theology and 'revealed' theology is a dialectic rather than an opposition. Reverence does not disqualify critical reason, revelation does not disqualify reasonableness and, as is already becoming clear, it is in the ('natural') being of particular beings that revelation occurs. How, then, does Macquarrie employ his early existential thought and his concern with ontology to construct an existential-ontological theism?

EXISTENTIAL-ONTOLOGICAL THEISM

Three points will illustrate the basic parameters of Macquarrie's natural theology: the human quest for God and human receptivity to the divine initiative, which together constitute the human pole; and the divine self-disclosure which constitutes the divine pole.

The human pole

Human transcendence and dialectical unity

Macquarrie begins his natural theology by recapping his analysis of human existence, showing again that the conditions for the quest for God lie in the very constitution of human nature.[18] In fundamental content, Macquarrie's discussion of human existence recapitulates that already set out in his Glasgow period, and does not need extensive comment at this point. The characteristic threefold understanding of human existence remains basic: man is both subject and object, man is possibility, and existence is always 'mine'. However, two important emphases are developed in *Principles of Christian Theology*.

First, a shift emerges which allows the existentialist analysis of human existence to occur within a natural theology framework. An account of *transcendence* is relocated from the divine to the human. In the revised edition, Macquarrie suggests that the characteristic *existence*, which he has termed following existentialist philosophy, might better be called transcendence. Although 'existence' emphasises that 'selfhood is not a ready-made "nature", or collection of properties, but a potentiality that has to be responsibly actualised, [such that] man can either attain to authentic selfhood or miss it', 'transcendence' better expresses the *dynamic* quality of this open, unfinished being.

'Transcendence' insists that it is in man's 'very nature to be always transcending or passing beyond any given stage of his condition'.[19] Understood in this way, the quest for grace arises not simply from a lack in human existence, but from an openness to, and drive towards, that which the sense of lack discloses, the possibility of authentic selfhood. More importantly, it establishes the existentialist analysis of human existence in an ontological framework. 'Faith', for example, is no longer to be conceived of as obedience to a divine summons which comes from beyond man in revealed confrontation, but is the existential commitment that the wider context in which man has his being is gracious to his being, does conjoin the polarities of his existence.

Secondly, and related, the summons to authenticity is located within a broad context of dialectical mediation between polarities. A minimal polarity recognised in existentialist philosophy between possibility and facticity extends to include a considerable variety of polarities. To possibility and facticity are added rationality and irrationality (as the capacity for right ordering and the disruption of order), responsibility and impotence, anxiety and hope, and individual and social. The dialectic movement between these poles becomes a characteristic feature of Macquarrie's theology, significantly applied to his doctrine of God, which I shall discuss in Chapter 5.[20]

In his article 'Revelation and Dialectical Theism' (written in the light of *In Search of Deity* when Macquarrie's dialectical method is more securely developed), P.S. Newey points out that Macquarrie's dialectic does not have the form 'X is A, X is not A', where not A is the logical negation of A. Rather, it has the form 'X is A and B', where B is not the negation of A 'but another positive quality, which, however, appears, at first sight at least, difficult to reconcile with A'.[21] This means that his dialectic is not logically absurd or simply proper to the *via negativa* involved in the use of analogical language. Rather, it is true Hegelian dialectic which 'pits word against word or thought against thought (*dia* as "separation") in order, by means of a necessary and mutually negating conflict, to find a way or to indicate a direction toward a mediating, synthesising position (*dia* as "transition")'.[22] Peter Hodgson points out that this form of dialectic does not involve pure negation, and therefore does not issue in irresolvable conflict. Thus, two terms in dialectical opposition 'mutually give and receive one another back from each other'.[23]

Newey's discussion concerns theism and balks at applying this dialectic to finite being, in order to give an account of how both characteristics can be affirmed simultaneously of the same object. However, it is precisely towards this possibility that Macquarrie's discussion of sin and grace points in establishing the groundwork of his natural theology. Sin is fundamentally an imbalance between the polarities in human existence, a failure to maintain the appropriate dialectic between poles which are not, ultimately, incompatible polar *opposites*.[24] The quest for grace, on the other hand, is exactly concerned with seeking 'support from beyond man such as would make sense of his existence and overcome its frustrations'.[25] Grace would be a 'further dimension in the situation', beyond man and nature, which provides the context and the condition for the possibility of maintaining the dialectic. In a key passage, Macquarrie describes the openness to grace, which sees

> the gulf between human resources (the heritage that is factically given) and the demands to which we are responsible (the potentialities that are disclosed). It seeks sense in this situation, and it sees that the condition that there is sense in it is that the being which we are given (the factical pole of existence) is of a piece with the existence to which we are summoned (the pole of possibility); that these are not accidentally conjoined or destined to be in perpetual and frustrating conflict with each other, but that they are both rooted in the wider context of being within which man has his being.[26]

This wider context of being, then, is *gracious* if it establishes a dialectic between the polarities in human existence.

Human receptivity

This much is a recapitulation of Macquarrie's account of the source of faith in the *human quest* for that which gives sense in existence. Fundamental to his understanding is also the way in which faith *finds that quest met* in human existence, since the man of faith

> speaks not so much of his own quest as of the object of this quest meeting him; or, better still, that he becomes the object of a search directed toward him; that the initiative comes from beyond himself, and that faith, while indeed it has roots within himself, is established only when he is grasped, as it were, by that for which he was dimly and ignorantly seeking.[27]

This grasp is experienced in various ways, for example as *grace* when it supports and strengthens man's existence, and as *judgement* in so far as it lays claim on him and exposes the distortions of his existence. *Revelation* points especially to the cognitive element of the experience, in so far as it brings him a new understanding both of himself and of his wider context. Rejecting criticisms that revelation can be defended on no rational grounds but only by an appeal to some private source of knowledge, Macquarrie again locates it by reference to the whole range of man's experience of knowing and to the type of capacity that makes it reasonable to think that he could be receptive to the religious confrontation with 'holy being'. This is, in brief, an 'epistemology of revelation', and shows the influence of Heidegger in the attention to truth as the unhiddenness of things as they are, to the role of affective states, and to the character of primordial thinking.

First, in the most general sense, revelation shares with all knowing some character of 'unveiling'. In a move typical of Heidegger, Macquarrie points to the Greek etymology of truth, ἀλήθεια, as 'unhiddenness':[28] 'We have attained truth when that which was concealed is made unhidden, brought out into the light.' That is to say, truth is not purely correspondent, but disclosive.[29]

This is key to Macquarrie's notion of revelation as it arises from the constitution of human existence: it does not involve seeing 'something extra' which can then be objectified, but seeing the same thing *in a different way*. The person who receives the revelation sees and hears no more than anyone in the situation could see and hear, but sees, as it were, in depth – sees not only the particular things that belong to the situation but becomes aware of the being that is present and manifest in them. This 'seeing' corresponds, for example, to Macquarrie's discussion of affective states which have their own understanding which points beyond the subject of the state. They refer not to objects, but to situations – and indeed to situations in which the person experiencing the state is a participant. This means that an affective state refers to something which is neither subject nor object but which is 'an unbroken unity of subject and object within a situation which is known from within'.[30] The relevance to the experience of revelation is made clear by the further clarification Macquarrie makes:

> A mood is something like an attunement to the environment, an awareness and response to the total situation in which one finds oneself and in which one participates. No amount of objective perceiving could ever disclose that of which we become aware in the mood. Yet the mood does not show us anything that does not show up in perceiving. It simply lets us be aware of the situation as a whole and permits us to notice dimensions of that situation which are disclosed to a participant but may be veiled from a mere beholder.[31]

What is distinctive about the religious use of the word is that the initiative is seen to lie with what is known: 'we do not bring it into the light or strip away what is concealing it, as we do in our researches into matters within the world, but rather that which is known comes into the light, or, better still, provides the light by which it is known and by which we in turn know ourselves.'[32]

Secondly, Macquarrie locates the revelatory experience in the range of man's general cognitive experience. Here Macquarrie uses Heidegger's distinction between calculative and primordial thinking, and a third type of thinking which he terms 'existential', to locate the kind of 'thinking' which best identifies revelation. Much discussion of revelation occurs, Macquarrie thinks mistakenly, under the category of *existential* thinking. Existential thinking means that kind of personal thinking which recognises that what is thought about is another subject. Typically, then, 'this kind of thinking involves participation, a thinking into the existence of the other subject that is thought about, and this "thinking into" is possible because of the common kind of being on both sides.'[33] Whilst this is more appropriate than the model of calculative thinking (for example, it replaces the notion of mastery and manipulation of what is known with the self-disclosure by what is known), Macquarrie points to three reasons for rejecting it as an unsatisfactory model. First, a personal encounter involves an essential physical aspect, which makes it difficult 'to suppose what a personal meeting or encounter could be like in the absence of the physical events which mediate it'.[34] Secondly, a personal encounter involves mutuality, whereas in a revelatory encounter 'the person who receives the revelation is utterly transcended by the holy being that reveals itself.'[35] Thirdly, a personal encounter involves two persons, that is, two beings, whereas in revelation the encounter is with *being* itself rather than with *a* being.

Macquarrie suggests that primordial, or essential, thinking is a more appropriate model for understanding the revelatory experience. Primordial thinking is not concerned with *encounters* with things or persons, but has a meditative rather than probing character. It waits and listens, and responds to the address of being itself, 'which communicates itself through all the particular beings by which it is present, by which it manifests itself, and not least through the depth of our own being, for we too are participants in being and indeed the only participants to which being opens itself, so that we not only are but we exist.'[36]

The knower is seized by what is known, and it impresses itself upon him, so that it has a gift-like character. Although it is the passive character of the knower that is emphasised in this explanation, he is not entirely passive because the capacity for revelation implies a degree both of appropriation and of kinship:

it is much more true to say that being grasps us than that we grasp being, yet it grasps us in such a way that we are not simply overwhelmed by it. In the religious experience of revelation, the overwhelmingness of being is matched by its grace, the *tremendum* by the *fascinans*, for being gives itself and opens itself, so that we stand in the grace and openness of being. It reveals itself not only in otherness but also in kinship, so that even as we are grasped by it, we can to some extent grasp it in turn and hold to it.[37]

Macquarrie likens the experience of primordial thinking and revelation to aesthetic experience: 'what is known in the aesthetic experience is not some additional thing, beyond what is open to universal inspection, but rather the depth of what confronts us, a structure or *Gestalt* that is noticed in the experience.'[38] It is this depth which is known rather than the things in themselves or something extra, which makes aesthetic experience an appropriate analogy for the revelatory experience, and, further, that it is not only a cognitive knowing but touches the whole of existence.

The divine pole

Revisiting Heidegger: Being's self-disclosure

The 'subjective' pole of Macquarrie's new-style natural theology harnesses his early existentialist commitments in a natural theology framework, then. The 'objective' pole reframes not only his early concern for ontology but, more significantly, his commitment to the kerygmatic summons in dialogue with Heidegger's later thought, to give an account of God's self-disclosure within the possibilities of natural theology. A brief review of ideas which occur especially in Heidegger's *Discourse on Thinking* and *Introduction to Metaphysics* will be helpful to clarify Macquarrie's thought.

I have already noted the theme of primordial, meditative thinking which Heidegger develops in his later work. In *Discourse in Thinking* (*Gelassenheit*, Releasement, in the original), meditative thinking is explored in the relatively uncomplicated forms of a memorial address and a 'conversation on a country road'. *Introduction to Metaphysics* investigates the same theme, but by the more convoluted means of etymology and an exposition of Heraclitus, Parmenides and Sophocles. Heidegger's aim in this latter work is to press back behind the Western philosophical tradition which understands the relation between thinking and being to be a relation between subject and object, to give an account of the relation such that being has the priority (indeed, is the active subject) and thinking is what is called forth.

Heidegger first argues that the domination of *logos* as logic, logical discourse, is etymologically suspect. Logos derives from λέγειν (Latin *legere*), to gather, collect: 'to put one thing with another, to bring together, in short, to gather'.[39] Alongside this, he places the derivation of *physis*, being, as 'the power that emerges. As contrasted with becoming, it is permanence, permanent presence. Contrasted with appearance, it is appearing, manifest presence.'[40] To make the connection between *physis* and *logos*, Heidegger interprets Heraclitus and Parmenides. From two fragments of Heraclitus, Heidegger gleans a use of *physis* and *logos* together which allows him to term *logos* as the primal gathering principle, the original 'collecting collectedness'. *Physis* and *logos*, then, are merged so that they come to mean the same: 'the steady gathering, the intrinsic togetherness of the essent', which does not merely dissolve into a freedom from opposition but 'maintains in a common bond the conflicting and that which tends apart ... [and] by uniting the opposites maintains the full sharpness of their tension'.[41]

From Parmenides' maxim *to gar auto noein estin te kai einai* (usually translated 'thinking and being are the same'), Heidegger reaches the translation 'there is a reciprocal bond between apprehension and being'. *Noein* is translated 'to apprehend' (*vernehmen*), which Heidegger notes has a double meaning of to hear and to question. Thus it means to accept, to let that which shows itself come to one, but not in a merely accepting attitude, but rather a *receptive* attitude. If, as Heidegger understands Parmenides, this apprehension is the same as being, being can now be explained thus:

> being means: to stand in the light, to appear, to enter into unconcealment. Where this happens, i.e. where being prevails, apprehension prevails and happens with it; the two belong together. Apprehension is the receptive bringing-to-stand of the intrinsically permanent that manifests itself ... To [*physis*] *belongs* apprehension, which shares in its power.[42]

What this connection between gathering, emerging power and apprehension allows Heidegger to assert is that apprehension 'is not a function that man has as an attribute, but rather the other way around: apprehension is the happening that has man.'[43] Man is the being in which being and apprehension occur together; this is the distinctive nature of human being. Where being prevails, apprehension must also prevail: being *requires* a place to appear, a place of disclosure, and this place is man. This is so because, for Sophocles, nothing surpasses man in his strangeness, in his contradiction between his overpowering of the world and his journeying into unfamiliar places which overpower him. In his grappling with this contradiction, man finds himself and shapes his world (that is, he becomes historical). It is being itself which drives man to become historical, 'which drives him beyond himself to venture forth toward being, to accomplish being, to stabilise it in the work, and so hold open the essent as a whole'.[44] Man is the site of openness, the site in which being is not only present but also manifest. Thus it is only as being's active self-disclosure through man, only in this accomplishment by being of unconcealment, that man 'thinks' being as the apprehension by being in man of being's appearance.[45]

The content of revelation

The influence of Heidegger's understanding of the self-disclosure and address of being emerges in Macquarrie's account of the content of divine initiative in revelation. To see how this can be the case, it is helpful to note three understandings of revelation from which Macquarrie distances himself.

First, he rejects the view that the content of revelation is 'a body of ready-made statements giving us information about matters inaccessible to our ordinary ways of knowing', that is to say, an esoteric knowledge in verbal, propositional form.[46] This popular misconception, Macquarrie suggests, is encouraged by the Church's preoccupation with verbal formulations in general. Just as faith is not primarily assent to propositions but an existential attitude of acceptance and commitment, so the corresponding revelation which seizes man in his whole being is not primarily verbal statement but the self-giving of being.

Secondly, Macquarrie rejects the view that the content of revelation can be 'transcribed into propositions or theories like those through which the sciences offer us a transcript of the phenomena of nature'.[47] He associates this view with traditional metaphysics, and although Heidegger is prepared to 'reclaim' the term metaphysics from its familiar meaning as the detached, speculative study of being (a task he rejects in *Being and Time*) and use it in his own sense as Dasein's 'going beyond' beings into nothing to find being itself (in *What is Metaphysics?*), Macquarrie still rejects the term as being too closely identified with an objective, pseudo-scientific style of enterprise.

Thirdly, Macquarrie repeats the inadequacy of the analogy of personal encounter with respect to the content of revelation. Just as the content of revelation cannot be deemed wholly objective, neither can it be considered through a subjective model, but must be articulated in a way that transcends the subject-object distinction.

The confrontation with being that constitutes the content of revelation is *sui generis*, but nevertheless, if it does have a cognitive aspect as Macquarrie has suggested, it must be expressible in verbal form, even if this is secondary and inadequate. Without verbal expression, revelation would appear vague and indeterminate, possibly contentless and hardly, indeed, revealing. It would also remain a private matter: 'in the absence of articulate communication, there could hardly be a sharing of the revelation; and without a sharing, there could be no community of faith founded upon the revelation; and thus in turn there could be no transmission and no repetitive appropriation of the revelation.'[48] The confrontation with being, then, must be articulated, and in such a way that overcomes the subject-object divide and, as Macquarrie has shown, this means in a way which indicates its participatory character: 'we ourselves *are*, and only through our participation in being can we think of it or name it, and only on the basis of its self-giving and self-disclosing to us can we know it.'[49]

Starting from existential analysis as Macquarrie does, Being must be understood in a non-speculative, existentially-oriented way.

Letting-be: ontological difference Being is *the prior condition that anything may be*, and as such, although it is not 'a' being, it is more 'beingful' than any thing which exists. It is a *transcendens*, transcending all usual categories, mysterious, incomparable, and yet not wholly incomprehensible. As the condition that particular beings may be, it has precisely the character of letting-be: that is, the positive and active 'enabling to be, empowering to be, or bringing into being'.[50] It is energy or, better, an *act* of unified, organised energy. As such, Being has priority over the beings which it lets-be: 'letting-be is the creativity of Being, and the dependence of the beings is their creatureliness.'[51] It is this capacity to let-be that constitutes the ontological difference between Being and the beings. The difference is absolute, but because the difference consists in conferring and sharing being it does not establish a distancing or alienating relation.

Presence and manifestation: ontological affinity Whilst this transcendent letting-be is mysterious at the ultimate level of why there should be something rather than nothing, it is not wholly inaccessible. Indeed, it is understandable at the *existential* level, in that man exists and knows that he exists. That is to say, man participates in being and knows therefore that he has been let-be, and even knows that he participates to a limited degree in letting-be as he engages concernfully with his world. Macquarrie notes that the religious man 'experiences the letting-be of beings as being's self-giving, the grace of being which pours itself out and confers being'.[52] Further, since being is present in every particular being – nothing can be unless it participates in being – it is open and accessible in its closeness in every being. Macquarrie asks, 'What do we mean by talk of seeing things in a new way or seeing them in depth or in a further dimension, except that we become aware of the *presence* of being, that is to say, of what lets the beings be and mediates itself through them?'[53] In part, this corresponds to the existential awareness of being which prompts ontological enquiry, but it also presses beyond the instrumental concern with objects to a more sacramental awareness of vehicles of being. This notion of *presence* becomes increasingly significant in Macquarrie's later work and, as well as being a key development in his sacramental emphasis, proves significant for the capacity of his theology to mediate between revealed and natural theologies by conceiving the self-giving *act* of God as *present in* as well as *present to* the realm of beings.

As well as the term 'presence', Macquarrie uses the notion 'manifestation'. He means by this a more general self-disclosure of being than the primordial revelation upon which a religious community is founded, which is nevertheless a making explicit of the being which is everywhere present. Manifestation may be latent; as Heidegger has pointed out, we tend to concern ourselves with beings rather then being. Therefore it does require an initiative, a self-opening, on the part of being. The relation of 'manifestation' and 'revelation' is ambiguous, though presumably revelation includes manifestation, whereas manifestation does not automatically mean revelation: everything has a revelatory capacity but not everything is revelation. Newey notes the ambiguity thus: 'On the one hand [Macquarrie] writes as if simply *being* were enough for a being to manifest a certain degree of Being, depending on its position within the hierarchy of being. Yet on the other hand he writes as if simply to be were not enough: manifestation is something more which happens on top of being.'[54]

Certainly Macquarrie has in mind levels of disclosure: in the hierarchy of being, human existence manifests being most fully, uniting material, organic and personal being; a hydrogen atom may manifest being, but to a lesser degree because it participates less fully in being. But even these levels of disclosure are dependent on the self-giving act of being in the beings, without which they would not be at all.

From Being to God

Macquarrie's introduction to being's self-disclosure, then, is this: 'being "is" the incomparable that lets-be and that is present and manifests itself in and through the beings.'[55] But how does he move from this general philosophical framework to a Christian understanding of God?

Holy Being   When he considers how this understanding of being helps to indicate the place of the religious term 'God', Macquarrie is careful to emphasise that 'being' and 'God' are not synonyms.[56] 'Being' is a neutral designation; it may be experienced positively or negatively, as gracious or as indifferent or alien to human existence, and no existential orientation can be inferred from it. 'God' does designate being, but it indicates a particular attitude to being – the attitude of faith, with 'important existential connotations of valuation, commitment, worship, and so on', again comparable with Otto's *mysterium tremendum et fascinans*.[57] 'God', then, might be said to refer to 'holy being'. Such an understanding unites the existential aspect, which *attributes* value and *takes up* the attitude of acceptance and commitment, with the ontological aspect which *discloses* value and *summons* acceptance and commitment.

Accordingly, Macquarrie identifies this position as *existential-ontological theism*, and suggests that it is the next important stage in the development of the idea of God from the primitive mythological and heavily anthropomorphic notion of a powerful God 'like us only more so', and the traditional theistic metaphysical God, existing beyond the self-regulating world. To perceive of God as holy being rather than as a being – albeit *ens realissimum* – would be theology's own engagement with Heidegger's challenge that Western culture has been characterised by the 'forgetting of being', emerging in theology as the thinking of God as *a* being. And it would be to continue a tradition found in both Augustine and Aquinas linking God with being, which finds some stirrings in contemporary theology in the attempt to conceive of God as *immeasurably* the greatest being: 'let it be said that if God is conceived as *immeasurably* the greatest being, so that he tends to be thought differently from particular beings altogether, then one is moving toward the thought of God as being.'[58]

Does such an understanding of God as present and manifest in all things leave Macquarrie open to a charge of pantheism? Certainly he is constructing a highly immanentist theology which explicitly guards against an exaggerated view of the transcendence of God, such as he reckons has dominated recent theologies. But is this tantamount to pantheism? Macquarrie himself makes a brief defence against the charge of pantheism, which he suggests 'rests on a gross misunderstanding' in the failure to understand his distinction between being and the sum of beings. Far from being the totality of beings, being is the *transcendens*, wholly other from the world which it lets-be, even though it is present and manifest in every being. It is important to note, then, that even at this stage, divine transcendence is not a quality *opposed to* divine immanence, but is *the condition by which* God can be immanent. Again, this is an example of his rejection of Kierkegaardian ontology in which the transcendence-in-immanence of divine Will confronts the finite will, and his use of Heideggerian ontology in which the transcendence-as-immanence of divine Being establishes and supports (lets-be) finite being.

Macquarrie is concerned to maintain these poles of transcendence and immanence in dialectic relation, and against pantheism holds that Being is of a different order to the beings and that 'the dynamic letting-be of being is prior to the derivative existence of the beings.'[59] This asymmetry of relationship between God and the world is the essential element in a rejection of pantheism. However, against traditional monarchical theism, which envisages God in a wholly asymmetrical relationship to the world (even though using the model of one being over others), he holds to the importance of a balancing 'organic' model which recognises the immanent pole and allows for a degree of symmetry and reciprocity in the relationship between God and the world. He insists that 'God cannot be conceived apart from the world, for it is of his very essence (letting-be) to create; God is affected by the world as well as affecting it, for creation entails risk and vulnerability; God is in time and history, as well as above them.'[60]

'God', then, has a double meaning:

> an ontological meaning, in so far as the word denotes being, and an existential meaning, in so far as it expresses an attitude of commitment to, or faith in, being. These two meanings belong together in the word 'God', and are inseparable. The word is the key word of religion because it already expresses the basic religious conviction – that fact and value belong together, that being which gives being is also gracious being. The assertion 'God exists' may be expressed in another way as meaning that being 'is' not alien or neutral over against us, but that it both demands and sustains, so that through faith in being, we can ourselves advance into fullness of being and fulfil the potentialities of selfhood.[61]

Again, this is the *grace of being*, but now given specific existential-ontological shape and content. Certainly, being is still understood as gracious to human existence, the meaning of the 'grace of being' derived from existential analysis. But here there is an additional emphasis: that this cannot be separated from the understanding that being is gracious *because it gives being*. Being as the giver of the gift of being is the ontological *transcendens* upon which finite being's experience of grace depends.

Triunity Although this account of God as holy being is clearly not equivalent to the traditional Christian understanding of God as Trinity, Macquarrie goes on to argue a 'convergence' of the doctrine of God as being with the doctrine of God as Trinity. Indeed, he suggests that

> the doctrine of the triune God gathers up in a remarkable way the findings of our philosophical theology ... if one is to think at all of holy being in dynamic rather than inert terms, as both transcendent and immanent and not just as one or the other, as the *mysterium* that is both *tremendum* and *fascinans*, then if God had not revealed himself as triune, one would need to have invented the idea of his three-in-oneness, or at least something like it.[62]

Macquarrie notes that these are not in practice rival accounts, for both sum up a long history of revelatory experience. On the one hand, trinitarian language is 'a language rooted in existence, in the community's experience of the approach of God'.[63] On the other hand, the doctrine of God as being has roots in Aquinas' teaching that the essence of God is to be, and in earlier Church fathers, stemming from the theophany recorded in Exodus 'I am who I am', and the Johannine 'I am' sayings.[64] So the 'nascent conception of God-as-Trinity' in the 'I am' parallelism, which expresses the unity of the Father and the Son, converges with the use of the language of being in thought about God.

In his trinitarian account of God as holy being (or, conversely, his existential-ontological account of God as triune) Macquarrie explains the three persons as movements. The Father is termed *primordial being*, to indicate 'the ultimate act or energy of letting-be, the condition that there should be anything whatsoever, the source not only of whatever is but of all possibilities of being'.[65] This understanding guards against the implication of remoteness and lack of differentiation in the transcendence of God, for it means that we do not conceive of primordial Being 'in isolation as an 'uncarved block' or whatever, but as a source of outpouring which is inseparable from the whole structure of Being and which is something like a 'movement' within it'.[66] That is to say, the first person of the Trinity cannot be known 'in himself' but only in so far as he pours himself out in the dynamics of being. The Son is termed *expressive* Being. It is through expressive Being that the energy of primordial Being is poured out 'and gives rise to the world of particular beings, having an intelligible structure and disposed in time and space'.[67] As expressive Being, the Logos is identified with Being, not with beings, but it is in and through beings that it expresses Being: 'the primordial being of the Father, which would otherwise be entirely hidden, flows out through expressive Being to find its expression in the world of beings.'[68] Although for Christians the fundamental expression of Being is in the finite being of Jesus ('and in such a way that his being is caught up into Being itself') and therefore at a specific point in history, the Logos – expressive Being – is co-eternal with the Father. This means that Christian theology does not think of 'an original static undifferentiated Being, from which the movements of Being started up as something subsequent ... If the Son is eternally begotten, so that there never was a time when the Son was not, then Being has always been dynamic, and primordial Being has always been united with expressive Being.'[69] Thus Macquarrie notes the unity and stability of Being even in its diversity and dynamism.

Because Being moves out from itself 'into a world of change and multiplicity and possibility' in the letting-be of beings, it involves itself in *risk* – that is to say, the risk that Being itself could become fragmented. This is particularly the case with the letting-be of man who has both freedom and responsibility and must choose whether or not to be faithful to Being. Rewording his earlier analysis of man as the one to whom Being is disclosed, and therefore as able not only to grasp his existence but also to fall from it, Macquarrie indicates the risk to Being in that human beings 'can choose to be for themselves, gathering up their being and ceasing to manifest that letting-be which is the essence of the Being of which they were constituted the guardians'.[70] That is to say, not only does man frustrate Being's letting-be of his own self in his failing to *exist*, but he fails to participate in the letting-be of other beings so that they slip back from being; Being is doubly frustrated.

It is on this understanding that Macquarrie deems the Holy Spirit *unitive* Being: 'it is the function of the Spirit to maintain, strengthen, and, where need be, restore the unity of Being with the beings.'[71] This results in a richer unity than could have been the case if primordial Being was undifferentiated and unexpressed, because the unity is one of diversity and of freedom. Macquarrie does not speculate about what this means for the lower levels of creation, but suggests that for man the action of the Spirit is unifying in that we see in depth Being as it manifests itself: 'this is a unifying operation because it relates the beings to Being, so that the beings that belong in the world are seen not as self-subsistent entities but as beings in which Being itself is present-and-manifest; while correspondingly we know ourselves not as autonomous beings, but as guardians of Being.'[72]

CONCLUSION

In these developments from his Glasgow period to his work in America, Macquarrie transforms his early concern with existentialism, moving it away from its typically Bultmannian context of revealed theology, into a natural theology framework. Without diminishing his emphasis that it is in the very constitution of human existence that the kerygmatic summons is received, Macquarrie's thought develops to give an account of the continuities of being which render the summons not only appropriatable, but also gracious to human being. The developing circles of relationality against which these continuities emerge now include the social and ecclesial, and already anticipate the cosmic relationality which deepens in the Oxford period. In this existential-ontological natural theology, the doctrinal heart of Macquarrie's theology comes to mature expression.

NOTES

1 The degree of this shift can be assessed by comparing Macquarrie's inaugural lecture at Union (1962) with his inaugural lecture at Oxford (1971). The former concerns how theological language can be meaningful to modern man; the latter is more confident in theology's role and influence in the contemporary context, and concerned that it should take the correct shape to make an appropriate influence. Compare 'How is theology possible?' in *SCE* 3–16 with 'Creation and Environment', *Expository Times* 83 (1971), 4–9.
2 *PCT* v
3 *PCT* 1, 2
4 *PCT* 3
5 See Macquarrie's account in *PCT* 21–33, and compare his *Twentieth Century Religious Thought* (London: SCM 1988[4], 2001[5]), hereafter *TCRT*, which is especially concerned with religious thought on the boundaries with philosophy. A persistent theme in *PCT* is that of 'seeing in depth' rather than seeing something additional or different.
6 *PCT* 43
7 *PCT* 57
8 *PCT* 55. Anselm's ontological argument is a key example, see *Proslogion* II and

IV (La Salle: Open Court 1957), 'I thank thee, gracious Lord, I thank thee; because what I formerly believed by thy bounty, I now so understand by thy illumination, that if I were unwilling to believe that thou dost exist, I should not be able not to understand this to be true.'

9   *PCT* 55–56
10 *PCT* 56, italics are Macquarrie's.
11 In contrast to the (supposedly) rational *a priori* of Anselm's *Proslogion* or Descartes' *Meditations on First Philosophy* (in *Philosophical Writings of Descartes* vol. 2 (Cambridge: CUP 1984), V, 65; and in contrast to the *a posteriori* method of Aquinas' Five Ways, *Summa Theologiae* 1a,2,3 (London: Eyre & Spottiswoode 1964).
12 'The problem of natural theology' in *Pittsburgh Perspective* 5 (1964) 10–19, 16, and see *PCT* 52, 56.
13 *PCT* 50. Macquarrie exaggerates his view to make his point. In practice, there is more common ground than he admits, in the understanding that reason is wrongly ordered (cf *PCT* 70) rather than wholly diminished. See John Calvin, *Institutes of the Christian Religion* I.III.1, I.IV.1, II.I.8, II.II.12.
14 *PCT* 50
15 *PCT* 51
16 *PCT* 52–53
17 *PCT* 53
18 In this sense, Macquarrie stands in the broad tradition of Luther and Calvin, Schleiermacher and Bultmann, that God is only known as he acts in human being, rather than in the Barthian insistence that God acts 'from above'. Such a tradition does not depend on a 'high' view of humanity; it agrees that only Christ is 'fully' human. Nevertheless, it starts with anthropology rather than christology because of the methodological necessity of starting 'where we are'.
19 *PCT* 61, 62. Note Rahner's influence here: see *Hearers of the Word* (New York: Seabury Press 1969) chapter 6.
20 Schubert Ogden criticises Macquarrie for his repeated use of 'not only ... but also', but Macquarrie welcomes Ogden's characterisation of his theology because it highlights a key method for preventing one-sided simplification and distortion.
21 P.S. Newey, 'Revelation and Dialectical Theism: Beyond John Macquarrie' in *Colloquium: the Australian and New Zealand Theological Society* 22 (1989), 37–44, 38.
22 Peter C. Hodgson, 'Georg Wilhelm Friedrich Hegel' in *Nineteenth Century Religious Thought in the West* vol. 1, eds Ninian Smart, John Clayton, Steven Katz and Patrick Sherry (Cambridge: CUP 1985), 81–121, 85. Macquarrie does not have the same concern with the role of reason in this process as Hegel, and claims no more than 'indicating a direction' as a reminder that there are limitations to finite being's understanding of God, *ISD* 172.
23 G.W.F. Hegel, *The Phenomenology of Mind* (London: George Allen & Unwin Ltd 1949), 234.
24 *PCT* 68–69. Macquarrie applies this not primarily to individual existence, but to the 'massive disorder' prevalent throughout human existence. In his exposition he is clearly indebted to Reinhold Niebuhr's analysis in *The Nature and Destiny of Man* vol. 1 (London: Nisbet & Co 1941).
25 *PCT* 73
26 *PCT* 79–80

27 *PCT* 83
28 That is, ἀ + λανθάνω (to escape notice).
29 *PCT* 86
30 *PCT* 98
31 *PCT* 98
32 *PCT* 86
33 *PCT* 92. The 'repetitive' thinking which appropriates a historical event or teaching or text is an example of this existential thinking, as is the 'solicitude', *Fürsorge*, with which *Dasein* recognises a fellow human being.
34 *PCT* 93
35 *PCT* 93
36 *PCT* 94
37 *PCT* 95. Here, as throughout *PCT*, the influence of Rudolf Otto's *The Idea of the Holy* is evident. Thus *mysterium tremendum et fascinans* points to the awe and 'overpoweringness' but also to the fascinating attractiveness of the wholly Other.
38 *PCT* 95
39 *Introduction to Metaphysics* 124
40 *Introduction to Metaphysics* 125
41 *Introduction to Metaphysics* 130, 134
42 *Introduction to Metaphysics* 139
43 *Introduction to Metaphysics* 141
44 *Introduction to Metaphysics* 163
45 This is a comparable shift of emphasis to that which Heidegger makes in *Being and Time*, where he insists that being is not in time, but time is in being.
46 *PCT* 104
47 *PCT* 105. Compare Macquarrie's consistent rejection of objectifying reason in theology.
48 *PCT* 105. Heidegger may be content with mystical communion, but Macquarrie seeks something more social.
49 *PCT* 106, italics are Macquarrie's.
50 *PCT* 113
51 *PCT* 211
52 *PCT* 114
53 *PCT* 114, italics are Macquarrie's.
54 P.S. Newey, 'Revelation and Dialectical Theism' in *Colloquium: The Australian and New Zealand Theological Society* 22 (1989), 37–44, 39; italics are Newey's.
55 *PCT* 115
56 Contrast Tillich for whom Being is the only non-symbolic language for God.
57 *PCT* 115
58 *PCT* 117, italics are Macquarrie's. This way of speaking means that it is inaccurate to say that 'God exists'. Beings exist, but God lets-be, which is more primordial than to be. To say that God exists is, in this sense, to reify God.
59 *PCT* 120
60 *PCT* 121
61 *PCT* 121–22
62 *PCT* 188. Macquarrie does admit that since his theology had to be constructed from a context rather than in a neutral sphere of observation, and in practice was constructed within the perspective of the Christian experience of God, the convergence is unsurprising!
63 *PCT* 191

64 See W. Eichrodt, *Theology of the Old Testament* vol. 1 (London: SCM 1961), 187–92 for the implication of active existence in the Hebrew *Yahweh*.
65 *PCT* 199
66 *PCT* 199
67 *PCT* 199
68 *PCT* 199–200
69 *PCT* 200
70 *PCT* 201
71 *PCT* 201
72 *PCT* 202

Chapter 5

The Grace of Being

INTRODUCTION: *IN SEARCH OF HUMANITY* AND *IN SEARCH OF DEITY*

The development of Macquarrie's thought into an existential-ontological natural theology culminates in his Oxford period in an anthropological argument for the existence of God.[1] The argument reaches cumulative expression in the two volumes *In Search of Humanity* (1982) and *In Search of Deity* (1984). Here Macquarrie's natural theology, based on the study of human being as a centre of freedom, is charted, as it were, from both directions: from the phenomenological analysis of the human condition and from the theological and philosophical concepts provided in various traditions of natural theology (that is, from a typically existentialist perspective and a traditionally ontological perspective, though dialectically qualified and enriched).

Since the books are companion volumes in many respects, their lack of similarity and continuity in other respects is disconcerting. Not only are they fundamentally different in style (*In Search of Humanity* is a collection of short essays on various themes, *In Search of Deity* is a more closely worked integral argument), but *In Search of Humanity* ends with a cue for a sequel, which *In Search of Deity* does not overtly provide. *In Search of Humanity* concludes with remarks on the concept of God, the point at which 'the search for humanity merges into the search for deity, [which] would call for another book',[2] so the very different starting point of *In Search of Deity*, in the discussion of classical theism, at first strikes a discordant note. Studied together, however, the two books present Macquarrie's consolidated anthropological argument for the existence of God, and an indication of its place in a tradition of theism which he reclaims as a valuable resource in the task of a natural theology for the present day.

In addition, the two volumes mark a further development in Macquarrie's thought, beyond the social and existential-ontological dimensions which characterised his New York period, to integrate the cosmos within the explicit scope of the grace of being. This development is best conceived as an additional concentric circle enlarging the scope of the grace of being beyond the two stages already charted. In Macquarrie's early work, the integrity of the individual existent was uppermost, even though he was already straining towards a greater emphasis on community than that typically found in existentialism and in Bultmann's theology in particular. Thus, in the Glasgow period, the grace of being was principally identified as the condition of unity between facticity and possibility in human existence, and this continues to provide the inner core to his theology. During the New York period, this core is enlarged by a surrounding concern with the corporate character of human existence and faith, shaped ecclesially by Macquarrie's growing commitment to Anglicanism, and politically under the ethos of Union Seminary. Here, the grace of being extends in scope to address the existence of the individual in its context of human institutions and community.

In the Oxford period, a still broader concern with the cosmos emerges, due in part to the influence of Macquarrie's colleague at Union, Daniel Day Williams, who looks for his categories of theological explanation to A.N. Whitehead. Macquarrie agrees that this allows Williams a much more adequate theology of nature than he had himself achieved under the influence of Heidegger's thought.[3] As will become clear in this chapter, this enlarged scope gives a new unifying dimension to the grace of being, which decisively overcomes the man-nature dualism inherent in existentialism.

In order best to illustrate this shift in Macquarrie's thought, and the new scope of meaning of the grace of being, it will be helpful to look first at *In Search of Deity* and then at *In Search of Humanity*. Although this is contrary to the order in which the books were written, the new insight into the character of human existence in relation to the whole created realm, and its role in the anthropological argument for the existence of God, appears most distinctively in the cumulative argument of the two books. Enough has already been said of Macquarrie's method to avoid any suggestion that his doctrine of God is *a priori* by considering it first. It remains Macquarrie's conviction that the best approach to many of the questions of theology is through the study of our humanity.

Initially, it will be sufficient to emphasise that Macquarrie's analysis of human existence in *In Search of Humanity* is for the most part a thematic recapitulation of his earlier thought, with its concern for existentialist themes in a broader corporate and existential-ontological framework, and its attention to embodiment in the sphere of the material and spatio-temporal. One divergent theme which will prove important for the anthropological argument, however, concerns the relation of human being to objects in the world.

Whereas in existentialist thought the fundamental relation between a human being and a material thing is of *concern*, in the sense of concern with equipment or a tool ('What is this *for*?'), in *In Search of Humanity* it is *having*.[4] Although this is not a wholly fortunate term, since it implies disposal, Macquarrie's exposition is concerned with the fundamental material necessities which raise life beyond survival to a distinctively human existence, and the way in which these resources are managed. His exposition is principally in terms of economics as the institutionalised (that is, corporate, public and ordered) form of having, wealth distribution, and planetary resources. The significance of this is that the *individualistic dualism* of instrumentality is replaced by the *socially responsible continuity* of stewardship within creation, in explicit agreement with Aquinas' teaching that human duty is 'to care for and distribute the earth's resources'.[5] This emphasis on responsible participation in one world which comprises persons and things, 'the one world of God', proves an important anticipation of the role in the cosmos accorded to human being in the full anthropological argument derived from both volumes. Not least, this depends on a renewed emphasis on embodiment.

Although existentialist philosophy insists that human being is *embodied* in the sense of being-in-the-world, in its explicit opposition to the Cartesian dualism of *res cogitans* and *res extensa* the physicality of this embodiment tends to be almost hidden behind the meaning of 'world' as the total context of significance. Although this world of significance cannot be apart from material reality (or man's engagement in it separate from his physical being in the world), the sphere of the material *as material* is not the key to significance. The hiddenness of physicality is further emphasised by the distinction of human *Existenz* from the *Vorhandenheit* of material and organic objects, which establishes a dualism between humanity and the rest of the material world. In his early works, as I have shown in Chapter 1, Macquarrie accepts this understanding of embodiment, and Bultmann's rendering of σῶμα to refer to it. By *In Search of Humanity*, however, Macquarrie is much more concerned to locate humanity as part of the universe. Embodiment does refer explicitly to the 'material organism' in its unity with freedom, transcendence and rationality. The human being is neither separated from, nor equated with, the material body, but lives a life which is 'incarnate', that is to say, which 'takes place "in the flesh", in the sphere of the material and spatio-temporal'.[6]

CLASSICAL AND DIALECTICAL THEISM

Originally the St Andrews Gifford Lectures for 1983–84, *In Search of Deity* places Macquarrie's new-style natural theology in relation not to the existential-ontological analysis of human being but to the traditional natural theology of classical theism, and to an alternative tradition which Macquarrie terms 'dialectical theism'.[7] Macquarrie's fundamental concern is to establish an understanding of God which will answer the question, 'What must God be, if he is to be both the focus of human worship and aspiration, and at the same time to be seen as the source, sustainer and goal of all that is?'[8]

Classical theism: the distant monarch

From his fundamental tenet that natural theology is 'natural' not because God is treated in the same way as a phenomenon of nature, but because 'the enquiry is to be carried out by the natural human resources that are common to all without appeal to some special source of knowledge', Macquarrie offers a critique of traditional natural theology, typified by classical theism.[9]

In beginning with the question, 'Does God exist?', classical theism inevitably objectifies God, considering God as (at best, *akin to*) one item amongst those which exist. Even though the definitions of God are 'fundamentally qualified', it remains ambiguous whether God is in fact removed by this from the various series of items. Furthermore, the Thomistic tradition of 'proofs' points to the concept of God principally as 'the efficient cause of the universe and also its intelligent ruler'.[10] This one-sided monarchical concept is, Macquarrie suggests, no longer *intellectually credible* in an age concerned with the organic integrity of the cosmos and with questions of human scope and autonomy. Nor is it *religiously satisfying*, since the religious consciousness seeks a God corresponding to the sense of affinity and immanence, rather than one who represents the 'cosmic forces' and 'reality of a higher order' as wholly external and other.

The teaching of classical theism on the attributes of God has compounded this monarchical starting point. The identification of the attributes as impassibility, immutability, eternity and perfection has served only to emphasise its one-sidedness: a God who is invulnerable, static and self-contained. The attributes function effectively to remove God from the series of 'things that exist' by emphatic qualification, but in so doing they exaggerate the distance and difference between God and the world without addressing the fundamental issue of how ontological difference is (mis-)conceived.

Even the account of God's *relation to the world* in the doctrine of creation further exaggerates the model of isolated, distant monarch. Creation *ex nihilo* by sovereign will separates the world from God. The created world is external to God and has a measure of independence, albeit wholly derivative. The act of creation, as wholly non-necessary and voluntaristic, holds open the implication of caprice and arbitrariness. God's continuing action in the world, which distinguishes classical theism from deism, is principally by means of 'secondary causes', but classical theism does, nevertheless, also allow for God's sovereign action beyond (and contrary to) secondary causes. This concept of a God *external* to the world but *intervening* in its affairs is, for Macquarrie, problematic to modern understanding.[11]

Further, Macquarrie suggests that the model of such an external God, who acts on and affects the world but is neither acted upon nor affected by it, swiftly moves to either acosmism or atheism. On the one hand, if God neither is increased by the world nor would be diminished by its disappearance, the world has no ultimate value, and 'only the invisible God or spiritual being is real; all else is illusion.'[12] On the other hand, if the world makes no difference to God, creation is little more than a capricious act with no continuing significance, and there is little practical difference between theism and atheism.[13]

Dialectical theism: clues in the cosmos

Against this classical tradition which emphasises divine transcendence *over* the created realm, whilst using language which objectifies God as one existent among others, Macquarrie seeks an alternative tradition which will share his own concerns both to express the kinship between God and the world by grounding it in a *different model of transcendence* derived from human being, and to safeguard the ontological difference in the *capacity to let-be*. Macquarrie finds in dialectical theism a more adequate account of God, which unites the existential and ontological poles in mutually informing relation.

Dialectic

The tradition Macquarrie explores lies between two one-sided extremes. On the one hand, it is posed against the one-sided transcendence of classical theism. On the other hand, it is posed against the one-sided immanence of pantheism, and the identification of God with the world-process. Dialectical theism claims that the being of God 'is both transcendent and immanent, both impassible and passible, both eternal and temporal'.[14] In adopting this position, Macquarrie concedes that the notion of God is, in a preliminary sense, *a priori*: the conditions of human existence prompt a search for a God who is already perceived to be the condition for affinity with the environing reality (or, the source of unity between possibility and facticity). In this sense, God 'must be' both transcendent and immanent in order to be religiously and intellectually satisfying. This 'must be' refers to the conditions which must be met if God-language is to be deemed appropriate.

The concept of God which Macquarrie develops in discussion with dialectical theism takes the form of 'a series of dialectical oppositions within God'.[15] These are neither contradictions nor sheer paradox, but take the Hegelian method described above in Chapter 4, moving from an account of the polarities of human existence to an account of the being of God.

The dialectical oppositions which Macquarrie discusses, in conversation with Plotinus, Dionysius, Eriugena, Nicolas of Cusa, Leibniz, Hegel, Whitehead and Heidegger, are as follows: being and nothing, one and many, knowability and incomprehensibility, transcendence and immanence, impassibility and passibility, eternity and temporality. Although each of these oppositions invites discussion, an indication of a particular cluster of concepts which emerge in the tradition must suffice in order to establish the concept of God which lies at the heart of Macquarrie's anthropological argument, and to anticipate the corresponding character and role of human being.

The One and the many

Since the starting point of the exploration is with Plotinus, the fundamental question which determines the enquiry is not 'Does God exist?', but 'What is the relation between the One and the many?' In answer, the tradition asserts firstly that the One is the *source* of the many, whether as the ultimate in (and yet beyond) the series (Leibniz) or wholly beyond the series (Dionysius), and that it is the source because of the superabundance of its being which overflows in creativity. In so far as the created realm can know the divine transcendence, it knows it as this going-beyond itself in creativity. Thus, creation is not an act of will in this tradition, but a consequence of the divine nature, and has the character less exclusively of 'making' and more of 'emanation' or 'fulguration' (Leibniz), or even of 'ultimate giving' (Heidegger). This means that the created realm bears considerable affinity to the Creator, whose own self is in some sense imparted in the creative act, even while remaining 'in himself'.[16] It also means that there is a continuity and dynamism both in the creative act and in the affinity: God is co-eternal with his creating.

Secondly, the tradition asserts that the One is the *goal* of the many, that the many are a dynamic hierarchy of being, transcending to union with (and likeness to) the One, a process which might be termed a move towards 'deiformity' or, in its ultimate form (for human being) 'deification', 'a process whereby we are made like to God and are united to him, so far as these things may be'.[17]

Three important points emerge from this twofold relation of the One to the many, emphasising the dynamic nature of God in this tradition, and the affinity and mutuality of God and the world, in contrast to the static and distant relation of classical theism.

First, there is an implicit *natural* theology of a triune God. God has three 'modes' in his relation to creation. The first, a primordial mode, is prior to creation, wholly other and hidden; second is an expressive mode, in which superabundant being overflows in order to be known and to give relation; and third, a unitive mode by which all of creation is eternally gathered into union with its source and destiny.

Secondly, there is a sense in which God can be said to 'create himself' in creation. Macquarrie locates this point in Eriugena's teaching. God is *not* himself created, but since his willing, acting and being are the same, he is in that which he makes and it is possible to say that the divine nature, 'although it creates all things and cannot be created by anything, is in an admirable manner created in all things which take their being from it.'[18] This is akin to Whitehead's notion of the consequent aspect of God. Macquarrie is careful to make the distinction that God does not '*evolve*', but that he is '*enriched*', so that perfection is no longer a static concept but something which moves on into richer levels. The dynamism of God is thus passible and temporal in its affinity to the cosmos.

Thirdly, there is a strong doctrine of internal relations in the hierarchy of being since it has a single source and a common goal. For Plotinus this is simple sociality, but for Leibniz and, following him, Whitehead, it amounts to a philosophy of organism in which the whole is in some sense present in each part, and each part both derives its character from its place in the whole and contributes to the whole from which all the (other) parts derive their character. There is implicit in this doctrine a mutual responsibility (though not a conscious one) for the process towards union with God, 'a reciprocal communication among the different grades of being', which Dionysius describes as 'two holy tasks, those of receiving and transmitting purification free from mixture, divine light and the science (ἐπιστήμη) that makes perfect'.[19]

What these three pointers to the affinity of God and the created world underscore is that the tradition of dialectical theism might prove to be religiously and intellectually satisfying at precisely the points at which classical theism has failed the modern understanding. Certainly, the tradition has a significant resonance with Macquarrie's own drafting of a natural theology in *Principles of Christian Theology*.

Microcosm and theophany

Along with a revised understanding of God, this alternative tradition also provides a fruitful understanding of the nature of human being, fundamentally as the culmination of the created realm and, by extension, in relation to God. In relation to the whole hierarchy of being, human being is understood as *microcosm*: 'in him the universal creature is contained. For he understands like an angel, reasons like a man, is sentient like an animal, has life like a plant and subsists in body and soul. There is no creature that he is without.'[20] Nicolas of Cusa draws attention to the importance of this: 'Hence is it a nature that, raised to union with the maximum, would exhibit itself as the fullest perfection of the universe and of every individual in it, so that in this humanity itself all things would achieve their highest grade.'[21] This points again to the mutual responsibility within the hierarchy of being, and is a far more intimate notion than that of stewardship, which can tend to mirror the external model of creation and sovereignty of classical theism.

As well as manifesting the cosmos, however, human being manifests God, and is therefore *theophany* as well as microcosm. Within the alternative tradition there are three overlapping expressions of how this is so.

Already in the understanding of man as microcosm, there are contained two aspects. First, as microcosm, man *reflects the cosmos* which already itself exhibits God, since God imparts something of himself in bringing it into being. Secondly, as microcosm, man includes the whole spectrum of being *including that of the Creator*, 'containing in miniature all the hierarchical structure of reality, from vestiges of the divine from which he has come to involvement in the material at the other end of the scale'.[22]

However, more directly, man reflects God, both in general as a spiritual, rational being, and, as for Augustine, in the threefold nature of his soul. Thus, for Eriugena, for example, as essence, power and operation, or intellect, reason and sense. In this sense, human being has 'in his own soul a mirror (*speculum*) in which the triune God is manifested. It is from this image that the truth of which it is an image must be sought.'[23] For Leibniz, too, human being not only enhances God in the process of response and becoming, but mirrors God. All monads mirror the universe, but 'minds are also images of the Deity or Author of nature Himself, capable of knowing the system of the universe and to some extent of imitating it through their own *échantillons* (subsidiary creations).'[24]

This understanding of human being as microcosm and theophany is scarcely an account of the *dynamism* of human transcendence comparable to that derived from existentialist analysis. But it is a vital account of the cosmos producing from its own resources a microcosm by which it sums itself up and brings itself to a new level of expression – a level which, crucially, points beyond itself. This is the heart of the cosmological argument: 'the conviction that the cosmos or universe points beyond itself to some more ultimate reality as its ground, and this more ultimate reality is claimed to be "God".'[25] The reason for looking beyond the cosmos is that the cosmos *itself* is perceived to point beyond itself, and it is Macquarrie's contention that in human being the cosmos is doing just this:

> Within the cosmos and brought forth by the cosmos there is a being whose horizons are not limited to the cosmos and who has the temerity to ask 'Why are there beings at all, and not just nothing? ... Since man is himself a product of the universe, we can say that in and through this product, the universe is questioning itself, transcending itself and pointing beyond itself.[26]

HUMAN BEING

It is timely, now, to return to Macquarrie's understanding of human being in *In Search of Humanity*, to show how this preliminary grounding for a cosmological argument is met in an anthropological argument. Macquarrie's understanding of human being at this mature stage in his thought embraces the aspects of existentialist thought that he regards as essential to a true analysis of human being, and now fully integrates the divergent emphases which he has maintained from the beginning: the *kerygma* (both as a transcendent summons from beyond man, and as embodying a minimum core of 'factuality' in the public realm), a regard for *ontology*, and the *corporate aspect* of human being.

Freedom and directedness

Fundamental to Macquarrie's thought is the understanding of human being as *a centre of freedom*. By freedom he means not a narrow freedom of the will but a 'primordial openness', by which human being 'is almost like a hole or a breach in the *plenum* of the world of things'.[27] Freedom, then, is not a 'something' with describable properties or even a state of mind, to which human being has a 'right' and may take hold. Rather, Macquarrie suggests, 'freedom is nothing at all. It is the absence of constraints, it is an open space not yet filled up, it is an empty horizon where nothing blocks the way ... Freedom is the empty space, the room that is still left for manoeuvre and has not yet been filled up and determined.'[28]

Although existentialist thought typically expresses this dualistically as a distancing of human being from nature (a 'standing-out'), Macquarrie increasingly emphasises its more positive character as an analogy of, and indeed a sharing in, God's creation. Freedom is known only in its exercise as creativity which shapes the space. Human being is confronted with what is not yet determined and must bring forth something of a definite shape. It must let-be. Thus, creativity rather than will is the fundamental form of the exercise of freedom. This is evidenced both in the human capacity to adapt the environment to itself (rather than adapting itself to the environment, which every other creature does in order to survive) and, most significantly, in the capacity to shape humanity itself.

A cluster of concepts follows from understanding human being as a centre of freedom which retains Macquarrie's persistent concern with existentialist themes. If freedom is the primordial openness which characterises human being, human *transcendence* is the 'continuing process of creativity and development which flows from that freedom', by which the human being gives himself shape and 'becomes more' in confronting the openness of freedom.[29] This is more than merely futurity, but is a pushing back of the horizons of human existence itself. An essential aspect of this is *temporality*, not simply that the human being endures through time, but that he exists over a particular stretch of time. This includes duration, of course, but more fundamentally it means that the human being must exist with an awareness of living within a *span* of time with specific limits. This is provided by the awareness of the existential significance of *death*, as the boundary which demarcates the 'space' in which a life can achieve a unifying pattern and meaning. The significance of the boundary is that 'human life in time can have a meaning and unity only if there is an end to it, a boundary that gives the perspective within which priorities can be set and the various events and possibilities of life seen in their interrelationships as part of a sense giving whole.'[30] Macquarrie describes this as the task of 'producing a biography' as well as of 'becoming a person, of sculpting the raw material of life into a truly human shape'.[31]

What is emerging here is that freedom is not only openness but also *directedness*. Sheer openness would be merely chaos, but there is in human being a principle of direction and unity, a *hegemonikon*, or leading edge, which gives the necessary shape in the openness of freedom. The notion of unity is firmly attached to the notion of directedness in order to indicate its dynamic character: unity is not a property or simply rationality, but involves the whole self in intentional action. The determining focus of this action Macquarrie identifies as *egoity*, the 'being a self'. Egoity corresponds to the pole of individuality in the human being – that inward, private, unique and irreplaceable aspect of the self, in which the self is self-aware, but which nevertheless is not the Cartesian *ego* but is dynamic and has, as Macquarrie puts it, very indefinite edges. Its edges are indefinite in the sense that it is always projecting itself into its possibilities, which also 'belong to' the self as much as what is already actual, 'so that we can say that the self is always more than it is, or, in another sense, less than it is. It never quite coincides with itself; that is to say, it never fits entirely within a definite boundary, but keeps spilling over.'[32]

Two functions of the self in particular focus the dynamic process of becoming fully human: the conscience and commitment. The *conscience* retains the existentialist analysis discussed in Chapter 1, and need not be revisited. Additionally, *commitment* is the means by which the self is given direction by the development of stable attitudes and policies of action. As such it involves will, emotion and intellect in unified action. Commitment is the projection of the *whole person* on the future, in a particular set of goals or relations. It is, in this sense, risky and unknown in its outcome, as well as definite and single-minded. It is a further indication of the nature of freedom that a bond or obligation such as commitment should not be contrary to it but, rather, essential to it, in so far as the energies which shape the self in the openness of freedom are not 'capriciously dissipated' but directed into specific channels which contribute to the development of personhood. Thus, Macquarrie suggests, 'commitments give shape to the raw material out of which character and personhood are to be built, and they give direction to our constructive energies.'[33] In this sense, commitment is self-forming, but Macquarrie also notes that in order to be truly self-forming it must as well be both self-transcending and self-limiting, or it will stifle in narcissism in the search for the ideal self.

In the first place, commitment must *transcend* the self by taking the self into stable relations with others. Macquarrie writes, 'The more a human being pledges himself and engages himself beyond himself, the more firmly he is established as a truly personal being; whereas the more he seeks to defend and consolidate the inner centre of his being, the less personal he becomes and the more he resembles a subhuman form of life.'[34]

In the second place, *limitation* is an unavoidable aspect of finitude, however transcending human existence may be; this means that 'every commitment, if it is a commitment in any depth, must also be a renunciation, for if one's time, energies and capacities are limited, one can only commit them in a certain direction by diverting them away from another direction.'[35] Commitment is not a decision of the will but an attitude of the whole person, and, indeed, is not a wholly asymmetrical relation between the person making the commitment and the object of that commitment. This stress on total engagement, and the recognition that commitment is evoked and is therefore a gift as well as a task, are relevant to the character of human being as a product of the cosmos and, *precisely as such*, a psychosomatic unity of matter and mind; and also as having an affinity with Being itself which, both in the individual's experience and in its wider organic context, evokes and invites commitment.

Continuity with the cosmos

This double character of freedom as openness and directedness remains fundamental to Macquarrie's understanding of human nature, but in this later stage of his work now also proves essential to man's role in relation to the cosmos.

In his Oxford period, Macquarrie's mature concern is with the organic unity of the cosmos, and the continuity of human being with the cosmos in contrast to the dualism of existentialist understanding. Macquarrie increasingly indicates an interest in the degree to which human being is continuous with the rest of creation as well as distinct, so that he comes to agree with Whitehead that 'it is a false dichotomy to think of Nature *and* man. Mankind is that factor *in* Nature which exhibits in its most intense form the plasticity of nature.'[36]

There is an anticipation of this interest in his essay 'The Natural Theology of Teilhard de Chardin' (1961). Although unextravagant in his praise of Teilhard, Macquarrie's analysis of his work anticipates significant themes in *In Search of Deity*, not least the idea that an evolutionary process produces a hierarchy of being which embraces the rational and non-rational, the living and non-living, and in which a series of thresholds or critical moments occurs, at which a genuinely novel and yet wholly continuous stage emerges. The continuity is grounded by Teilhard thus, 'In the world, nothing could ever burst forth as final across the different thresholds successively traversed by evolution (however critical they may be) which has not already existed in an obscure and primordial way.'[37] Macquarrie is critical of Teilhard's 'emerging' God, who is found at the end of the evolutionary process as its goal but not at the beginning as its creator, and the mind/body dualism that creeps in if the physical process ends in a purely rational existence liberated from its material matrix. These criticisms are maintained into *In Search of Deity* wherever these tendencies appear in the tradition of dialectical theism. Macquarrie admits that this is probably not the interpretation that Teilhard would have wished of his work, but suggests that it is the most obvious one to be consistent with his stated premises and aims.

What is particularly significant for its anticipation of Macquarrie's later work is the identification of the emergence of man 'as the bearer of reflective thought' as a critical epoch, and one in which 'evolution becomes conscious of itself and within limits able to direct itself'.[38] It is exactly this understanding, though with the recognition that God is the source as well as the goal of the developing cosmos, which Macquarrie traces in the notion of man as microcosm in the tradition of dialectical theism. Human being sums up in himself all the levels of the hierarchy of being; although he is a wholly new level of being, distinctively 'personal' in a way in which no other level is, he is also thoroughly continuous with all the levels of being which are below him or precede him in the hierarchy, and reflects in himself the whole structure of the universe.

This is the core of Macquarrie's anthropological argument. It is fundamental that the universe itself, out of its own resources (however 'obscure and primordial' they may have been), has produced human being, if *human* capacity is to be said to be the *universe* in some sense being conscious of itself, directing itself, transcending itself, and pointing beyond itself in the Leibnizian question, 'Why is there something rather than nothing?' It is important to recognise that it is human *transcendence* which is a product of the universe, as well as human facticity, so that it cannot be misunderstood that a mind-matter dualism has been reinstated. Even in *Principles of Christian Theology*, there is a lingering tendency to see man's relational context as a limiting factor in an individual's existence rather than as an occasion of transcendence, so that human transcendence must be in some sense *over* or *from* its relational context. Here, it is explicit that human transcendence is the embodied transcendence of its relational organic context.

Macquarrie's understanding of embodiedness in *In Search of Humanity* is appropriate to this position. He utterly rejects both the Cartesian dualism which holds that human rationality is an independent substantial entity 'inhabiting' the body, and the empiricist response to this dualism which holds that rationality is simply an epiphenomenon of the body. He affirms that freedom, transcendence and rationality in human being are not found apart from the material organism, which can be both threatening *and supportive*. Part of the task of becoming fully human in relation to the hierarchy of being from which human being emerges is that 'such biological phenomena as sexuality and death, without in the least ceasing to be bodily, are at the human level, transformed from *merely* biological phenomena into profoundly meaningful events of personal life.'[39]

Affinity with Being

Previously, Macquarrie has indicated the affinity between human being and Being itself in a number of ways. In the first place, he has grounded the search for Being in the very constitution of human nature, in the search for a wider context of being which will be 'gracious' to the human condition of possibility conjoined with facticity. And second, he has located human affinity with Being not in rationality or a model of stewardship over creation, but precisely in the conjunction of possibility and facticity: in the openness of human existence and the capacity for shaping that which remains open in the givenness of the world of things. That is to say, it is human creativity and love in which the affinity of human being with Being is shown, so that the affinity is with Being's superabundance and generosity of self-giving, in its character of letting-be, in the strongest possible sense.

In this mature period of Macquarrie's thought, human being has a new degree of affinity with Being because it is doubly grounded: not only in humanity's distinctive affinity with Being, but also in its affinity with the cosmos, which itself has affinity with Being as the outcome of Being's Expressive mode.

Cosmic transformation

Human being's role in the created realm follows from its character as freedom-as-openness/directedness and from its continuity with the cosmos, as well as from its affinity with Being, and it has a distinctive form in Macquarrie's mature thought. In his earlier writings, human transcendence is the culmination of creation, but with a degree of separation. The human capacity to 'let-be' is directed to bringing the rest of creation into the human world of instrumentality, so that as human existence becomes more truly human and exerts its influence on the world of things, they are drawn into the human horizon and reach a higher level of significance as 'equipment'. In Macquarrie's concern with community, letting-be gives love its distinctive character and spaciousness, in contrast to a model of love as a desire for union. But in the mature work, the relation of human letting-be to the cosmos is considerably more organic, so that man's task is the bringing of the whole of creation to 'deiformity' in his own process of 'deification': 'since human nature embraces within itself all levels of being in the universe, then if it could be raised to union with God, all things would be brought to their perfection in it.'[40]

It is not simply that human being, as personal, is where Being is most present-and-manifest. Certainly, this remains the case, as Macquarrie notes in the understanding of man as theophany. But, in addition, it is that in human being as a product of the universe the universe both transcends itself, and is itself a theophany, pointing beyond itself to an ultimate source of being. In the same way, then, that the task of becoming fully human involves transforming the merely biological, the human task in the cosmos is the transformation of the merely inanimate, organic, animal into union with Being.

This is not an external role which human being exerts on a passive cosmos. Not only is there human continuity with the cosmos, but also there is already in every entity some capacity to become what it truly is: 'a tendency to strive towards the realisation of its own potentiality for being; it strives to develop its own perfection as that thing which it is.'[41] This does not contradict the givenness of the beings, since their being is not truly open, but is akin to Leibniz' notion of unconscious appetition: 'An acorn embraces in itself the entelechy of the mature oak.'[42] The human task in the cosmos, then, is bringing to fuller fruition (and indeed to consciousness in his own understanding of the process) this universal presence of entelechy. From the alternative tradition of theism in *In Search of Deity*, Macquarrie notes this as a rudimentary, primordial potentiality for mind in the cosmos: 'Wherever there is order, pattern, organism, form, there is the rudiment of mind, though it may be far below the level of consciousness.'[43] Human being, as conscious, rational and able to create order and pattern to some extent himself, is the ultimate expression of this in the created order. As Dionysius indicates, the hierarchy of being is not simply static gradation, but dynamic and reciprocal; in Macquarrie's words, 'hierarchy is the coming down from God through the various levels and, in reverse order, the rising up to God.'[44] This is again, then, the mutual responsibility in the hierarchy of being: without the lower levels, human being could not have evolved, and without the emergence of human being the hierarchy as a whole would be diminished and the lower levels would have failed to transcend into their ultimate potentialities.

In this concern with the cosmos, the existential dimension has not been lost in human transcendence. It remains true for the human existent that there is a summons to existence, and that existence consists of possibility as well as facticity, and that existence is always 'mine'. But now, as the human existent pursues his possibilities, the implications are more profound for the cosmos which is, as it were, contained and carried in human transcendence.

THE ANTHROPOLOGICAL ARGUMENT

Here, then, is Macquarrie's anthropological argument for the being of God, a grace-full account of ontological difference and ontological affinity between the cosmos, human being and God. Within the tradition of dialectical theism, an account of the cosmos emerges which conceives of the universe as producing from its own resources a microcosm, human being, by which it brings itself to new self-expression. The *personal* character of this new expression points beyond the cosmos, asking 'why is there being rather than nothing?' In raising the question of being, and in pushing back the horizons of human existence, and in shaping the world, human being provides an analogy for what it points to beyond the cosmos: a God both immanent (as human being is microcosm) and transcendent (as human being lets-be).

Further, 'Human beings show a natural trust in the wider being within which their existence is set.' This basic trust in the order of things, while not the same as faith in God, is a predisposition to it. It points to a fundamental affinity between God and the cosmos. Negative factors do not always merely contradict this trust, but in extreme form 'when one comes to the limit of the human situation', may be the occasion of *encounter* with transcendent being.

Finally, from these deep roots in the human constitution and situation, these various strands emerge in worship. Overwhelmingly, this is a claim to experience the reality of God, 'and this claim has a *prima facie* case for its validity as one deeply rooted in the human condition and one which has never been disproved and perhaps never could be.'[45]

In this anthropological argument for the being of God, the various meanings of the grace of being find expression in the broad scope of its application to the individual, the relational and the cosmic. *It is grace-full to be human because it is here not only that the quest for God begins for the individual existent, but also that the cosmos reaches beyond itself to its personal, spiritual telos. Being is gracious to human being because in its letting-be of the beings it discloses its immanence and transcendence, confers participation and summons into responsibility.* As Macquarrie concludes, 'a God so conceived as deeply involved with his creation is no oppressive God, but one whose transcendence is a goal and encouragement to the transcendence of humanity.'[46]

CRITICAL INTERLUDE: THE GRACE OF BEING AND THE PROBLEM OF EVIL

Space precludes a comprehensive critical analysis of Macquarrie's use of the tradition of dialectical theism in his anthropological argument. But in so far as that tradition is derived fundamentally from neo-Platonism, one critical question must be raised, and that concerns the nature of evil. As Macquarrie himself admits, this is the cause of frequent criticism of the tradition. Most of the thinkers considered in *In Search of Deity*, from Plotinus to Whitehead, have been accused by some of not taking evil sufficiently seriously. Macquarrie is somewhat dismissive of this particular accusation, contending 'what would it mean to take evil with more seriousness than they have done? Would it not mean setting up a dualism in which evil is given positive ontological status as a realm of Satan over against the kingdom of God?'[47] But it remains the case that, precisely from the motivation to avoid a dualistic account, the Christian tradition has been perennially occupied with the problem of evil and the need to provide a theodicy to show that the presence of evil does not falsify a belief in a good and sovereign God. Macquarrie's disinclination to offer a robust theodicy, in spite of his own commitment to resist the temptations to dualism in Christian theology and to give an account of the reasonableness of Christian faith, thus raises a question of whether his own use of the neo-Platonic influenced tradition fails to take the question of evil with due seriousness. Is Macquarrie's account of evil based on an impersonal understanding of reality which falsifies the claim that the grace of being is directed to the good of human being?

In the first place, it must be admitted that within his entire corpus, Macquarrie's material on evil is scant.[48] It is also cautious. In *Principles of Christian Theology*, for example, Macquarrie addresses evil in relation to a belief in providence, in the context of the consideration of whether the presence of evil in the world might be the point at which the reasonableness of Christian faith is falsified. Although at every other step in *Principles of Christian Theology* Macquarrie begins from the existential aspect and proceeds reductively to consider what can only be known from the outside, in his discussion of evil he reverses the procedure and considers evil which arises from natural factors. His justification for this reversal is that 'evil is a reversal of the positive, affirmative tendency toward being, a reversal of the very creative act of letting-be ... Evil is essentially negative and destructive, and thus the enemy of beings.'[49] For Macquarrie, then, the important issue is how to give an ontological account of evil which accords with his understanding of Being, rather than an existential account which risks attributing undue positive reality to evil. The danger of beginning with an existential account is precisely this: that to proceed from the existential experience of evil to the external observation of evil *and thence to an ontological account* is itself to reverse the negative non-becoming of evil into a positive reality. Evil is negation, *privatio boni*, the standing threat to created beings, which 'have been created out of nothing, and it is possible for them to slip back into nothing or to advance into the potentialities for being which belong to them. Evil is this slipping back toward nothing, a reversal and defeat of the creative process.'[50]

Macquarrie's account of evil arises from his understanding of the basic character of the created world as a sharing of being, a *self-giving* outpouring of Being's own being. This is the heart of Macquarrie's balancing of the classical doctrine of creation with the notion of

The Grace of Being 139

emanation. In neo-Platonic terms, this relates to the principle of *plenitude*. It is not, however, a pure Plotinian neo-Platonic plenitude, which argues that the world contains all possible species in an exact hierarchy: 'divine plenitude overflows, pouring itself outwards and downwards in a teeming cascade of ever-new forms of life until all the possibilities of existence have been actualised and the shores are reached of the unlimited ocean of non-being.'[51] The risk of creation is exactly that the outpouring of Being to determinate beings means that they are finite and limited, poised between being and non-being and capable of slipping back into non-being. Macquarrie deems this the 'tragic element' of creation, an 'inevitable accompaniment in the creation of a universe of particular beings'.[52] Only if this is recognised to be a metaphysical account and not an account of human anguish, can this be an adequate comment.

What can be said, however, about the lack of an account of human anguish? John Hick's criticism of the neo-Platonic tradition is that it is fundamentally *impersonal*. God's goodness and love are understood 'primarily as His creative fecundity, His bestowing of the boon of existence as widely as possible'.[53] Therefore creation as a whole exists for divine self-expression, and human being in particular exists because otherwise there would be a gap in the hierarchy of being that would mar the divine self-expression. Hick objects that 'the emphasis is not that man is created for his own sake as finite personal life capable of personal relationship with the infinite divine Person, but upon the thought that man is created to complete the range of a dependent realm which exists to give external expression to God's glory.'[54]

Furthermore, evil as privation, embraced by human will, is seen as the principle that what can fail will fail, and thus human being is rendered a 'fragile' metaphysical substance. Sin as a personal act is disregarded, and grace is 'a metaphysical force that repairs the defect in being, rather than a gracious personal relationship'.[55]

It is certainly the case that Macquarrie tends not to use explicitly 'personal' terms. But it is equally the case that his thought does not have the chilling impersonal note that Hick draws from the Augustinian approach. What reason can be given for this, from the resources of Macquarrie's own thought?

It is here that, once again, Macquarrie's dialectical method becomes significant. Although his discussion of evil takes place in ontological mode, and makes little reference to its existential impact, the total context of the discussion is principally determined by existential interest. From the starting point that Being is gracious because it brings into being by sharing its own Being, and thus ensures that possibility and facticity are of a piece, the question about evil is raised ontologically concerning the conditions under which transcendence is a matter of directed freedom and not metaphysical necessity. It is raised existentially not in a form which admits the positive reality of evil (in case that should be interpreted ontologically *rather than* existentially), but in a way that emphasises that this transcendence is a matter of responsibility in an ambiguous world. Human being tends to forget Being and immerses itself instead in beings. The result is a stunting and distorting of human being. In this sense, the existential aspect of Macquarrie's account of evil is more Irenaean than Augustinian. For although the stunting element appears in neo-Platonism as the preferring of a lower place in the hierarchy of being, here it has a more perverse character as the rejection of the gift of being and the call into (comm)union. Being is summoned into its possibilities, and must take responsibility. Whilst this is not couched in personal language, the dynamic is personal. Transcendence is the distinctively personal aspect of human being. This is the aspect which in Macquarrie's early thought distinguishes human being *from* the natural realm, and which in his later thought is the cosmos' own means of transcendence. Since God is the source, ground and goal of this transcendence, he is said to be personal or, better, more than personal.

Macquarrie admits that his view comes close to an instrumental view of evil in this respect. Although he denies that evil is an instrument of God's justice, he agrees that

> there is more to be said for the view that natural evil can be understood as an instrument of God's *education* of the human race, for it surely is true that in a universe where no one could suffer or get hurt, there would not be possible any development in depth of character or of personal relations; or, to put the matter in another way, *without the threat of nullity and frustration, there could be little development of selfhood*.[56]

NOTES

1 Macquarrie is not thereby claiming to 'prove the existence' of God. I have already noted the parameters he sets for talk of God's existence. However, the phrase provides a pleasing symmetry with the 'proofs' of classical theism, and establishes Macquarrie's desire to work in some degree of continuity with at least the aims of traditional natural theology.
2 *ISH* 261
3 *ISD* 146. Macquarrie does note, too, that Williams acknowledged that

Macquarrie's use of Heidegger provided a more profound understanding of the human person than his preference for Whitehead.
4   See, for example, *BT* 97; *ET* 48; *ISH* 72. Macquarrie's discussion refers to an *external* object, not to the existent's own body, which principally he *is*.
5   See, for example, Thomas Aquinas, *Summa Theologiae* 2a 2ae q66 a7 (London: Eyre & Spottiswoode 1974).
6   *ISH* 46. This is exactly what Gundry and also Gareth Jones in *Bultmann* (Cambridge: Polity Press 1991) have identified as the necessary corrective to the weaknesses in Bultmann's position noted above.
7   On occasions, Macquarrie uses the term 'panentheism' rather than dialectical theism, but generally prefers the latter because it is less easily confused with 'pantheism', from which he is anxious to distinguish himself.
8   *ISD* 55. Here, then, is Macquarrie's existential-ontological concern carried forward into his Oxford period.
9   *ISD* 12. Space prohibits a full discussion on the relation between Macquarrie's 'new' natural theology and traditional Thomism, and in particular the grounds on which it might be argued that Macquarrie revitalises Aquinas' work in a contemporary philosophical and theological context. Indeed, Macquarrie's writings display an ambiguity towards Aquinas that confuses this question. However, Macquarrie does affirm Aquinas' perspective on the grace of God which bestows being, *PCT* 225 and compare *Summa Contra Gentiles* III.21.3 (London: University of Notre Dame 1975), and his criticism of Aquinas can be explained as a polemical use to represent a position he is arguing against, rather than from a genuine incompatibility of content. In any case, Macquarrie's argument is not dependent on the extent to which Aquinas represents classical theism; he is concerned with the monarchical characteristics of classical theism itself, and with satisfying his claim that it is possible to construct a natural theology which does *not* objectify God.
10 *ISD* 34
11 *ISD* 39
12 *ISD* 40
13 Macquarrie develops this thesis in *God and Secularity* (London: SCM 1968), where he traces the development of atheism and religionless Christianity from neo-orthodox theologies which have exaggerated the distance between God and the world.
14 *ISD* 54
15 *ISD* 172
16 On the self-imparting of God in modern theology compare Friedrich Schleiermacher, *The Christian Faith* (Edinburgh: T&T Clark 1989), 732; Karl Barth, *Church Dogmatics* I/2 (Edinburgh: T&T Clark 1956), 377–401, IV/2 (Edinburgh: T&T Clark 1958), 730–35; Jürgen Moltmann, *The Coming of God* (London: SCM 1996), 337.
17 *ISD* 84. See Dionysius, *Celestial Hierarchy* I.4.86 in J.P. Migne's *Patrologia Graeca* vol. 3.
18 *ISD* 93. See Eriugena, *On the Division of Nature* Book I Col 454C in J.P. Migne's *Patrologia Latina* vol. 122.
19 *ISD* 74–75, Dionysius, *Celestial Hierarchy* VII.2.A, in J.P. Migne's *Patrologia Graeca* vol. 4.
20 *ISD* 95, see Eriugena, *On the Division of Nature* Bk. III 733B in *Patrologia Latina* vol. 122.

21 Nicolas Cusanus, *Of Learned Ignorance* (London: Routledge & Kegan Paul 1954), III.3. In modern theology compare Jürgen Moltmann, *Man: Christian Anthropology in the Conflicts of the Present* (London: SPCK 1971), 108–11; Reinhold Niebuhr, *Nature and Destiny of Man* vol. 1 (London: Nisbet 1941), 203; Wolfhart Pannenberg, *Systematic Theology* vol. 2 (Edinburgh: T&T Clark 1994), 203ff.
22 *ISD* 70
23 *ISD* 95, Eriugena, *On the Division of Nature* Book 2 579A.
24 *ISD* 122, Leibniz, *Monadology*, 266.
25 *ISD* 206
26 *ISD* 209
27 *ISH* 26, 12
28 *ISH* 11, 13
29 *ISH* 26, 32
30 *ISH* 238
31 *ISH* 43
32 *ISH* 44
33 *ISH* 143
34 *ISH* 144
35 *ISH* 145
36 A.N. Whitehead, *Adventures of Ideas* (Cambridge: CUP 1933), 99.
37 Pierre Teilhard de Chardin, *The Phenomenon of Man* (London: Collins 1959), 71; *SCE* 185.
38 *SCE* 185
39 *ISH* 48, italics are Macquarrie's. See also 7–8.
40 *ISD* 110
41 *ISD* 115
42 *ISD* 116, compare Leibniz, *Monadology* para 15, 18.
43 *ISD* 143
44 *ISD* 74, compare Dionysius, *Celestial Hierarchy* VII.2A, in J.P. Migne's *Patrologia Graeca* vol. 4.
45 *ISH* 261
46 *ISH* 261
47 *ISD* 182–83
48 The two main sources are *PCT* 253–59 and *ISD* 182–84, though *ISH* 222–32 contains some relevant material.
49 *PCT* 254
50 *PCT* 255
51 John Hick, *Evil and the God of Love* (Basingstoke: Macmillan 1985³), 75.
52 *PCT* 258
53 Hick, 193
54 Hick, 194
55 Hick, 195. Compare John Oman, *Grace and Personality* (Cambridge: CUP 1931).
56 *PCT* 258, italics are mine. Compare J.V. Langmead Casserley's conclusion: 'Pain is only a stark, unrelieved evil if we allow it to become so', *Evil and Evolutionary Eschatology* (Lewiston: The Edwin Mellen Press 1990), 11.

Chapter 6

A Christology of Self-Giving

INTRODUCTION: RECIPROCAL MOVEMENTS OF SELF-GIVING

Macquarrie's grace of being finds concrete expression in the self-giving love of Jesus Christ, understood as the point of meeting between two convergent movements of self-transcendence. In Jesus Christ, the human capacity for self-transcendence towards God and the divine self-transcendence as Expressive Being meet. This is the thesis of *Jesus Christ in Modern Thought* (1990), particularly the constructive third part, 'Who really is Jesus Christ for us today?'[1] Here Macquarrie outlines his own christological position, drawing on 'the findings of the earlier two books on humanity and deity ... to make sense in modern terms of the conception of the God-man, as applied to Jesus Christ'.[2]

In this chapter, I shall consider this constructive christology of Macquarrie's, and the account of the humanity and divinity of Christ which he offers. This will provide the opportunity to raise a number of critical issues. First, I shall assess Macquarrie's emphasis on the humanity of Christ, and its outcome in a somewhat adoptionist account of christology, in relation to his discussion of kenotic christologies. Secondly, in discussion with Stephen Sykes, I shall suggest that Macquarrie's christology points to the way in which his rejection of the monarchical model of divine power does not entail a rejection of divine power *per se*.

WHO REALLY IS JESUS CHRIST FOR US TODAY?

Macquarrie's christology is constructed in response to the challenges raised against classical christology by the Enlightenment: biblical criticism, confidence in human being and especially human reason, the challenge to the 'external' authority of Church and scripture, the 'heteronomous' rule of a transcendent God. In the light of these challenges, and in the light of other post-Enlightenment attempts to reformulate christology for the modern situation, Macquarrie notes the ways in which a present-day christology will differ from classical christology: its approach to the historical question, its starting point in the humanity of Christ, its account of metaphysics, its account of the way in which Christ is related to the whole human race, and its approach to the uniqueness of Christ.

The historical question

After three centuries of historical and literary criticism, a christology must now address explicitly the 'historical question'. That is to say, it must address the question of how much can be reliably known about the formative events of the Christian faith, and take a position on the prior question of whether such historical information is necessary, or if a mythical Christ would be adequate.

The what *and* how *revisited*

I have already noted in Chapter 2 that Macquarrie distinguishes himself from various narrowly existentialist christologies, in maintaining that it is not enough simply to affirm the fact of the historical existence of Jesus of Nazareth. For Bultmann, sceptical about what can be known about the historical Jesus, it is enough to affirm *das Dass*, the fact that Jesus lived (and was crucified) without exploring the content of his history (*ihr Was*).[3] Against Bultmann, Macquarrie agrees with the 'plain common sense' view of Donald Baillie, that it is the content which gives significance to the fact. So, for example, 'the meaning of the cross cannot be understood apart from what we know about the one who dies on the cross.'[4] It is not the resurrection alone which gives meaning to the cross, but the being of the one who was crucified.

For a somewhat different reason, Macquarrie distinguishes himself from Kierkegaard's position. Although not sceptical about the availability of historical information about Jesus, Kierkegaard holds that it is of no value in relation to the claim that Jesus is God because it belongs to a different realm of discourse. Because of his insistence on an 'infinite qualitative difference' between God and human being, Kierkegaard exaggerates the degree to which God is veiled in his revelation in Jesus Christ, and uses the language of 'incognito'.[5] For Macquarrie, once again following Baillie's lead, there must be a genuine revelation of God in the incarnation or 'what would be the gain of believing that God therein became man?'[6] And, more pertinently to

Macquarrie's position, what ground would there be at all for assessing the claim that Jesus is God? So, although for Kierkegaard it would suffice for Jesus' contemporaries to say, 'We have believed that in such and such a year God appeared among us in the humble figure of a servant, that he lived and taught in our community, and finally died', because faith could not be distilled from any amount of historical detail, for Macquarrie something more is required.[7] It is not that Macquarrie requires a biography of Jesus to offer a proof of his divinity, because he notes that '"flesh and blood" will not reveal anything more than flesh and blood', and has often insisted that in revelation nothing in addition to the historical event is seen.[8] However, he rejects the gulf that Kierkegaard asserts between God and the created realm. Therefore he maintains that 'a personal existence made to the image of God and having therefore some affinity to God might in the mysteries of love and obedience and faithfulness point us beyond the realm of flesh and blood', and that some historical remnant is needed to assess the claim that Jesus was such a person living such a life.[9] This, then, is Macquarrie's familiar insistence that an existentialist approach alone is inadequate, because existential significance is attributed for good reason not chance, and therefore some account can be given of the reason.

Macquarrie's approach to the historical question also distinguishes his intention, if not always his content, from that of distinctively Enlightenment christologies, such as those of Lessing, Kant and Hegel. He insists on the importance of the real existence of the historical figure Jesus of Nazareth because the Christian claim is that the ideal of human being, the archetype has been realised in history and embodied in an actual life, not simply that there is such an ideal. It is the central value given to this claim that distinguishes Macquarrie from Kantian rationalism or Hegelian idealism. Neither Kant nor Hegel (nor, for example, Strauss or Caird in the Hegelian school) deny that the archetypal human being has been realised in the person of Jesus Christ, but they stress that the archetype exists either within the structure of reason in human consciousness, or in the realm of eternal ideas. The realisation of the archetype gives a concrete example which excites the imagination or provides a pictorial pointer towards an eternal truth. But once the idea is grasped, the historical instance is dispensable. In contrast, Macquarrie emphasises the importance of the historical reality of Jesus in disclosing that full human existence is possible under historical conditions and is precisely not an unattainable ideal in the eternal realm, whether the eternal realm in this sense is immanent (Kant) or transcendent (Hegel, Strauss, Caird).

Thus while Macquarrie could be said to be in agreement with both rationalist and idealist christologies in so far as he recognises that the concrete example does in fact operate as a dispensation for human weakness in regard to actualising true human being, for Macquarrie the importance of the concrete embodiment is precisely that it occurs in the same realm that all human existence occurs in, and therefore affirms the priority of this realm.

It is important to note too, though, that Macquarrie is not *denying* that the archetype does also exist in what may be deemed in a particular sense the eternal realm of ideas and in the very constitution of human being. First, he allows for the 'pre-existence' of Christ at least in the mind and purpose of God, which is 'to enjoy a very high degree of reality even if it is different from the reality of existing in space and time'.[10] And, because of God's self-expression in creation, there is another sense in which Christ as the archetype of human being pre-exists within the potentiality of the universe which 'from its own resources' brings forth human being. Secondly, Macquarrie is in full agreement with Kant that an awareness of the archetype is present within our human constitution because it is only as such that we are able to recognise the existential significance of the concrete realisation of the archetype: 'there could be an endless succession of saviour figures and we could remain blind to their significance were there not something within us (conscience? practical reason? mystical awareness? religious consciousness? or however one may describe it) which enables us to recognise in the saviour-figure our own highest good.'[11] This coherence between historical reality, ontological structure, and human constitution is a central feature of Macquarrie's grace of being theology.

The formative event: self-giving

As I indicated in Chapter 2, from his earliest writings Macquarrie has asserted the possibility of establishing a 'minimal core of factuality'. Initially, this is a very narrow core in terms of its content, but reveals the importance that self-giving will come to have in his thought. In *The Scope of Demythologizing* the core is simply 'that there was someone who once exhibited in history the possibility of existence which the kerygma* proclaims.'[12] In *Studies in Christian Existentialism*, it is expanded slightly to clarify that it is not simply that Jesus lived and died, but that in the manner of his life and death he 'did manifest the self-giving that the tradition ascribes to him', and to which the kerygma summons all human existence.[13] In *Jesus Christ in Modern Thought*,

Macquarrie hazards a fuller content, but becomes correspondingly hesitant about the term 'core of factuality'. A diffuse outline of a life of Jesus to which Macquarrie points is derived from Paul's writings, and bears close correspondence to the eight points made by John Bowden in his *Jesus: The Unanswered Questions* and approved by the historian E.P. Sanders.[14]

Of particular relevance to my concern with the grace of being is Macquarrie's account of Jesus' understanding of his own death. Despite the fact that he is antagonistic to 'psychologising' attempts to establish Jesus' self-understanding about his mission and possible death in Jerusalem, Macquarrie makes a cautious suggestion about Jesus' self-understanding which is important specifically because of Christ's role as mediator in salvation. Macquarrie insists that salvation cannot happen 'behind our backs', without our conscious involvement and appropriation, as if we were so many sheep and not responsible personal beings. Here he argues, 'if this is true of the Christians who experience salvation or the beginning of salvation through the cross of Christ, must it not be even more true of Christ himself? He is the central character in what is going on, the mediator between God and the human race and we can hardly suppose that he is unconscious of the meaning of the events in which he is involved.'[15] What Macquarrie attempts is to retain the voluntary character of Jesus' death, to safeguard the motif of self-giving love, whilst not accepting that the decision to go to Jerusalem was made in the full knowledge that he would die there. Predictions of his death can be regarded as the hindsight of the disciples who knew the outcome of the journey and the theological significance of the death. Macquarrie follows Bornkamm (and Bultmann) in suggesting that Jesus 'went up to Jerusalem to confront the religious establishment with his message of the kingdom in the hope that even at that late hour they would hear the message and repent, or perhaps in the hope that the kingdom would break in at that time'.[16] This view has the benefits of maintaining the voluntary character of Jesus' death while also maintaining the non-predictive limits of his genuine humanity; it also accords with Macquarrie's valuing in *Principles of Christian Theology* of the agony in the garden as the real moment of self giving to his mission.

Jesus Christ: human transcendence

It is fundamental to Macquarrie's thought that, in a secular age, christology must begin with the humanity of Jesus, because humanity is still familiar in a way that divinity no longer is. Starting from 'below', the key christological question is not 'How does God become man?', but '"How does a man become God?" or "How does a human life embody or manifest the divine life?"'[17] Again, in accordance with his method of natural theology, and his concern that faith is seen to be reasonable, in order to establish the *possibility* of such an occurrence, Macquarrie reviews various secular transcendent anthropologies which establish a view of human nature not as a fixed essence but as an openness that might allow for a continuum of development.

As well as the familiar *existentialist* insistence that 'the human being not only *is* but knows that he or she is, and because of this knowledge has some say and some responsibility in determining what he or she will become',[18] Macquarrie notes the corporate dimension of transcendence in *Marxism and neo-Marxism*. In particular he acknowledges the social theories of Marcuse, in which 'transcendence takes place as an "overshoot" within a society of the existing structures and institutions', and of Bloch who identifies a principle of 'hope' in all things – a drive or tendency to realise its possibilities of being such that (with Aristotle) it is not enough to ask what a thing is without also asking what it is capable of becoming.[19] This provides a resonance with *philosophies of process* in which 'mankind is that factor in nature which exhibits in its most intense form the plasticity of nature.'[20]

From these secular anthropologies, four pointers reappear from Macquarrie's anthropological argument which are key for his christology.

Openness

The openness of human nature to go beyond itself implies that 'there is always something *more* to a human being, that which he or she may become and which is not yet determined.'[21] This is the starting point for an adoptionist christology. Grounded in the 'pre-history' of understanding human being as made in the image of God, and of that image as the self-communication of God, there arises the possibility that 'if there ever came into existence a human being in whom that image was not defaced but manifested in its fullness, would not that human being, precisely by being fully human, be God's existence into the world, so far as the divine can be manifest on the finite level?'[22] This 'deification' of human being is present in the patristic tradition in Irenaeus and, more especially, the Eastern theology of Maximos. It is expressed in the modern period in the transcendental theology of Rahner, for whom divinity is the ultimate horizon of humanity.

Directedness

The directedness of the openness of human existence emerges initially in the modern period in Schleiermacher's early use in his *Speeches* of the idea of the 'sense and taste for the infinite' which finds reasonable grounding in the human capacity for indefinite going out from itself in becoming, in knowledge, and in relationality. Macquarrie notes the importance of this strand in the transcendental Thomism of Lonergan and Marcel, as well as that of Rahner who has taken the Thomist use of Aristotelian categories and given them a more 'fluid, dynamic quality'. For Rahner, then, God is the 'whither' of human transcendence, and the spirit is the desire for this absolute being: 'There is that in the human being which, so to speak, opens out toward God and finds its completion in God.'[23] In terms of christology, this is a way of saying 'all this is from God' from the perspective of the humanity of Christ.

Corporate event

The corporate dimension is significant for two aspects of Macquarrie's christology. In the first place, it accords with his use of the notion the *Christ-event*: Jesus Christ is always mediated to the Church in a corporate context. He is inseparable not only from the family and friends and culture of his upbringing but also from the faith of the early disciples.

More significantly at this stage, the notion of the Christ-event emphasises its *dynamic* character, and moves christology away from speculative, metaphysical and interventionist interpretations of the incarnation, towards the complex human reality in which God has expressed himself. So, Macquarrie writes that the incarnation 'was not just the work of a moment; it did not happen in a flash on the day of the annunciation; it was a lengthy process which had been long preparing in the history of Israel and then continued in the life of the church – the coming into being of a new humanity.'[24]

This last phrase links to the second aspect of Macquarrie's christology raised by the corporate dimension of transcendence. That is, the understanding of Christ as *representative*, the representative human being, which is intended to answer the question of the relation of Christ's person and work to the whole human race. With regard to his *person*, Christ is representative because 'we recognise him as the fulfilment of our humanity, one with us in the whole spectrum of human experience, yet different from us in having brought the most central possibilities of humanity to a new level of realisation.'[25] With Kant, Macquarrie acknowledges that this recognition is only possible because the archetype of humanity which Christ fulfils exists within us, as an ideal which lures us forwards. Christ's fulfilment of the archetype is not an isolated event, but 'as the true human being who has fulfilled in his humanity the image of God, he is representative of that authentic humanity which is striving for expression in every human person.'[26]

With regard to his *work of atonement*, Christ is also our representative and not our substitute. In the saving event of his passion and death, Christ 'steps in for us, but he holds the place open for us so that we can step in ourselves. The Christian must consciously appropriate the work of Christ on his or her behalf, and take up the cross.'[27]

Cosmological significance

The cosmological dimension stresses human transcendence as manifesting the 'plasticity of nature', in Whitehead's expression. I have already noted the broadening of Macquarrie's theology to cosmic relationality, and the overcoming of existentialist man/nature dualism by understanding human transcendence as the transcendence *of* the universe itself, rather than of human being *out of* the universe. Macquarrie makes the connection with christology in his remarks on pre-existence. As well as accepting that pre-existence might mean existing in the intention of God, he notes a possible cosmological interpretation brought to light by modern evolutionary understandings of the world. In so far as what becomes actual is previously potential within the cosmos, it is possible to say that Christ has always existed in potential in the cosmos from the very beginning, 'that, (however one may interpret the matter), this earth, the human race, yes, Jesus Christ himself were already latent, already predestined, in the primaeval swirling cloud of particles.'[28] This view is anticipated by Schleiermacher in his view that 'Christ even as a human person was ever coming to be simultaneously with world itself', and emerges again in Rahner's understanding of Christ as the entelechy of the whole creation.[29] In this sense then, the evolution of the cosmos itself produces the human race and, at its ultimate horizon, Jesus Christ. Once again, this is Macquarrie's desire to give an account of the incarnation which minimises its interpretation as an instantaneous metaphysical event, and which places it securely within its physical and historical matrix.

These points derived from Macquarrie's review of modern transcendent anthropologies all serve to establish the possibility of the incarnation: that is to say, that transcendent human being in its historical and physical context does indeed have the capacity for growing towards God and manifesting the divine life.

Jesus Christ: divine self-giving

The possibility that Christ's humanity was raised to its ultimate horizon of divinity is, for Macquarrie, an important and essential part of the kerygma, and the vital starting point for a twentieth-century christology. But he insists that it does not constitute a complete christology, and that 'the raising of a human life to the level at which it manifests God is possible only through the descent of God into that life.'[30] These are complementary perspectives on the same event or, in Kähler's expression, 'a reciprocity of personal movements'.

Macquarrie admits that the movement 'from above' is more speculative than 'the idea of an indefinite capacity for "transcendence" in the humanity which we all experience at first hand'.[31] He is critical of nineteenth-century kenotic christologies for a supposed 'detailed inside knowledge' of the pre-existent Logos, and of Barth for 'pressing the limits, if not over-stepping them' in his attempt to specify the asymmetrical participation between Christ's two natures. However, despite being wary of the temptation to indulge in unanswerable speculation, Macquarrie is also opposed to 'every kind of anti-intellectualism' and consistently maintains the need to give an ontological account of christology in order to ensure that the account of Jesus Christ is intellectually well-founded.

In this sense, Macquarrie seeks to be true to the intention of Chalcedon, whilst recognising that the technical metaphysical terms which were accessible in the Hellenistic world need to be replaced by new philosophical languages for the twentieth century. He notes that this is what the Hegelians have attempted with idealism, Bultmann with existentialism, and Pittenger with process philosophies. However, I have already noted Macquarrie's criticisms of Hegelian idealism in so far as it weakens the value of history. Likewise, I have noted that Macquarrie does not regard Bultmann's use of existentialism as an adequate philosophical grounding for christology precisely because he does not address the underlying ontological issues. In *Jesus Christ in*

Modern Thought, Macquarrie is cautious about the value of engaging the technical aspects of process philosophy for theological use. He notes the broad value of Pittenger's emphasis on a process of incarnation in which Jesus is 'a fresh intensification of the divine *nisus* in action in the creation', but is rightly unconvinced that his 'somewhat naturalistic' stress on process genuinely coheres with the Chalcedonian intention to express that 'all this is from God' (2 Cor 5:17). He argues that Ogden fails in his attempt to integrate existentialist philosophy and process philosophy because while his doctrine of God draws on process philosophy his christology continues to derive from a Bultmannian existentialism, stressing the significance of who Christ *is* for us, without grounding that significance in his doctrine of God.

For Macquarrie, then, it is important that the ontological component of christology does actually give account of the person of Jesus Christ *in relation to the doctrine of God from which the ontology is derived*. Macquarrie does this by revisiting the dialectical theism with which he concerns himself in *In Search of Deity*. He acknowledges that the Christian community does not initially develop an explicit doctrine of divine immanence, which would have been inimical to the Jewish tradition of a transcendent God in contradiction to pagan and polytheistic immanent gods, and too reminiscent of a 'vague universal presence of God in everything' to be an adequate expression of the specific revelation encountered in the person of Jesus Christ.[32] Instead, it is through the doctrine of the Trinity that the specific immanence of God in Jesus Christ finds expression. This does, however, have a particular 'pre-history' in the Old Testament. Macquarrie agrees with Barth that the God of the Old Testament is a God who speaks, who communicates himself, and has already established the pre-history of the dialectical relation between God and the world in first-century Judaism.

This same strand, however, is found in the neo-Platonic tradition which lies behind the dialectical theism of *In Search of Deity*. From Plotinus' triad of divine hypostases and, for example, Dionysius' use of these ideas in Christian theology, there emerges another tradition of God coming forth from himself to create the world and dwell at its heart. It is from this perspective that Macquarrie suggests that 'the incarnation is to be seen as the culminating moment in this descent ... not as an isolated or anomalous happening, but as the focus of what God is always doing and has always been doing, that is to say, coming into his creation.'[33] This is reminiscent of Kierkegaard and Barth on the lowliness of God, that is, that 'God is always God, even in His humiliation. The divine being does not suffer any change, any

A Christology of Self-Giving

diminution, any transformation into something else, any admixture of something else, let alone any cessation.'[34] Macquarrie's use of this theme is very different from Barth's, and he is rightly critical of Barth's 'poor view of the human race' and of the historical realm, even in his later work. But they are at least agreed on the fundamental importance for Christian theology of 'the idea of a God who does not dwell in some kind of frozen perfection, far from the material world, but a God who comes out of his transcendence in a generous overflow of love so as to identify with the world'.[35]

In fact, for Macquarrie, it is not so much that God 'comes *out of* his transcendence' but that his transcendence *is* his coming out from himself. Just as self-transcendence in human being is the capacity to go beyond the self in directed openness, so divine transcendence can be understood as the dynamic reaching out in creation and redemption.

This, then, is the ontological grounding for Macquarrie's christology, and provides the same element of dynamic process that his attention to transcendent anthropology gives to his understanding of the humanity of Jesus Christ. He writes:

> As we ourselves move toward a more dynamic conception of God and think of him not as dwelling in a distant heaven in untroubled bliss but as transcending in the sense of constantly coming forth from himself, then the idea of incarnation will not seem to be some improbable speculation or some fragment of a fantastic mythology. Rather, we can see it as the meeting point at which the transcendence of humanity from below ... is met by the divine transcendence from above.[36]

For Macquarrie, then, the grace of being comes to concrete expression in Jesus Christ, where the transcendent movement of human being and the transcendent movement of divine being converge. In *Principles of Christian Theology*, Macquarrie writes:

> Jesus Christ may properly be understood as the focus of Being, the particular being in whom the advent and epiphany take place, so that he is taken up into Being itself and we see in him the coming into one of deity and humanity, of creative Being and creaturely being. And what we see in Christ is the destiny that God has set before humanity; Christ is the first fruits, but the Christian hope is that 'in Christ' God will bring all men to God-manhood ... He is definitive in the sense that for Christians he defines in normative fashion both the nature of man (which he has brought to a new level) and the nature of God (for the divine Logos, expressive Being, has found its fullest expression in him).[37]

This is an affirmation of faith, but one made within history rather than claiming to be from some vantage point above history. It is also an affirmation which combines the existential significance of Jesus Christ with an ontological account which locates him in relation to the ultimate reality of divine and creaturely being.

ADOPTIONISM AND INCARNATIONISM

Despite couching his christology in terms of the convergence of two personal movements, Macquarrie remains emphatic that the consideration must *start* with Jesus Christ's *humanity*, if it is to be intelligible. Further, if the humanity of Jesus Christ is fundamental to the summons to the authentic life which is exhibited as a genuine possibility because it has been lived under the conditions of human existence, all tendencies to docetism must be rigorously resisted.

Macquarrie therefore accepts adoptionism as a model of christology which must be retained. However, since he insists that this is only 'half the story', and that adoptionism must be completed in incarnationism, it is important to ensure that this is indeed the case in his own christology. Certainly, in places his terminology is unfortunate. Despite rejecting John Knox's conclusions, he draws on his pattern of movement from adoptionism to incarnationism to docetism in a way which might suggest (contrary to his insistence) a decreasing scale of validity and an increase in corruption of the earliest experiences of Jesus Christ. Further, his rejection of traditional understandings of preexistence, together with reservations expressed in his review of nineteenth-century kenotic christologies in *Jesus Christ in Modern Thought*, may prompt similar anxieties. So then, does Macquarrie verge too close to adoptionism in his commitment to rid christology of its docetic tendencies?

I shall address this question in two ways. First, I shall consider Macquarrie's approach to the transition from adoptionism to incarnationism in classical christology, in contrast to the modern adoptionist approach of, for example, Schleiermacher. Secondly, I shall explore Macquarrie's writings on pre-existence and kenosis in the two essays 'The pre-existence of Jesus Christ' (1966) and 'Kenoticism Reconsidered' (1974) which offer a more in-depth discussion than *Jesus Christ in Modern Thought*, in order to show that although Macquarrie's christology begins from below, it does not thereby fail to give an account of christology from above.

From adoptionism to incarnationism

In the first part of *Jesus Christ in Modern Thought*, Macquarrie traces the development of christology from its 'pre-history' and earliest biblical expression, to its formulation at Chalcedon. He establishes that in this early period there was a shift from adoptionism to incarnationism, and both that incarnation completes adoption, and that it does not thereby supersede it. The formulation of Chalcedon must not be allowed, therefore, to stand high and dry as an end point in a process, but as a particular point in a process which continues, and continues according to the earliest pattern of christological development. Although christology must always move towards incarnation, both safeguard important aspects of christological affirmation: 'Incarnationism teaches the priority of God, and that the event of Jesus Christ is not just an arbitrary or natural evolution; adoptionism guards against a docetic distortion of Christ by insisting on his humanity and on the need for human obedience and co-operation in fulfilling the potentialities of God's creation.'[38]

As I have indicated in Chapter 3, Macquarrie places the beginnings of christology with the point at which his followers began to make at least a minimal confession of faith: 'There must have been a time when the first somewhat vague attachment of the disciples to their teacher began to take the form of a more definite faith that he was a theologically significant figure ... at this point an explicitly theological content appeared in what the disciples had to say about Jesus.'[39] This means that the task of christology (like that of the gospels themselves) is not merely to *replicate* an original event for future generations, but to *recognise and re-present the essence* of that event.

The person and career of Jesus 'comprise a moment in universal history so impressive that after two thousand years it is still "revelation"' in the purely human sense that Nietzsche acknowledges, 'that something which profoundly convulses and upsets one becomes suddenly visible and audible with indescribable certainty and accuracy.'[40] Even so, for such a novel revelatory event to be recognised – for its impact to be felt from the first – there must already be a context in which it can be interpreted. For Macquarrie, the horizons for understanding the revelation of the person of Jesus were already established within first-century Judaism, in a framework of beliefs and expectations constituted by a dialectical relation between God and the world: the condescension of God in choosing a nation of the obscurity of Israel for spiritual leadership among the nations, the transcendent monarchy of God who nevertheless manifests himself by entrusting his image to his human creation, the intimacy of God with the prophets through his Spirit and Word, the covenant relationship between God and his people which is an open process of (in Gerhard von Rad's expression) 'ever increasing anticipation'. These motifs in contemporary Judaism, whilst not being an explicit prediction of Christ, prepared the ground for understanding an event as the condescension and self-communication of the transcendent God in his creation through an incarnation or hypostatisation to establish the new reign of God on earth.

The availability of this imagery and associated messianic titles explains for Macquarrie the extraordinarily rapid development of an explicit christology in the early Church, a development he likens to a cosmological 'big bang', in which the whole subsequent development of christology was established in essence within the first twenty or so years after the crucifixion. For Macquarrie, the *availability* of imagery which was *adapted* to the revelation in Christ allowed for this early attribution of divinity to Jesus, and the subsequent rapid development within the New Testament from adoptionism to incarnationism to give expression to that divinity, in the understanding of the theological significance of the person and work of Jesus Christ.

Development or evolution?

The point that must be assessed is whether this is a properly *developmental* account, or *evolutionary* in a way which implies a degeneration from the earliest accounts of Jesus' humanity to a later supernaturalising tendency towards docetism. Moule distinguishes developmental from evolutionary as an intention 'to explain all the various estimates of Jesus reflected in the New Testament as, in essence, only attempts to describe what was there from the beginning. They are not successive additions of something new, but only the drawing out and articulating of what is there.'[41]

Certainly, Macquarrie recognises the development in early christology. In much the same way as Reginald Fuller, he traces the development from a human Jesus with an earthly ministry to a 'full-blooded' incarnation and use of the divine man concept, via a certain struggle to express an increasing reverence couched in supernatural terms.[42] However, Macquarrie's account of the development appears somewhat exaggerated in comparison with Fuller's, because of his insistence that Paul's theology does not have a developed doctrine of pre-existence and is therefore, in effect, exclusively adoptionist. Macquarrie is highly dependent on James Dunn for his interpretation, and a comparison of Macquarrie and Dunn's divergence from Fuller on the Christ-hymn of Philippians will serve to illustrate the point, and to address the question of whether Macquarrie's account is developmental in a sense that allows for a diversity of christological models to coexist, or evolutionary in a sense that does not.

For Fuller, the origin of the hymn is in the Hellenistic Jewish Christian mission to Hellenistic gentiles, and not the earlier Semitic culture to which Lohmeyer assigns it, or the Gnostic redeemer myth which Bultmann and Käsemann read in it. Fuller retains the syncretistic situation of Bultmann and Käsemann, but without the dependence on Gnostic mythology, arguing that the hymn uses materials which would have been sympathetic to the new situation without constituting a thoroughgoing 'Hellenization' of christology. The *incarnation* of the Redeemer (rather than his *fall* into the material world) is a distinctively Christian adaptation of the myth to the history of Jesus of Nazareth, even though set in a borrowed context of pre-existence.

The significance of Fuller's interpretation is that it ascribes a cautious acceptance of incarnation to Paul by his inclusion of the hymn in his epistle. This means that although Fuller traces a developmental christology in three stages from primitive Palestinian christology (two foci: Jesus' earthly ministry and an imminent *parousia*) to the Hellenistic Jewish mission (two stages: Jesus' earthly ministry and his current exalted ministry) to the Hellenistic gentile mission (three stages: pre-existence, incarnation, exaltation), it is a moderate *developmental* (rather than evolutionary) account. James Dunn's work, although judicious and careful, is more *evolutionary* in approach. Dunn places the Christ-hymn firmly in the dominant Adamic christology of the 40s and 50s, and argues that it is two-stage (earthly-exalted) rather than three-stage christology. The diadic pattern contrasts 'form of God' with 'form of a slave', and 'equality with God' with 'in likeness of men', in parallel with Romans 1:23 and 7:7–11. Thus:

> Christ faced the same archetypal choice that confronted Adam, but chose *not* as Adam had chosen (to grasp equality with God). *Instead* he chose to empty himself of Adam's glory and to embrace Adam's lot ... *The Christ of Phil 2:6–11 therefore is the man who undid Adam's wrong*: confronted with the same choice, he rejected Adam's sin, but nevertheless freely followed Adam's course as fallen man to the bitter end of death; wherefore God bestowed on him the status not simply that Adam lost, but the status which Adam was intended to come to, God's final prototype, the last Adam.[43]

Macquarrie follows Dunn's interpretation, emphasising that the Christ-hymn is not Paul's acknowledgement of pre-existence and incarnation, but a comparison of giving or grasping. Macquarrie is concerned to safeguard Jesus' true humanity, which he insists is diminished if he had 'prior to his birth a conscious, personal pre-existence in heaven'.[44] He accepts the scholarship of Dunn, admittedly against a 'host of other scholars', to argue that Paul does not have a developed doctrine of pre-existence and is therefore, in effect, exclusively adoptionist. From this starting point, Macquarrie traces what does appear to be a significantly *evolutionary* account of christological development in the remainder of the New Testament. 'from the early adoptionism which told of a crucified man being made Lord and Christ by God, to the later incarnationism which told of the divine Word living as a human being in the midst of the human race'.[45] So far, Macquarrie's account appears largely evolutionary, but three points can be noted which suggest that his account is, in practice, *developmental* in a way that allows for a *diversity* of christological models.

Diversity and mutual completion

The perennial task of balance   First, Macquarrie draws attention to the perennial task of christology, that of giving justice to two different sets of data, along with the perennial danger that 'the balance is tipped one way or the other. Either we end up with a man, who may indeed tower in incomparable moral and spiritual superiority over his fellows, but only by a misplaced courtesy could such a man be called God; or else we have an alien being from heaven who, whatever human qualities he may manifest or simulate, is finally of a different origin and kind.'[46]

It is the earliest history of this balance-keeping which culminates in the formulae of Nicea and Chalcedon, and the particular new conditions of the patristic period which determine the degree to which the balance is allowed to fall towards incarnationism, at least in so far as classical christology comes to begin with the divinity of Christ and only subsequently to inquire of his humanity. The patristic task of formulating into a coherent body of teaching the disparate material received from the New Testament witness occurred when the membership of the Church was becoming increasingly Gentile and educated, so that the ideas engaged to express christological truths came more naturally from the philosophy of the prevailing Hellenistic culture. Thus the ideas of the Logos and the incarnation in John were taken up as conducive to dialogue with the Greek philosophical tradition.

Macquarrie, like Rahner, regards formulae such as those of Nicea and Chalcedon as milestones in a continuing process of reflection, 'not end but beginning, not goal but means, truths which open the way to the – ever greater – Truth'.[47] Certain dead ends are recognised, but the community is 'incited to pursue more promising ways in the hope of getting a fuller vision of truth'.[48] However, Macquarrie's estimate of the legacy of Chalcedon is pessimistic; he suggests that an imbalance towards an intellectualising *over-emphasis* on doctrinal formulae has diminished the existential and soteriological understanding of faith, and has left open a danger of slipping into artificial debate of the minutiae of metaphysical scholasticism. Macquarrie's christological construction, therefore, whilst arguably balanced towards Christ's humanity, is an explicit attempt to rebalance classical christological tendencies by a re-emphasis of an under-valued aspect.

Schleiermacher: a test case   Secondly, if Macquarrie was too strongly biased towards adoptionism, it might be expected to show in an unreserved approval of a wholeheartedly humanistic christology such as Schleiermacher's. This is not the case. Certainly, Macquarrie has much to say that is positive about Schleiermacher's christology. He dismisses claims that it is reductionist, arguing that it attempts to be true to Chalcedonian orthodoxy whilst beginning from a 'fairly definite anthropology ... [which] is the clue to the particular status which Christians ascribe to Jesus as the Christ'.[49] Schleiermacher's dual emphasis on human finitude and a 'sense and taste for the infinite' matches Macquarrie's own: 'a human being is finite, severely limited in power, intelligence, moral capacity, finally given over to death. Yet this finitude is contradicted by that same being's reaching out beyond himself, and though finite, setting his sights, so to speak, on the infinite.'[50]

Macquarrie agrees that Schleiermacher shares his intention in insisting that the appearance of Jesus Christ in history must be regarded as a *natural fact*, and that his difference from other human beings lies in the *potency* of his God-consciousness, a potency which is present to a degree in all human being. He agrees further that this is fundamentally expressed in Second Adam christology, and acknowledges the importance of 'an affirmative understanding of redemption (better, perhaps, salvation) as bringing the human person not only to the state of being freed from sin but also to the state of having fulfilled his or her potentiality for being'.[51]

However, despite areas of agreement with Schleiermacher over the task of post-Enlightenment christology, Macquarrie expresses significant reservations about Schleiermacher's work. In particular, he insists that 'it is decidedly odd to speak of the *incarnation* as a "natural fact". We try to think of it as something that has come about within the texture of world-happening, yet we also want to say that something new and decisive has appeared at this point.'[52] Macquarrie agrees that Schleiermacher attempts to do this, but regards his solution as inadequate because it falls back on precisely the supernatural account avoided by emphasising Christ's humanity, but does not thereby offer an *ontological* account.

Two stories: a British theme One final point can be noted to suggest that Macquarrie's account is not a fundamentally adoptionist approach to which has been added an ill-fitting ontological component. Macquarrie's stress on the incarnation as two converging personal movements, though derived from continental perspectives, coheres remarkably well with the approach taken by Maurice Wiles and others in the British *Christ, Faith and History* symposium (1972). Wiles notes the tendency to attribute to significant doctrines a singular act, divine or human. Thus, especially in the doctrines of the creation and fall, 'it was for a very long time felt that a certain specific action in history was essential to the possibility of affirming the doctrine.'[53] Where this tendency to tie a doctrine to a particular event meets the doctrine of the incarnation, there is an attempt to describe logically a single point at which the two natures are conjoined in an act of incarnation upon which redemption is predicated. Contrary to this tendency, Wiles advocates a 'two story' approach: 'in the first place a human story of the partial overcoming in human lives of that repudiation of the fellowship with God of which the doctrine of the fall speaks. And also a mythological story of God's total self-giving, God's compassionate acceptance of pain and evil whereby that overcoming is made possible and effective.'[54] The two stories are then interwoven in various ways at various times, achieving a loose fit, but enough coherence to retain credibility. Macquarrie's two personal movements perform the same function.

Pre-existence and kenosis

A second means by which to assess whether or not Macquarrie is unduly adoptionist in his desire to safeguard Christ's humanity is his account of pre-existence and kenosis. As might be expected, Macquarrie considers nineteenth-century kenotic christologies too dependent on the speculative, metaphysical claim that 'a divine, pre-existent Being, the Logos or second person of the Trinity, had surrendered some of His

A Christology of Self-Giving

divine prerogatives and accepted the limitations of an embodied existence, so that He might manifest the life of God in the flesh.'[55] More surprisingly, he is critical of the christologies of the twentieth century which have preserved the valuable notion of self-emptying from the earlier tradition and recast it in a humanistic framework. He deems these christologies, which include and develop Bonhoeffer's 'man for others', a 'new-style kenoticism'.[56] But he is critical of their tendency to a one-sided adoptionism in their enthusiasm for Jesus' full humanity, and recommends that whilst the mythological associations of pre-existence must certainly be abandoned, its essential meaning must be emphasised as a safeguard against adoptionism.

The essential meaning of pre-existence is *God's initiative*: his presence in the event of the incarnation and, most particularly, his authorship of the event. Thus Macquarrie writes:

> the idea of pre-existence is one of the ways in which the New Testament writers tried to bring to expression their conviction that the initiative in the event of Jesus Christ lay with God; or, to put the matter in another way, that this event is understood on a more fundamental level when we see it as God's coming among men than when we think of it as a man's exaltation to Godhood.[57]

Within Macquarrie's two convergent paths of self-giving, this is expressed as the continual activity of God in going out from himself to confer being (the tradition of the Logos, or Expressive Being). As the supreme manifestation of the presence and action of God in the world, the incarnation *recapitulates* the creation which is 'already a self-emptying, a self-giving and self-spending on the part of God. He does not maintain Himself in some remotely serene aloofness, but shares the mystery of being, conferring the gift of existence upon a creation – yes, conferring upon it even something of his own freedom and creativity, and accepting the risk which this self-emptying necessarily brings with it.'[58] The other path, the human person of Jesus Christ as the culmination of the unfolding of creation, meets and brings to expression this primary self-giving, 'as if the unfolding of the creation has been directed toward bringing forth the Christ who would make explicit the meaning that has been hidden in the creation from the beginning'.[59]

It is Christ who brings to light the hidden meaning of creation because, although all creation participates in God since God has shared his own existence with it, when creaturely being lives not for itself but is '*utterly careless of its own existence and pours itself out in creative love*, then indeed it is participating most in God and realising the highest potentialities that God has conferred.'[60] God's activity of creating is itself a self-emptying and self-giving, and so the creature who most truly empties himself brings the creation nearest to God and is indeed 'the image of the invisible God, the first born of all creation'. What Macquarrie insists on, then, is that 'theological reflection upon the self-emptying Man for others, Jesus of Nazareth, is bound to lead into an exploration of the ontological depths of this encounter', and that these depths concern the self-giving love of God.[61]

In 'Kenoticism Reconsidered' (1974), Macquarrie begins from the self-giving of the human Jesus Christ. By this stage (post-*God and Secularity* (1967)) Macquarrie has become more critical of the humanising trend in theology and is concerned to prevent the humanistic agenda in theology from slipping towards thoroughgoing secularism. In this context he acknowledges nineteenth-century kenotic christology as a mediating theology which attempted to retain both the *true humanity* of Jesus and the *traditional framework* of christology against the growing positivism of Strauss and atheism of Feuerbach. His criticism is now focused not on its metaphysical speculations, but on its failure of nerve to return radically to Christ's humanity (a failure he admits was understandable against the 'extreme lengths of dissolution' engendered by Strauss and Feuerbach). He argues that the nineteenth-century kenoticists attempted to begin with a fully wrought conception of God and to show how much of the divine being could be brought within the limits of a human existence, rather than to allow Christ to be the revelation of God which renews our conception of divine being. Instead, he advocates a return to the pattern of early Church christology which starts with a 'full and unambiguous acceptance of Christ's humanity' and only then proceeds to an incarnational statement as the *end* of a process of reflection.[62]

Once again, the motif of self-emptying is all important, but now Macquarrie begins with the humiliation of the human Jesus Christ, with his self-abasement as he goes obediently to the cross – the humility of the Second Adam explored in *Jesus Christ in Modern Thought*. The paradox is that Christ's humiliation on the cross is his exaltation: it is on the cross that he is 'lifted up'. And it is precisely this self-offering and self-outpouring that 'constitutes his glory and that transfigures him so that God-Language becomes a necessity if we are to speak of him with any adequacy ... When we use God-language about him, we mean that the self-emptying of Jesus Christ has not only opened up the depth of a true humanity but has made known to us the final reality as likewise self-emptying, self-giving, self-limiting.'[63] So, then, the convergence of the two personal movements in the incarnation discloses that

> *kenosis* is not the dimming down, as it were, of the divine nature in an atypical act of condescension but is the very expression of that nature at its deepest and most significant level ... This is the paradox of personal existence, that emptying and fulfilling, *kenosis* and *plerosis*, are the same; and he who utterly emptied himself, Jesus Christ, is precisely the one who permits us to glimpse that utter fullness we call divine.[64]

The importance of these two essays is that they indicate again that Macquarrie does not stop with an adoptionist christology, but always sees it completed in incarnation, because the incarnation is always already characteristic of the ultimate reality of God's being. Far from failing to give an account of the self-emptying pre-existent Logos, Macquarrie places the incarnation in a whole history of divine self-giving. These essays provide the link between the notion of the grace of being as developed in *Principles of Christian Theology*, *In Search of Humanity* and *In Search of Deity* and its concrete expression in the life and work of Jesus Christ, in the motif of self-giving love. Human being is grace-full because its ultimate horizon is deification; divine being is gracious to human existence because it is in human being that it comes to its fullest presence and manifestation in creation; these two complementary movements are solely possible because of the gift of existence (again, the grace of being) imparted in the self-offering of the ground and goal of all existence, Being itself.

SELF-GIVING AND POWER

The issue of kenosis, and especially the notion that *kenosis is plerosis*, suggests an approach to a further critical question that might be raised against Macquarrie's theology: does his rejection of the monarchical model of divine power and of irruptive divine action entail an abandonment of the idea of divine power altogether, or does his understanding of self-giving include an account of divine power? In his essay, 'The Strange Persistence of Kenotic Christology', Sykes agrees with Macquarrie that the self-giving quality of God's love, in which kenosis is plerosis, is of fundamental significance. But he raises a specific difficulty which emerges precisely because of this emphasis, which will shed a critical light on an aspect of Macquarrie's theology and which, if defensible, will be of some significance. The crux of

Sykes' argument for my purpose is this: that despite its emphasis on the *emptying of power*, the notion of kenosis persists as a significant motif precisely because it is experienced as *empowering*; and that this gives cause for some suspicion about the rhetoric of powerlessness in Christian theology.

The difficulty that Sykes notes with regard to new-style kenotic christologies is the persistent danger of a facile identification of kenosis with plerosis. He begins his enquiry by suggesting that 'after all, humility is not humility if it cannot be contrasted with exaltation, weakness is not weakness if it cannot be contrasted with power, limit is not limit if it cannot be contrasted with plenitude.'[65] The significance of this blurring is that 'a theology which abandons all reference to the power of God with the result that the death of one called the Son of God becomes one more act of divine love is to miss its uniquely scandalous character.'[66] To fail to attend to the *reality of the death* of Christ is to ignore two important things. First of all, it is to ignore the degree to which the need to give an account of this death has been a key force in christological development from the beginning, and remains a fundamental issue with regard to the question of the power and identity of God. Secondly, it is to ignore an important distinction between the relative powerlessness of the human Jesus who teaches and heals, and the absolute powerlessness of the dead Jesus; in this sense, to characterise the death of Jesus as an act of love *per se* is somehow to miss the point by rendering it a minor act of love divested of ongoing power. Ultimately, for Sykes, this threatens to be a loss of distinction between creation and redemption. This poses a second (though related) critical question for Macquarrie's theology: is his grace of being fundamentally a theology of creation, or is it also a theology of redemption?

Sykes tackles his enquiry by noting that the motif of self-emptying is not merely *ethically* compelling (the merits of humility in personal relations) but is, first and foremost, *religiously* compelling as divine out-pouring. To explore why this is so, Sykes turns to the insights of social anthropology. He notes that the Christ-hymn plausibly derives from a baptismal setting, and that whether or not this is its *Sitz im Leben* it has the same structure as a baptismal rite, with two symmetrical movements of descent and separation followed by ascent and reintegration. Understood in its religious, ritual context, two aspects become important: the use of metaphor and the experience of community.

First, the power of the motif of kenosis survives all critical onslaught because it is reinforced in a religious context in association with the much more powerful imagery of baptism and eucharistic sacrifice. Sykes makes two points here. First, the hymn employs a *double metaphor* – that of baptism itself, and that of Christ's 'supposed self-abasement in his identification with the human condition'.[67] In baptism, the believer participates in the death of Christ and thereby in the new life of Christ: a new identity is bestowed and the whole process is to the glory of God. The power of the metaphor of kenosis is derived from the primary metaphor of baptism as the participation in Christ's participation in our condition. A further point can be made about the way in which identification with Christ in a baptismal dying 'effect[s] the transition to a new life of higher status'.[68] Sykes refers to James Fernandez' work on the *progression of metaphors*, each of which locates the believer in a particular place, so that the effect of the progression is to *relocate* the believer. In the case of kenosis there is a relocation of the believer from a 'lower' life to a 'higher' life by participation in the death of Christ; this 'works' by the (non-rational) 'logic' of sacrifice, 'according to which metaphysical power is released by putting to death a living gift, and thus separating its essence from its material body. Sacrifice is thus a process of communication between the deity and humanity, in which the "bridge" is a gift.'[69] This model of sacrifice is constantly reinforced in a eucharistic context, and linked to this context the motif of kenosis gains power, *and becomes empowering*, from the sacramental life of the community.

Secondly, drawing on the work of Victor Turner, Sykes notes the experience of *communitas*, an immediacy of relationship, a comradeship which is not dependent on convention, which is part of the common yearning of every human being but is experienced principally by those in a position of 'structural inferiority', typically the poor or those passing from one mode of being to another. Kenosis not only is linked to the initiatory rite of baptism, but is also a metaphor of poverty. In becoming poor, Christ identifies with all humanity, and those who participate in him by baptism enjoy *communitas* with him and with fellow believers: 'This new immediacy and intimacy of relationship is precisely what is meant by kenotic love.'[70]

In both these aspects, Sykes is emphasising that the theme of kenosis persists and is empowering precisely because it is mediated in the Christian tradition within the pre-theological ritual of the Christian community. Its persistence and power lie in the self-involving corporate life, rather than in its conceptual triumph. Rather than an objectified programme of enquiry, Sykes argues, kenotic christology was intended to express belief in a participation in a new redeemed community, and cannot therefore be separated from the baptismal identity of the

Christian. In the same way, for Macquarrie kenotic christology as an account of the self-outpouring of Expressive Being, and the corresponding self-giving of transcendent human being at its ultimate horizon, is of concern only because of its *effective* empowering of human transcendence as letting-be.

This existential account is not without ontological significance in relation to the question of the power of God. Although he does not pursue this insight here, Sykes raises suspicions about the fashionable interest in the powerlessness of God, particularly characterised by dealing with kenosis as an issue for the doctrine of God rather than christology *per se*. Sykes points out that for the baptised human being, unity with Christ in his renunciation of power is not at all straightforward in relation to the exercise of power in the realm of human institutions. It is by no means clear that 'a Christian who has participated in the kenosis of Christ by baptism into his death [is] permanently marked by that humility, so that the exercise of human power can never again be a feature of his or her life.'[71] It is the *identity* of the being of the baptizand which causes this ambiguity, and so, translated to the matter of God's identity of being in Christ, invites suspicion of the rhetoric of divine powerlessness. Self-abandonment, then, might not be equivalent to the total abandonment of power.

What Sykes proposes is that, even if the 'tidy' two-nature scheme is abandoned, its achievement of holding together self-abandonment and power in the Logos can be retained in a differentiated treatment of divine power. The motif Sykes articulates shows the extent to which Macquarrie's theology meets his proposal: 'the true lifting up of humanity by the majesty of divine condescension'.[72] What this motif expresses is that the divine self-giving *is effective in lifting up humanity*, and is not a mutual immersion in weakness. This is Macquarrie's criterion of the reasonableness of belief in God, expressed variously as the condition that there is something rather than nothing, or that facticity and possibility are of a piece so that human being may be transcendent under the conditions of human existence. The self-giving of God is 'powerful' in that it gives being and summons into possibility. Further, as I have already indicated, this capacity is the heart of Macquarrie's understanding of ontological difference, which reaches its fulfilment in the convergence in the incarnation of two movements of self-giving, one ultimate and unconditioned, the other purely graced. Macquarrie's christology, then, contributes an account of the self-abandonment of the Logos, Expressive Being, but also of the power of the Logos precisely in the gift of being and the summons into possibility which makes *incarnation* possible as a reciprocal movement.

Finally, with regard to the question of whether Macquarrie's christology is simply a theology of creation and not also a theology of redemption, some defence can now be offered. Sykes suggests that such a confusion arises when the love of God is invoked, especially as self-limiting, in such a way that denies divine power. Although Macquarrie is resistant to the description of the person and work of Christ as a unique event, and in that sense accords with Wiles above in rejecting the assumption that a doctrine rests on a single event, and he shares with Rahner the understanding of the incarnation as the horizon of the cosmos' evolutionary transcendence, his christological account of God's self-giving is decidedly not an invitation to ethically supportive weakness in a mutual created state. Rather, it is an account of the effectual power of transformation: the transforming gift of being which effects transcendence of individual human being within a corporate (and institutional/ritual) context.

NOTES

1. This is an explicit borrowing of Bonhoeffer's question, which Macquarrie finds as 'real and oppressive' a question today, *Christology Revisited* (London: SCM 1998), 10; Dietrich Bonhoeffer, *Letters and Papers from Prison* (London: SCM 1971), 279.
2. *JCMT* ix
3. Rudolf Bultmann, *Theology of the New Testament* vol. 2 (London: SCM 1955), 66.
4. *JCMT* 328; compare D.M. Baillie, *God was in Christ* (London: Faber & Faber 1948), 52.
5. Søren Kierkegaard, *Training in Christianity* (London: OUP 1946), 27, 127.
6. *God was in Christ*, 49. Neither Baillie nor Macquarrie deny that the revelation of the incarnation is in some sense also a veiling, but both wish to maintain that it is *less* veiled here than elsewhere.
7. Søren Kierkegaard, *Philosophical Fragments* (London: OUP 1936), 87.
8. *JCMT* 352, compare *PCT* 89.
9. *JCMT* 352
10. *JCMT* 391, *Christology Revisited* 64, 67
11. *JCMT* 183
12. *SD* 93
13. *SCE* 48
14. *JCMT* 51–52, and 425n15. Compare E.P. Sanders, *Jesus and Judaism* (London: SCM 1985), 11, 321.
15. *JCMT* 355
16. *JCMT* 356. Günther Bornkamm, *Jesus of Nazareth* (London: Hodder & Stoughton 1960), 155.
17. *JCMT* 360
18. *JCMT* 364. Compare J.P. Sartre 'Existentialism is a Humanism' in ed. Walter

Kaufman *Existentialism from Dostoyevsky to Sartre* (Cleveland: World Publishing Co 1956), 287–311, 290.
19 *JCMT* 366, Ernst Bloch, *The Principle of Hope* vol. 1 (Oxford: Basil Blackwell 1986), 246.
20 A.N. Whitehead, *Adventures of Ideas* (Cambridge: CUP 1933), 99.
21 *JCMT* 364, italics are Macquarrie's.
22 *JCMT* 371
23 *JCMT* 369, 370. Compare Karl Rahner, *Theological Investigations I*, 184; *Hearers of the Word* (London: Sheed & Ward 1969), 79.
24 *JCMT* 22
25 *JCMT* 373
26 *JCMT* 401
27 *JCMT* 402. Compare Dorothee Sölle's *Christ the Representative* (London: SCM 1967).
28 *JCMT* 392
29 *The Christian Faith* 402; compare Karl Rahner, *Theological Investigations V* (London: DLT 1966), 157–192; *Foundations of Christian Faith* (New York: Crossword 1978), 178–203.
30 *JCMT* 376
31 *JCMT* 376
32 *JCMT* 378
33 *JCMT* 379
34 *Church Dogmatics* IV/1 (Edinburgh: T&T Clark 1956), 179.
35 *JCMT* 380
36 *JCMT* 380
37 *PCT* 303, 305
38 John Macquarrie, 'The Pre-existence of Jesus Christ', *The Expository Times* 77 (1966), 199–202, 202.
39 *JCMT* 3–4
40 Friedrich Nietzsche, *Ecce Homo* (London: George Allen & Unwin 1911), 102.
41 C.F.D. Moule, *The Origin of Christology* (Cambridge: CUP 1977), 1–10, 2–3.
42 Reginald Fuller, *The Foundations of New Testament Christology* (London: Collins 1969); the felicitous phrase 'full-blooded incarnation' is Fuller's, 206.
43 James D.G. Dunn, *Christology in the Making* (London: SCM 1980), 117–19, italics are Dunn's.
44 *JCMT* 57; in place of this mythological account, Macquarrie accepts that Christ pre-existed in the mind and purpose of God.
45 *JCMT* 147
46 *JCMT* 126
47 Karl Rahner, *Theological Investigations I* (London: DLT 1965), 149.
48 *JCMT* 165
49 *JCMT* 192
50 *JCMT* 197; Friedrich Schleiermacher, *On Religion: Speeches to its cultured Despisers* (New York: Harper & Row 1958), 39.
51 *JCMT* 205; see *Christian Faith* 64, 385.
52 *JCMT* 206; italics are mine.
53 Maurice Wiles 'Does christology rest on a mistake?' in eds S.W. Sykes and J.P. Clayton *Christ, Faith and History* (Cambridge: CUP 1972), 3–12, 4.
54 Wiles, 9
55 John Macquarrie 'The Pre-existence of Jesus Christ', *The Expository Times* 77

(1966), 199–202, 199. See, for example, Charles Gore, *Lux Mundi* (London: John Murray 1891), 265 n2, 360.
56 See, for example, Dietrich Bonhoeffer, *Letters and Papers from Prison* (London: SCM 1971), 380ff; Paul Tillich, *Systematic Theology* vol. 1 (Chicago: University of Chicago Press 1951), 148; J.A.T. Robinson, *Honest to God* (London: SCM 1963), 64–83.
57 *Pre-existence* 200
58 *Pre-existence* 201
59 *Pre-existence* 202
60 *Pre-existence* 202, my italics.
61 *Pre-existence* 200
62 John Macquarrie 'Kenoticism Reconsidered', *Theology* 77 (1974), 115–24, hereafter *Kenoticism*, 121.
63 *Kenoticism* 123–24, compare 'Pre-existence' 202.
64 *Kenoticism* 123
65 S.W. Sykes, 'The strange persistence of kenotic christology' in *Being and Truth* eds Alistair Kee and Eugene T. Long (London: SCM 1986), 349–75, hereafter *Kenotic Christology*, 359
66 *Kenotic Christology* 359
67 *Kenotic Christology* 362
68 *Kenotic Christology* 364
69 *Kenotic Christology* 364; Sykes notes in passing that this shows that Lohmeyer had at least a 'sound instinct' in locating the Philippians Christ-hymn in a eucharistic rather than a baptismal context.
70 *Kenotic Christology* 363
71 *Kenotic Christology* 371
72 *Kenotic Christology* 372, compare Augustine, *Confessions* 7, xviii (London: JM Dent & Sons 1907), 139–40.

Concluding Remarks

Macquarrie's thought is too complex to allow for easy summary. With these concluding remarks I shall simply review the direction of the preceding discussion and point up selected observations which coincide with my specific interests and with the more distinctive aspects of Macquarrie's work.

First, I have traced the development of Macquarrie's thought from his early focus on existentialist thought in his Glasgow period, to the existential-ontological theism of his later work. In doing so, I have indicated that his concerns move in increasing concentric circles of relationality, from anthropocentric focus on the individual (albeit moderated in emphasis), through social and ecclesial relationality and embodiment in the shared public realm, to attention to the role of human being within the organic wholeness of the cosmos. I have discussed this development in the context of influences on Macquarrie's thought, and the positions from which he distinguishes his work. The way in which he develops his distinctive approach to natural theology in dialogue with the theological community but unfettered to a single school of thought allows him to bring together divergent traditions in a creative synthesis.

I have argued that the cohesiveness of Macquarrie's thought throughout its development lies not only in his commitment to express the truth of the Christian faith intelligibly to its context but, more significantly, in his insistence that this must be done with attention to human being as an ontologically rich resource for understanding the reality of God and the nature of the cosmos. By means of the hermeneutical phrase *the grace of being*, I have argued for a threefold core to this divine-human relationality. That is, firstly, human being is the locus of grace because it is in the very constitution of human existence that the quest for God begins and is answered. Secondly, God as holy Being is gracious to human being as its source, support and goal. Thirdly, the reason for this is that being (existence) is precisely a divine act of self-giving. The concentric circles of developing relationality provide the broadening scope for the account of the grace of being: individual, social, cosmic. These transitions do not render obsolete the previous stage. Rather, each emphasis is incorporated into a more inclusive horizon.

In particular, the phrase *the grace of being* has indicated that the distinctive mediating thrust of Macquarrie's theology is between *gift* and *being*. This lies at the heart of his existential-ontological mediation, and is of interest for its capacity to unify the wholly other summons from beyond human existence with an account of continuity and kinship of being, divine and created. I have shown that Macquarrie thereby provides an account of human being which does not need to cling to Enlightenment models of autonomy in order to provide a high view of what it means to be human in terms of dignity, responsibility and agency. Equally, he is able to provide a high view of God's ontological difference and of the divine imperative which does not thereby conceive of God as an isolated monarchical monad distant from and alien to the created realm. In so doing, Macquarrie holds together two fields of theological endeavour which are more typically opposed: revealed theology and natural theology. The pivotal point of opposition, epistemology, is shown to be a false polarity. It is not the case that we have knowledge of God *either* as a gift received as wholly other *or* from the human capacity for the divine, since human capacity (and, indeed, existence) is itself divine self-gift.

Further, the phrase *the grace of being* has allowed the concept of giving to take its central stand in Macquarrie's doctrines of human being, God and Christ. The personal movement of God as self-giving in creation, and the personal movement of human being as letting-be in participation with God and bringing the cosmos to new expression, meet in the person of Jesus Christ. The transcendence of God and the transcendence of human being coinhere in him, giving an account of power which is neither monarchical nor co-ordinate with weakness. The focusing of these movements in Jesus Christ once again grounds the existential-ontological in that realm where it must prove significant: concrete embodiment in the shared public realm.

Although this book is not intended to cast Macquarrie's theology polemically as 'ripe for rediscovery', it is notable how infrequently his work is cited as a conversation partner in contemporary dogmatics, and yet how resourceful it might be in such a context. At a point when constructive theology is recovering confidence, the capacity to articulate God-talk in terms accessible to secular culture must be joyfully safeguarded. Macquarrie's theology offers both a methodological method and enduring examples of content for this task. More than this, his work offers cogent resources for that cluster of doctrines so prevalent at present: trinity, creation, eschatology. These doctrines are concerned with questions of the nature of God and its specific relevance to the shape of human living; questions of the nature of the relation of God to the world, and of the relation of the activity of God to history. Macquarrie's attention to these issues, and to the ontological and epistemological issues underlying them, makes him a resourceful partner in the continuing systematic conversation.

Beyond this immediate relevance, Macquarrie's corpus provides a landmark example of British theology. It is grounded, balanced and gracious. It gives attention to the experience of Christian believing which lies at the heart of theology, while engaging scrupulously with the philosophical questions inherent in (and levelled against) this experience. It offers a coherent and systematic stance in its persistent commitment to dialectical theism; and yet it summons the reader to engage in a broader exploration and application of its resources rather than a narrower discussion of its technical minutiae. It is, in this sense, a model example both of Anglican 'restraint' and of postmodern contextualisation.

For all these reasons (as well as for those which others will themselves bring to the texts), Macquarrie's work merits careful attention and will continue to stimulate its readers to pursue their own conversation about the nature of human and divine being in the world.

Bibliography

A NOTE ON THE BIBLIOGRAPHY

The bibliography gives a full list of Macquarrie's published works and extensive references to the thinkers and communities of ideas used in this exploration of his thought. For a more general introduction to Macquarrie's thought, the following can be considered as the key texts:

- For his existentialist period: *An Existentialist Theology* and *Studies in Christian Existentialism*. *An Existentialist Theology* explores the way in which Martin Heidegger's existentialist philosophy can be used to commend the Christian faith, and analyses the way in which Rudolf Bultmann has attempted to do this. It traces 'inauthentic' and 'authentic' existence in relation to major Pauline themes such as sin, the flesh and life in the spirit. *Studies in Christian Existentialism* is a collection of essays which develop Macquarrie's own use of existentialist thought, and demonstrate his commitment to balancing significance for the human person with a grounding in 'objective' reality. His own distinctive theological position begins to emerge clearly, tested out in relation to the doctrine of the atonement, the nature of death, and the work of the Holy Spirit.

- For his new expression of natural theology: *Principles of Christian Theology*. This is a one-volume systematic theology in three parts. It lays out how the quest for God arises from our human condition and shows what this means for understanding God as Being which is gracious to the contradictions and desires of being human. It interprets the traditional doctrines of the Christian faith in the light of this kind of natural theology. And it locates the practical implications in terms of liturgical practice, ethics and prayer.

- For the doctrinal heart of his work: *In Search of Humanity*, *In Search of Deity* and *Jesus Christ in Modern Thought*. These three books form a 'trilogy' laying out the culmination of Macquarrie's theology in the nature of human being, the nature of God, and a christology for the present day. In each case, the notion of self-giving (or self-transcendence) is a key motif. The human capacity to go beyond the self in openness to God and the divine capacity to go beyond the self in creation and communication meet in the person of Jesus Christ.

A summary of each of Macquarrie's major works can be found in *On Being a Theologian: John Macquarrie*, ed. John H. Morgan (London: SCM 1999), 178–213.

PRIMARY SOURCES

Macquarrie, John, *An Existentialist Theology* (London: SCM 1955)

Macquarrie, John, 'Changing Attitudes to Religion in Contemporary English Philosophy', *The Expository Times* 68 (1957), 298–301

Macquarrie, John, *The Scope of Demythologizing* (London: SCM 1960)

Macquarrie, John, *Twentieth-Century Religious Thought* (London: SCM 1963, 1988^4, 2001^5)

Macquarrie, John, 'Theologians of our Time: Karl Rahner', *The Expository Times* 74 (1963), 194–97

Macquarrie, John, 'Second Thoughts: The Philosophical School of Logical Analysis', *The Expository Times* 75 (1963), 45–48

Macquarrie, John, 'The Problem of Natural Theology', *Pittsburgh Perspective* 5 (1964), 10–19

Macquarrie, John, 'How can we think of God?', *Theology Today* 22 (1965), 194–204

Macquarrie, John, 'A Dilemma in Christology', *The Expository Times* 76 (1965), 207–10

Macquarrie, John, 'Rudolf Bultmann' in *A Handbook of Christian Theologians*, eds Martin E. Marty and Dean G. Peerman (Nashville: Abingdon 1965), pp. 445–63

Macquarrie, John, *Studies in Christian Existentialism* (London: SCM 1966)

Macquarrie, John, *Principles of Christian Theology* (London: SCM 1966, 1977^2)

Macquarrie, John, 'Philosophy and Theology in Bultmann's Thought' in *The Theology of Rudolf Bultmann*, ed. Charles W. Kegley (London: SCM 1966), pp. 127–43

Macquarrie, John, 'The Pre-existence of Jesus Christ', *The Expository Times* 77 (1966), 199–202

Macquarrie, John, 'I Recommend You to Read', *The Expository Times* 78 (1967), 292–96

Macquarrie, John, 'Heidegger's Earlier and Later Work Compared', *Anglican Theological Review* 49 (1967), 3–16

Macquarrie, John, *God-Talk* (London: SCM 1967)

Macquarrie, John, 'Will and Existence' in *The Concept of Willing*, ed. James Lapsley (Nashville: Abingdon Press 1967), pp. 73–87

Macquarrie, John, *God and Secularity* (London: SCM 1968)

Macquarrie, John, *Martin Heidegger* (London: Lutterworth 1968)

Macquarrie, John, 'Bultmann's Understanding of God', *The Expository Times* 79 (1968), 356–60

Macquarrie, John, 'The Doctrine of Creation and Human Responsibility' in *Knowledge and the Future of Man*, ed. Walter J. Ong (New York: Holt, Rinehart & Winston 1968), pp. 125–38

Macquarrie, John, 'Subjectivity and Objectivity in Theology and Worship', *Theology* 72 (1969), 499–505

Macquarrie, 'Schleiermacher Reconsidered', *The Expository Times* 80 (1969), 169–200

Macquarrie, John, *Three Issues in Ethics* (London: SCM 1970)

Macquarrie, John, 'What is the Gospel?', *The Expository Times* 81 (1970), 296–300

Macquarrie, John, 'Word and Idea', *International Journal for the Philosophy of Religion* 1 (1970), 65–76

Macquarrie, John, 'Creation and Environment', *The Expository Times* 83 (1971), 4–9

Macquarrie, John, 'The Humanity of Christ', *Theology* 74 (1971), 243–50

Macquarrie, John, 'John McLeod Campbell 1800–72', *The Expository Times* 83 (1971), 263–68

Macquarrie, John, *Paths in Spirituality* (London: SCM 1972)

Macquarrie, John, *Existentialism* (London: Penguin 1972)

Macquarrie, John, *The Faith of the People of God* (London: SCM 1972)

Macquarrie, John, 'God and the World: One Reality or Two?', *Theology* 75 (1972), 394–403

Macquarrie, John, *Mystery and Truth* (Milwaukee: Marquette University 1973)

Macquarrie, John, 'A theology of alienation' in *Alienation: Concept, Term and Meanings*, ed. Frank Johnson (New York: Seminar Press 1973), pp. 311–20

Macquarrie, John, *The Concept of Peace* (London: SCM 1973)
Macquarrie, John, 'Kenoticism Reconsidered', *Theology* 77 (1974), 115–24
Macquarrie, John, *Thinking about God* (London: SCM 1975)
Macquarrie, John, *Christian Unity and Christian Diversity* (London: SCM 1975)
Macquarrie, John, 'The idea of a theology of nature', *Union Seminary Quarterly Review* 30 (1975), 69–75
Macquarrie, John, 'Recent Thinking in Christology', *The Expository Times* 83 (1976), 36–39
Macquarrie, John, *The Humility of God* (London: SCM 1978)
Macquarrie, John, *Christian Hope* (London: SCM 1978)
Macquarrie, John, 'Existentialism and theological method', *Communio: International Catholic Review* 6 (1979), 5–15
Macquarrie, John, 'Foundation Documents of the Faith: The Chalcedonian Definition', *The Expository Times* 91 (1979), 68–72
Macquarrie, John, 'Tradition, Truth and Christology', *Heythrop Journal* 21 (1980), 365–75
Macquarrie, John, *In Search of Humanity* (London: SCM 1982)
Macquarrie, John, 'Celtic Spirituality' in *A Dictionary of Christian Spirituality*, ed. Gordon Wakefield (London: SCM 1983), pp. 83–84
Macquarrie, John, *In Search of Deity* (London: SCM 1984)
Macquarrie, John, 'Pilgrimage in Theology' in *Being and Truth*, eds Alistair Kee and Eugene Thomas Long (London: SCM 1986), pp. xi–xviii
Macquarrie, John, *Theology, Church and Ministry* (London: SCM 1986)
Macquarrie, John, 'Enlightened about Enlightenment', *The Expository Times* 97 (1986), 218–19
Macquarrie, John, 'A Theology of Personal Being' in *Persons and Personality*, eds Arthur Peacocke and Grant Gillett (Oxford: Blackwell 1987), pp. 172–79
Macquarrie, John, 'The Papacy in a Unified Church', *Pacifica* 2 (1989), 123–34
Macquarrie, John, *Jesus Christ in Modern Thought* (London: SCM 1990)
Macquarrie, John, *Mary for all Christians* (London: Collins 1991; Edinburgh: T&T Clark 2001)
Macquarrie, John, 'Updatings on the Trinity', *The Expository Times* 103 (1992), 249
Macquarrie, John, 'Natural Theology' in *The Blackwell Encyclopaedia of Modern Christian Thought* (Oxford: Blackwell 1993), pp. 402–5
Macquarrie, John, *Heidegger and Christianity* (London: SCM 1994)

Macquarrie, John, *Invitation to Faith* (London: SCM 1995)
Macquarrie, John, *The Mediators* (London: SCM 1995)
Macquarrie, John, 'Theological Reflections on Disability' in *Religion and Disability*, ed. Marilyn E. Bishop (Kansas: Sheed & Ward 1995), pp. 27–45
Macquarrie, John, 'Ebb and Flow of Hope: Christian Theology at the End of the Second Millennium', *The Expository Times* 107 (1996), 205–10
Macquarrie, John, *A Guide to the Sacraments* (London: SCM 1997)
Macquarrie, John, *Christology Revisited* (London: SCM 1998)
Macquarrie, John, 'Current Trends in Anglican Christology', *Anglican Theological Review* 79 (1997), 563–70
Macquarrie, John, *On Being a Theologian* (London: SCM 1999)
Macquarrie, John, 'Postmodernism in philosophy of religion and theology', *International Journal for Philosophy of Religion* 50 (2001), 9–27

SECONDARY LITERATURE

Abbott, Walter M., *The Documents of Vatican II* (New York: Association Press 1966)
Adam, Karl, *The Christ of Faith* (London: Burns & Oates 1957)
Adams, Marilyn McCord and Robert Merrihew Adams, eds, *The Problem of Evil* (Oxford: OUP 1990)
Anselm, *Proslogion* (La Salle: Open Court 1951)
Apel, Karl-Otto, *Towards a Transformation of Philosophy* (London: Routledge & Kegan Paul 1980)
Aquinas, St Thomas, *Summa Theologiae* (London: Eyre & Spottiswoode 1963–74)
Aquinas, St Thomas, *Summa contra Gentiles* (London: University of Notre Dame Press 1975)
Augustine, *City of God* (Washington, DC: Catholic University of America Press 1952)
Augustine, *Confessions and Enchiridion* (London: SCM 1955)
Augustine, *de Trinitate* in *Fathers of the Church*, Vol. 45 (Washington, DC: Catholic University Press of America 1963)
Avis, Paul, 'Does Natural Theology exist?', *Theology* 87 (1984), 431–37
Baillie, D.M., *God was in Christ* (London: Faber & Faber 1948)
Baillie, John, *Our Knowledge of God* (London: OUP 1939)
Baker, John Austin, *The Foolishness of God* (London: DLT 1970)

Barrett, C.K., *From First Adam to Last* (London: A&C Black 1962)
Barrett, William, *The Illusion of Technique* (New York: Anchor Press 1978)
Barth, Karl, *Church Dogmatics* (Edinburgh: T&T Clark 1957–75)
Barth, Karl, *The Humanity of God* (*Scottish Journal of Theology*, Occasional Paper 8, 1956)
Barth, Karl, *Anselm: Fides Quaerens Intellectum* (London: SCM 1960)
Barth, Karl, *The Word of God and the Word of Man* (Gloucester: Peter Smith 1978)
Barton, John, *Love Unknown* (London: SPCK 1990)
Bartsch, Hans-Werner, ed., *Kerygma and Myth*, vols. 1 & 2 combined (London: SPCK 1972)
Bauckham, Richard, *Moltmann: Messianic Theology in the Making* (Basingstoke: Marshall Pickering 1987)
Blackham, H.J., *Six Existentialist Thinkers* (London: Routledge 1961)
Bloch, Ernst, *The Principle of Hope*, Vol. 1 (Oxford: Blackwell 1986)
Bloesch, D.G., 'Christ and Culture: Do they connect?', *Christianity Today* 28 (1984), 54–58
Bonhoeffer, Dietrich, *Life Together* (London: SCM 1954)
Bonhoeffer, Dietrich, *Ethics* (London: SCM 1955)
Bonhoeffer, Dietrich, *The Cost of Discipleship* (London: SCM 1959)
Bonhoeffer, Dietrich, *Act and Being* (London: Collins 1962)
Bonhoeffer, Dietrich, *Sanctorum Communio* (London: Collins 1963)
Bonhoeffer, Dietrich, *Letters and Papers from Prison* (London: SCM 1971)
Bornkamm, Günther, *Jesus of Nazareth* (London: Hodder & Stoughton 1960)
Bowden, John, *Jesus: The Unanswered Questions* (London: SCM 1988)
Braaten, Carl E. and Roy A. Harrisville, eds, *The Historical Jesus and the Kerygmatic Christ* (New York: Abingdon Press 1964)
Bracken, Joseph A., 'The Holy Trinity as a Community of Divine Persons', *Heythrop Journal* 15 (1974), 166–82
Bracken, Joseph A., 'Process Philosophy and Trinitarian Theology', *Process Studies* 8 (1978), 217–30
Bracken, Joseph A., 'Process Philosophy and Trinitarian Theology II', *Process Studies* 11 (1981), 83–96
Bracken, Joseph A., *The Triune Symbol: Persons, Process and Community* (Lanham: University Press of America 1985)
Bracken, Joseph A., 'Process Perspectives and Trinitarian Theology', *Word and Spirit* 8 (1986), 51–64
Bradley, F.H., *Appearance and Reality* (Oxford: Clarendon Press 1930)

Bradley, F.H., *Essays on Truth and Reality* (Oxford: Clarendon Press 1930)
Bradley, F.H., *The Principles of Logic*, 2nd edn (London: OUP 1922)
Bradley, F.H., *Aphorisms* (Oxford: Clarendon Press 1930)
Braithwaite, R.B., *An Empiricist's View of the Nature of Religious Belief* (Cambridge: CUP 1955)
Brandt, Richard, *The Philosophy of Schleiermacher* (New York: Greenwood Press 1968)
Brindley, T. Herbert, *The Oecumenical Documents of the Faith* (London: Methuen & Co. 1950)
Brown, Colin, συνείδησις in *The New International Dictionary of New Testament Theology*, ed. Colin Brown (Exeter: Paternoster 1975)
Brümmer, Vincent, *The Model of Love* (Cambridge: CUP 1993)
Brunner, Emil, *The Mediator* (London: Lutterworth Press 1934)
Brunner, Emil, *Man in Revolt* (London: Lutterworth Press 1939)
Brunner, Emil, *The Divine-Human Encounter* (London: SCM 1944)
Brunner, Emil and Karl Barth, *Natural Theology* (London: Geoffrey Bles 1946)
Bultmann, Rudolf, 'To Love Your Neighbour', *Scottish Periodical* (1947), 42–56
Bultmann, Rudolf, *Theology of the New Testament*, Vol. 1 (London: SCM 1952)
Bultmann, Rudolf, *Theology of the New Testament*, Vol. 2 (London: SCM 1955)
Bultmann, Rudolf, *Essays: Philosophical and Theological* (London: SCM 1955)
Bultmann, Rudolf, *Jesus and the Word* (London: SCM 1958)
Bultmann, Rudolf, *Existence and Faith* (London: Hodder & Stoughton 1961)
Bultmann, Rudolf, 'The Primitive Christian Kerygma and the Historical Jesus' in *The Historical Jesus and the Kerygmatic Christ*, eds Carl E. Braaten and Roy A. Harrisville (New York: Abingdon Press 1964), pp. 15–42
Bultmann, Rudolf, *New Testament and Mythology and other Basic Writings* (Philadelphia: Fortress Press 1984)
Bultmann, Rudolf, *Faith und Understanding*, Vol. 1 (London: SCM 1969)
Bultmann, Rudolf, 'New Testament and Mythology' in *Kerygma and Myth*, Vols 1 & 2 combined, ed. Hans-Werner Bartsch. (London: SPCK 1972), pp. 1–44
Burhenn, Herbert, 'Pannenberg's Doctrine of God', *Scottish Journal of Theology* 28 (1975), 534–49

Buri, Fritz, *Theology of Existence* (Greenwood: The Attic Press 1965)
Buri, Fritz, 'Theologie der Existenz' in *Kerygma und Mythos III* (Hamburg: Herbert Reich 1966)
Busch, E., *Karl Barth* (London: SCM 1976)
Calvin, John, *Institutes of Christian Religion* (Philadelphia: Westminster Press 1960)
Campbell, John McLeod, *The Nature of the Atonement* (London: Macmillan 1869)
Casserley, J.V. Langmead, *Evil and Evolutionary Eschatology* (Lewiston: The Edwin Mellen Press 1990)
Church of England Doctrine Commission Report, *Believing in the Church: The Corporate Nature of Faith* (London: SPCK 1981)
Cobb, John B., *A Christian Natural Theology* (London: Lutterworth 1966)
Coll, Niall, *Some Anglican Interpretations of Christ's Pre-existence* (Rome: Pontifica Universitas Gregoriana 1995)
Conzelmann, Hans, *An Outline of the Theology of the New Testament* (London: SCM 1969)
Cox, Harvey, *The Secular City* (London: SCM 1965)
Craighead, Houston, 'Rudolf Bultmann and the Impossibility of God-Talk', *Faith and Philosophy: Journal of the Society of Christian Philosophers* 1 (1984), 203–15
Croatto, J. Severino, *Exodus: A Hermeneutics of Freedom* (Maryland: Orbis 1981)
Cupitt, D., 'Mansel and Maurice on our Knowledge of God', *Theology* 73 (1970), 301–11
Cupitt, D., *Christ and the Hiddenness of God* (London: Lutterworth 1971)
Cupitt, D., *The Leap of Reason* (London: Sheldon Press 1976)
Cupitt, D., *Taking Leave of God* (London: SCM 1980)
Cusanus, Nicolas, *Of Learned Ignorance* (London: Routledge & Kegan Paul 1954)
D'Arcy, Charles, 'Trinity' in *A Dictionary of Christ and the Gospels*, ed. James Hastings (Edinburgh: T&T Clark 1913), 759–66
Daly, Mary, *Beyond God the Father* (Boston: Beacon Press 1973)
Davies, Brian, *The Thought of Thomas Aquinas* (Oxford: Clarendon Press 1992)
Derrida, Jacques, *Given Time: 1 Counterfeit Money* (Chicago: University Press 1992)
Descartes, R, *Meditations on First Philosophy* in *Philosophical Writings of Descartes* Vol. II (Cambridge: CUP 1984)

Dionysius, *The Divine Names* in J.P. Migne, *Patrologiae Graeca* Vol. 3 (Paris: Garnier frères 1857–66)
Dionysius, *Celestial Hierarchy* in J.P. Migne, *Patrologiae Graeca* Vol. 3 (Paris: Garnier frères 1857–66)
Dix, Gregory, *The Shape of the Liturgy* (Westminster: Dacre Press 1943)
Dreyfus, Hubert L. and Harrison Hall, eds, *Heidegger: A Critical Reader* (Oxford: Blackwell 1992)
Dumas, André, *Dietrich Bonhoeffer: Theologian of Reality* (London: SCM 1971)
Dunn, James D.G., *Jesus and the Spirit* (London: SCM 1975)
Dunn, James D.G., *Unity and Diversity in the New Testament* (London: SCM 1977)
Dunn, James D.G., *Christology in the Making* (London: SCM 1980)
Ebeling, G., *Word and Faith* (London: SCM 1963)
Eckstein, Hans-Joachim, *Der Beigriff Syneidesis bei Paulus* (Tübingen: JCB Mohr (Paul Sieberg) 1983)
Eichrodt, Walther, *The Theology of the Old Testament* Vol. 1 (London: SCM 1961)
Eriugena, *On the Division of Nature* in J.P. Migne, *Patrologiae Latina* (Paris: Garnier frères 1865)
Farmer, W.R., C.F.D. Moule and R.R. Niebuhr, eds, *Christian History and Interpretation* (Cambridge: CUP 1967)
Farrell Krell, David, ed., *Basic Writings: Martin Heidegger* (London: Routledge 1993)
Farrer, Austin, *The Freedom of the Will* (London: A&C Black 1963)
Feenstra, Ronald J. and Cornelius Plantinga, eds, *Trinity, Incarnation and Atonement* (Notre Dame: University of Notre Dame Press 1989)
Fenton, J.C., 'Matthew and the Divinity of Jesus' in *Studia Biblica 1978*, ed. E.A. Livingstone (Sheffield: JSOT Press 1980)
Fergusson, David, *Bultmann* (London: Geoffrey Chapman 1992)
Fernandez, James, 'The Mission of Metaphor in Expressive Culture', *Current Anthropology* 15 (1974), 119–45
Feuerbach, Ludwig, *The Essence of Christianity* (New York: Harper & Brothers 1957)
Flew, A.G.N., 'Hume' in *A Critical History of Western Philosophy*, ed. D.J. O'Connor (New York: Free Press of Glencoe 1964), 253–74
Ford, David F. and Dennis L. Stamps, *Essentials of Christian Community* (Edinburgh: T&T Clark 1996)
Ford, David, ed., *The Modern Theologians* (Oxford: Blackwell 1997²)
Foucault, Michel, *Power/Knowledge* (Sussex: Harvester Press 1980)

Freire, Paulo, *Pedagogy of the Oppressed* (Harmondsworth: Penguin 1972)
Freud, Sigmund, *Civilisation, Society and Religion* (London: Penguin 1985)
Fuller, Reginald, *The Foundations of New Testament Christology* (London: Collins 1969)
Gadamer, Hans-Georg, *Truth and Method* (London: Sheed & Ward 1989²)
Gerkin, Charles, *The Living Human Document* (Nashville: Abingdon 1991)
Gilson, Etienne, *Le Thomisme* (Paris: Libraire Philosophique J.Vrin 1942)
Godsey, John D., *The Theology of Dietrich Bonhoeffer* (London: SCM 1960)
Gollwitzer, Helmut, *The Existence of God as Confessed by Faith* (London: SCM 1965)
Gore, Charles, *Lux Mundi* (London: John Murray 1891)
Gore, Charles, *Dissertations* (London: John Murray 1895)
Gore, Charles, *The Incarnation of the Son of God* (London: John Murray 1896)
Goulder, M., ed., *Incarnation and Myth* (London: SCM 1979)
Grenz, S.J. and R.E. Olsen, *Twentieth-Century Theology* (Carlisle: Paternoster 1992)
Gresham, John L., 'The Social Model of the Trinity and its Critics', *Scottish Journal of Theology* 46 (1993), 325–43
Grey, Mary, 'Claiming Power-in-Relation', *Journal of Feminist Studies* 7 (1991), 7–18
de Gruchy, John, *Dietrich Bonhoeffer: Witness to Jesus Christ* (London: Collins 1987)
Grundmann, Walter, 'ἁμαρτία in the NT' in *Theological Dictionary of the New Testament* Vol. 1, ed. Gerhard Kittel (Grand Rapids: Eerdmans 1964), 302–16
Guigon, Charles B., ed., *The Cambridge Companion to Heidegger* (Cambridge: CUP 1993)
Gundry, Robert H., *SOMA in Biblical Theology* (Cambridge: CUP 1976)
Gunton, Colin, *Being and Becoming* (Oxford: OUP 1978)
Gunton, Colin E., *The Promise of Trinitarian Theology* (Edinburgh: T&T Clark 1991)
Gunton, Colin E., *The One, the Three and the Many* (Cambridge: CUP 1993)

Gunton, Colin E., *The Triune Creator* (Edinburgh: University Press 1998)
Gutiérrez, Gustavo, *A Theology of Liberation* (London: SPCK 1988)
Habermas, J., *Knowledge and Human Interests* (London: Heinemann 1972)
Hammerton-Kelly, R.G., *Pre-existence, Wisdom and the Son of Man* (Cambridge: CUP 1973)
Hardy, Daniel, *God's Ways with the World* (Edinburgh: T&T Clark 1996)
Harries, R., ed., *Reinhold Niebuhr and the Issues of our Time* (Oxford: Mowbray 1986)
Harvey, John, 'A New Look at the Christ Hymn in Phil 2:6–11', *Expository Times* 76 (1965), 337–39
Hefling, Charles C, 'Reviving Adamic Adoptionism: The Example of John Macquarrie', *Theological Studies* 52 (1991), 476–94
Hegel, G.W.F., 'Logic' in *Encyclopaedia of Philosophical Sciences* (Oxford: Clarendon Press 1892)
Hegel, G.W.F., *The Phenomenology of Mind* (London: George Allen & Unwin Ltd 1949)
Heidegger, Martin, *Vom Wesen der Wahrheit* (Frankfurt am Main: Vittorio Klostermann 1954)
Heidegger, Martin, *Introduction to Metaphysics* (New Haven: Yale University Press 1959)
Heidegger, Martin, *Being and Time* (Oxford: Blackwell 1962)
Heidegger, Martin, *Discourse on Thinking* (New York: Harper & Row 1966)
Heidegger, Martin, *Poetry, Language, Thought* (New York: Harper & Row 1971)
Heidegger, Martin, *Basic Writings*, ed. David Farrell Krell (London: Routledge 1993)
Henderson, Ian, 'Karl Jaspers and Demythologizing', *The Expository Times* 65 (1954), 2911–93
Hendrickson, Marion Lars, *Behold The Man! An Anthropological Comparison of the Christologies of John Macquarrie and Wolfhart Pannenberg* (Lanham: University Press of America 1998)
Hendry, G.S., 'The Freedom of God in the Theology of Karl Barth', *Scottish Journal of Theology* 31 (1978), 229–44
Heron, Alasdair, *A Century of Protestant Theology* (Cambridge: Lutterworth 1980)
Heyward, Isabel Carter, *The Redemption of God: A Theology of Mutual Relation* (New York: University Press of America 1982)
Hick, John, *Evil and the God of Love* (Basingstoke: Macmillan 1985)

Hick, John 'The problem of Evil' in *The Encyclopaedia of Philosophy*, ed. Paul Edwards (London: Collier-Macmillan 1967), 136–40

Hodges, H.A., *Wilhelm Dilthey: An Introduction* (London: Routledge and Kegan Paul 1944)

Hodges, H.A., *The Philosophy of Wilhelm Dilthey* (London: Routledge and Kegan Paul 1952)

Hodgson, Leonard, *The Doctrine of the Trinity* (London: Nisbet & Co 1943)

Hodgson, Leonard, 'The Glory of the Eternal Trinity', *Christianity Today* (1962), 827–29

Hodgson, Leonard, 'The Doctrine of the Trinity: some further thoughts', *Journal of Theological Studies* 5 (1954), 49–55

Hudson, W.D., 'Questions People Ask. An Updated Philosophy of Theism', *The Expository Times* 107 (1996), 132–37

Hume, David, *Dialogues Concerning Natural Religion* (Oxford: OUP 1993)

Illingworth, J.R., *The Doctrine of the Trinity* (London: Macmillan 1907)

Jantzen, Grace, *God's World, God's Body* (London: DLT 1984)

Jaspers, Karl, *The Perennial Scope of Philosophy* (London: Routledge & Kegan Paul 1957)

Jaspers, Karl, *Philosophy* Vol. 2 (Chicago: University of Chicago Press 1970)

Jenkins, David, *The Scope and Limits of John Macquarrie's Existential Theology* (Uppsala: University Press 1987)

Jenson, Robert, *God after God* (Indianapolis: Bobbs-Merrill Co 1969)

Jenson, Robert, *The Triune Identity* (Philadelphia: Fortress 1982)

Jewett, R., *Paul's Anthropological Terms* (Lieden: Brill 1971)

Johnson, Roger, *Rudolf Bultmann: Interpreting Faith for Modern Man* (London: Collins 1987)

Jones, Gareth, *Bultmann: Towards a Critical Theology* (Cambridge: Polity Press 1986)

Jüngel, Eberhard, *God as the Mystery of the World* (Edinburgh: T&T Clark 1983)

Jüngel, Eberhard, *Karl Barth: a theological legacy* (Philadelphia: Westminster Press 1986)

Jüngel, Eberhard, *Theological Essays* (Edinburgh: T&T Clark 1991)

Jüngel, Eberhard, *Theological Essays* II (Edinburgh: T&T Clark 1995)

Kant, Immanuel, *Critique of Pure Reason* (London: Dent 1934)

Kant, Immanuel, *Religion Within the Limits of Reason Alone* (New York: Harper & Row 1960)

Käsemann, Ernst, *Essays on New Testament Themes* (London: SCM 1964)
Käsemann, Ernst, *New Testament Questions of Today* (London: SCM 1969)
Käsemann, Ernst, *Perspectives on Paul* (London: SCM 1971)
Kaufman, Walter, ed., *Existentialism from Dostoyevsky to Sartre* (New York: Harper & Row 1956)
Kee, Alistair and Eugene T. Long, eds, *Being and Truth* (London: SCM 1986)
Kegley, Charles W., ed., *The Theology of Rudolf Bultmann* (London: SCM 1966)
Kegley, Charles W. and R.W. Brettall, eds, *Reinhold Niebuhr* (New York: Macmillan 1956)
Kekes, John, *Facing Evil* (Princeton: Princeton University Press 1990)
Kekes, John, 'Evil' in *Routledge Encyclopaedia of Philosophy*, ed. Edward Craig (London: Routledge 1998)
Kenny, Anthony, *The Five Ways* (London: Routledge & Kegan Paul 1969)
Kierkegaard, Søren, *Philosophical Fragments* (London: OUP 1936)
Kierkegaard, Søren, *The Point of View* (London: OUP 1939)
Kierkegaard, Søren, *The Sickness unto Death* (London: OUP 1941)
Kierkegaard, Søren, *Training in Christianity* (London: OUP 1946)
King, Magda, *Heidegger's Philosophy* (Oxford: Blackwell 1964)
Klooster, Fred H., 'Revelation and Scripture in Existentialist Theology' in *Challenges to Inerrancy*, eds G. Lewis and B. Demarest, (Chicago: Moody Press 1984), 175–214
Knox, John, *The Early Church and the Coming Great Church* (London: Epworth Press 1957)
Knox, John, *The Church and the Reality of Christ* (London: Collins 1963)
Knox, John, *Myth and Truth* (London: Carey Kingsgate Press Ltd 1966)
Küng, Hans, *Does God Exist?* (London: SCM 1991)
LaCugna, C.M., 'Re-conceiving the Trinity as the Mystery of Salvation', *Scottish Journal of Theology* 38 (1985), 1–23
Laird, John, *Problems of the Self* (London: Macmillan 1917)
Lampe, G.W.H., *God as Spirit* (Oxford: Clarendon Press 1977)
Landon, H.R., ed., *Reinhold Niebuhr; Essays in Tribute* (Greenwich: Seabury Press 1962)
Leach, Edmund, *Social Anthropology* (Oxford: OUP 1982)
Leibniz, G.W., *Monadology and Other Philosophical Writings* (London: OUP 1925)

Lessing, G.E., *Theological Writings* (London: A&C Black 1956)
Lohmeyer, Ernst, *Kyrios Jesus: Eine Untersuchung zu Phil. 2, 5–11* (Heidelberg: Carl Winters Universitätsbuchhandlung 1928)
Lonergan, Bernard, *Insight* (London: Longmans, Green & Co 1957)
Long, Eugene T., 'John Macquarrie on Ultimate Reality and Meaning', *Ultimate Reality and Meaning: Interdisciplinary Studies in the Philosophy of Understanding* 6 (1983) 300–20
Long, Eugene T., *Existence, Being and God* (New York: Paragon House 1985)
Lovejoy, Arthur, *The Great Chain of Being* (New York: Harper & Row 1936)
MacIntyre, Alasdair, 'Existentialism' in *A Critical History of Western Philosophy*, ed. D.J. O'Connor (New York: Free Press of Glencoe 1964), 509–29
Mackintosh, H.R., *The Doctrine of the Person of Jesus Christ* (Edinburgh: T&T Clark 1913)
Mackintosh, H.R., *Types of Modern Theology* (Welwyn: Nisbet & Co 1937)
Macmurray, John, *Persons in Relation* (London: Faber & Faber 1970)
Malet, A., *The Thought of Rudolf Bultmann* (Shannon: Irish University Press 1969)
Malevez, L., *The Christian Message and Myth* (London: SCM 1958)
Manser, Anthony and Guy Stock, eds, *The Philosophy of F.H. Bradley* (Oxford: Clarendon Press 1984)
Marcel, Gabriel, *Mystery of Being* Vol. 1 (London: The Harvill Press 1950)
Marion, Jean-Luc, *God without Being: Hors Texte* (Chicago: University Press 1991)
Maritain, Jacques, *Degrees of Knowledge* (London: Geoffrey Bles 1959)
Martin, D.B., *The Corinthian Body* (New Haven: Yale University Press 1995)
Martis, John, 'Thomistic *Esse* – Idol or Icon?', *Pacifica* 9 (1996), 55–68
Martis, John, 'Postmodernism and God as Giver', *The Way* 36 (1996), 236–44
Marty, Martin E., *The Place of Bonhoeffer* (London: SCM 1963)
Mascall, E.L., *Existence and Analogy* (London: DLT 1949)
Mascall, E.L., *He Who Is* (London: DLT 1966)
Mascall, E.L., *The Openness of Being* (London: DLT 1971)
McCabe, Herbert, *God Matters* (London: Geoffrey Chapman 1987)
McFadyen, Alistair, 'The Trinity and Human Individuality: the conditions for relevance', *Theology* 95 (1992), 10–18

McFague, Sallie, *Models of God* (London: SCM 1987)
McFague, Sallie, *The Body of God* (London: SCM 1993)
McGrath, Alister, *The Making of Modern German Christology* (Oxford: Blackwell 1986)
McGrath, Alister, ed., *The SPCK Handbook of Anglican Theologians* (London: SPCK 1998)
McIntosh, Mark, *Mystical Theology: The Integrity of Spirituality and Theology* (Oxford: Blackwell 1998)
Maurer, Christian, σύνοιδα, συνείδησις in *Theological Dictionary of the New Testament* Vol VII, ed. Gerhard Friedrich (Grand Rapids: Eerdmans 1971), 898–919
Metz, Johannes B., *Theology of the World* (London: Burns and Oates 1969)
Miegge, G., *Gospel and Myth* (London: Lutterworth 1960)
Mill, John Stuart, *Three Essays on Religion* (Westport: Greenwood Press 1969)
Mitchell, Margaret, *Paul and the Rhetoric of Reconciliation* (Westminster: John Knox Press 1991)
Moltmann, Jürgen, *Theology of Hope* (London: SCM 1967)
Moltmann, Jürgen, *Man: Christian Anthropology in the Conflicts of the Present* (London: SPCK 1971)
Moltmann, Jürgen, 'The Trinitarian History of God', *Theology* 78 (1975), 632–46
Moltmann, Jürgen, *The Trinity and the Kingdom of God* (London: SCM 1981)
Moltmann, Jürgen, 'The Unity of the Triune God' (and replies), *St Vladimir's Theological Quarterly* 28 (1984), 155–88
Moltmann, Jürgen, *The Coming of God* (London: SCM 1996)
Molnar, Paul D., 'Some Problems with Pannenberg's Solution to Barth's "Faith Subjectivism"', *Scottish Journal of Theology* 48 (1995), 315–39
Molnar, Paul D., 'God's self-communication in Christ: a comparison of Thomas F. Torrance and Karl Rahner', *Scottish Journal of Theology* 50 (1997), 288–320
Moule, C.F.D., *The Origin of Christology* (Cambridge: CUP 1977)
Mulhall, Stephen, *Heidegger and Being & Time* (London: Routledge 1996)
Murray, Michael, ed., *Heidegger and Modern Philosophy* (New Haven: Yale University Press 1978)
Myers, Christopher, 'The Paradoxical Character of Revelation: a sympathetic essay on dialectical Theism', *Colloquium: The Australian and New Zealand Theological Society* 23 (1990), 12–17

Neufeld, Vernon, *The Earliest Christian Confessions* (Lieden: Brill 1963)
Neville, Robert C., *God the Creator* (Chicago: University Press 1968)
Newey, P.S., 'Revelation and Dialectical Theism: Beyond John Macquarrie', *Colloquium: the Australian and New Zealand Theological Society* 22 (1989), 37–44
Niebuhr, Reinhold, *The Nature and Destiny of Man* Vol. 1 (London: Nisbet 1941)
Niebuhr, Reinhold, *Moral Man, Immoral Society* (London: Scribner's Sons 1942)
Niebuhr, Richard, *Schleiermacher on Christ and Religion* (London: SCM 1965)
Nietzsche, Friedrich, *Ecce Homo* (London: George Allen & Unwin 1911)
Nietzsche, Friedrich, *The Will to Power* Vol. 2 (Edinburgh: T.N. Foulis 1913)
Nietzsche, Friedrich, *Thus Spake Zarathustra* (London: Dent 1933)
Norman, Richard, *Hegel's Phenomenology* (Sussex: Harvester Press 1976)
Nygren, Anders, *Commentary on Romans* (London: SCM 1952)
Nygren, Anders, *Agape and Eros* (London: SPCK 1954)
O'Connor, D.J., 'Locke' in *A Critical History of Western Philosophy*, ed. D.J. O'Connor (New York: Free Press of Glencoe 1964), 204–19
Ogden, Schubert M., *Christ Without Myth* (New York: Harper & Row 1961)
Ogden, Schubert, *The Point of Christology* (London: SCM 1982)
Olsen, Roger, 'Trinity and Eschatology: the historical being of God in Jürgen Moltmann and Wolfhart Pannenberg', *Scottish Journal of Theology* 36 (1983), 213–27
Olsen, R., 'Wolfhart Pannenberg's Doctrine of the Trinity', *Scottish Journal of Theology* 43 (1990), 175–206
Oman, John, *Grace and Personality* (Cambridge: CUP 1931)
O'Meara, Thomas F., 'Thomas Aquinas and Today's Theology', *Theology Today* 55 (1998), 46–58
Ott, H., *Reality and Faith: the theological legacy of Dietrich Bonhoeffer* (Philadelphia: Fortress Press 1972)
Otto, Rudolf, *The Idea of the Holy* (London: OUP 1923)
Owen, H.P., *Revelation and Existence* (Cardiff: University of Wales Press 1957)
Owen, H.P., *Concepts of Deity* (London: Macmillan 1971)
Paillin, David A., 'Herbert of Cherbury and the Deists', *The Expository Times* 94 (1983), 196–200

Pannenberg, Wolfhart, 'The revelation of God in Jesus of Nazareth' in *Theology as History*, eds James M. Robinson and John B. Cobb (New York: Harper & Row 1967), 101–33
Pannenberg, Wolfhart, *Systematic Theology* Vol. 1 (Edinburgh: T&T Clark 1988)
Pannenberg, Wolfhart, *Systematic Theology* Vol. 2 (Edinburgh: T&T Clark 1991)
Pax, Clyde, *An Existential Approach to God* (The Hague: Nijhoff 1972)
Peacocke, Arthur and Grant Gillett, eds, *Persons and Personality* (Oxford: Blackwell 1987)
Peters, Ted, 'God as Trinity: Relationality and Temporality in Divine Life', *Theology Today* 51 (1994), 174–76
Philo, *On the Account of the World's Creation Given by Moses* in *Philo* Vol. 1 (London: William Heinemann Ltd 1929)
Pittenger, Norman, *The Word Incarnate* (Welwyn: Nisbet & Co 1959)
Pittenger, Norman, *Christology Reconsidered* (London: SCM 1970)
Plantinga, Alvin C., *God, Freedom and Evil* (Grand Rapids: Eerdmans 1974)
Plantinga, Alvin and Nicholas Wolterstorff, eds, *Faith and Understanding: Reason and Belief in God* (Notre Dame: University of Notre Dame Press 1983)
Plato, *Timaeus and Critias* (London: Penguin 1977)
Polanyi, Michael, *Personal Knowledge* (Chicago: University of Chicago Press 1962)
Polanyi, Michael, *The Tacit Dimension* (London: Routledge & Kegan Paul 1967)
Porter, Jean, 'The Feminization of God: Second Thoughts on the Ethical Implications of Process Theology', *St Luke's Journal of Theology* 24 (1986), 251–60
Pratt, Douglas G., 'Existential-Ontological Theism and the question of the relatedness of God: Macquarrie revisited', *Colloquium: The Australian and New Zealand Theological Society* 17 (1984), 26–33
Pratt, Douglas G., 'The imago Dei in the thought of John Macquarrie: a reflection on John 10.10', *Asian Journal of Theology* 3 (1989), 79–83
Quick, Oliver Chase, *Doctrines of the Creed* (London: Nisbet 1938)
Rahner, Karl, *Theological Investigations I & IV* (London: DLT 1965)
Rahner, Karl, *Theological Investigations V* (London: DLT 1966)
Rahner, Karl, *Hearers of the Word* (London: Sheed & Ward 1969)
Rahner, Karl, *The Trinity* (Tunbridge Wells: Burns and Oates 1970)
Rahner, Karl, *Foundations of Faith* (New York: Crossword 1978)

Ramsey, Ian T., *Religious Language* (London: SCM 1957)
Rassmussen, L., *Reinhold Niebuhr: Theologian of Public Life* (Philadelphia: Fortress Press 1991)
Reardon, B.M.G., 'Demythologizing and Catholic Modernising', *Theology* 59 (1956), 445-51
Reardon, B.M.G., *Religious Thought in the Nineteenth Century* (Cambridge: CUP 1966)
Reardon, B.M.G., *Roman Catholic Modernism* (London: A&C Black 1970)
Reardon, B.M.G., *Religion in the Age of Romanticism* (Cambridge: CUP 1983)
Richardson, Herbert, *Theology for a New World* (London: SCM 1967)
Richardson, John, *Existential Epistemology* (Oxford: Clarendon Press 1986)
Richardson, William, *Heidegger: Through Phenomenology to Thought* (The Hague: Nijhoff 1963)
Rickman, H.P., ed., *Meaning in History* (London: George Allen & Unwin Ltd 1961)
Ricoeur, Paul, *Oneself as Another* (London: University of Chicago Press 1992)
Robinson, H. Wheeler, *The Christian Doctrine of Man* (Edinburgh: T&T Clark 1958)
Robinson, James M., *A New Quest of the Historical Jesus* (London: SCM 1959)
Robinson, James M. and John B. Cobb, eds, *The Later Heidegger and Theology* (New York: Harper & Row 1963)
Robinson, James M. and John B. Cobb, eds, *Theology as History* (New York: Harper & Row 1967)
Robinson, J.A.T., *The Body* (London: SCM 1952)
Robinson, John, *Honest to God* (London: SCM 1963)
Root, H.E., 'Beginning all over again' in *Soundings*, ed. A.R. Vidler (Cambridge: CUP 1964)
Royce, Josiah, *The Problem of Christianity* Vol. 2 (Chicago: Gateway 1968)
Russell, Robert John, 'Does "the God who acts" really act? New Approaches to Divine Action in the Light of Science', *Theology Today* 54 (1997), 43-65
Ryle, Gilbert, 'Critical Notice: Sein und Zeit', *Mind* XXXVIII (1929), 355-70
Sanders, E.P., *Jesus and Judaism* (London: SCM 1985)
Sarot, Marcel, *God, Passibility and Corporeality* (Kampen: Kok Pharos 1992)

Savage, Timothy, *Power Through Weakness* (Cambridge: CUP 1996)
Saxena, Sushil Kumar, *Studies in the Metaphysics of Bradley* (London: George Allen & Unwin 1967)
Schleiermacher, Friedrich, *On Religion: Speeches to its cultured Despisers* (New York: Harper & Row 1958)
Schleiermacher, Friedrich, *The Christian Faith* (Edinburgh: T&T Clark 1989)
Schmittals, Walther, *Introduction to the Theology of Rudolf Bultmann* (London: SCM 1968)
Schütz, J.H., *Paul and the Anatomy of Apostolic Authority* (Cambridge: CUP 1975)
Schweizer, E., σῶμα in *Theological Dictionary of the New Testament* Vol. 7, ed. Gerhard Friedrich (Grand Rapids: Eerdmans 1971)
Schwöbel, Christoph, 'Die Rede vom Handeln Gottes im Christlichen Blauben. Beiträge, zu einem systematisch-theologischen Rekonstruktionsversuch' in *Vom Handeln Gottes. Marburger Jahrbuch Theologie I*, eds W. Harle and R. Preul (Marburg: N.G. Elwert 1987), 56–81
Schwöbel, Christoph, 'Theology in Anthropological Perspective?', *Kings Theological Review* 10 (1989), 21–25
Schwöbel, Christoph and Colin E. Gunton, eds, *Persons, Divine and Human* (Edinburgh: T&T Clark 1991)
Searle, John R., ed., *Speech-Act Theory and Pragmatics* (London: D. Reidel Publ. Co. 1980)
Smart, Ninian, John Clayton, Steven Katz and Patrick Sherry, eds, *Nineteenth Century Religious Thought in the West* Vol. 1 (Cambridge: CUP 1985)
Sölle, Dorothee, *Christ the Representative* (London: SCM 1967)
Sölle, Dorothee, *Choosing Life* (London: SCM 1981)
Sölle, Dorothee, *Thinking about God* (London: SCM 1990)
Sölle, Dorothee, *Theology for Sceptics* (London: Mowbray 1995)
Sontag, Frederick, *A Kierkegaard Reader* (Atlanta: John Knox Press 1979)
Soskice, Janet Martin, 'Trinity and the "Feminine Other"', *New Blackfriars* (1994)
Soskice, Janet Martin, 'God of Power and Might', *Theology Today* 54 (1997), 1928
Surin, Kenneth, *Theology and the Problem of Evil* (Oxford: Blackwell 1986)
Sykes, S.W. and J.P. Clayton, eds, *Christ, Faith and History* (Cambridge: CUP 1972)
Sykes, S.W., 'Sacrifice in the New Testament and Christian Theology'

in *Sacrifice*, eds M.F.C. Bourdillon and Meyer Forbes (London: Academic Press 1980)

Sykes, S.W., 'The strange persistence of kenotic christology' in *Being and Truth* eds Alistair Kee and Eugene T. Long (London: SCM 1986), 349–75

Teilhard de Chardin, Pierre, *The Phenomenon of Man* (London: Collins 1959)

Tertullian, *Disciplinary, Moral and Ascetical Works* (Washington, DC: Catholic University of America 1957)

Thatcher, Adrian, 'The Personal God and a God who is a Person', *Religious Studies* 21 (1985), 61–73

Thielicke, H., 'Reflections on Bultmann's Hermeneutic', *The Expository Times* 67 (1956), 154–56, 175–77

Thiselton, Anthony C., *The Two Horizons* (Exeter: Paternoster 1980)

Thiselton, Anthony C., 'Barr on Barth and Natural Theology: A Plea for Hermeneutics in Historical Theology', *Scottish Journal of Theology* 47 (1990), 519–28

Thiselton, Anthony C., *New Horizons in Hermeneutics* (London: Harper Collins 1992)

Thiselton, Anthony C., 'Gareth Jones, Bultmann: Towards a Critical Theology', *Journal of Theological Studies* 43 (1992), 317–19

Thiselton, Anthony C., *Interpreting God and the Postmodern Self* (Edinburgh: T&T Clark 1995)

Thomson, J.F., 'Berkeley' in *A Critical History of Western Philosophy*, ed. D.J. O'Connor (New York: Free Press of Glencoe 1964), 236–52

Thornton, Lionel, *The Incarnate Lord* (London: Longmans Green & Co 1928)

Thornton, Lionel, *The Common Life in the Body of Christ* (Westminster: Dacre Press 1944)

Thunberg, Lars, *Microcosm and Mediator: The theological anthropology of Maximus the Confessor* (Lund: C.W.K. Gleerup & Ejnar Munksgaard 1965)

Thurmer, J.A., 'The Analogy of the Trinity', *Scottish Journal of Theology* 34 (1981), 509–15

Tillich, Paul, *Systematic Theology* Vol. 1 (Chicago: University of Chicago Press 1951)

Tillich, Paul, *Systematic Theology* Vol. 2 (Chicago: University of Chicago Press 1957)

Tillich, Paul, *Love, Power and Justice* (London: OUP 1954)

Tillich, Paul, *Perspectives on Nineteenth-century and Twentieth-century Protestant Theology* (London: SCM 1967)

Torrance, Alan, *Persons in Communion* (Edinburgh: T&T Clark 1996)

Torrance, Thomas F., 'The Goodness and Dignity of Man in the Christian Tradition', *Modern Theology* 4 (1988), 309–22

Turner, Victor, *Dramas, Fields and Metaphors* (Ithaca: Cornell University Press 1974)

Van den Brink, G., *Almighty God* (Kampen: Kok Pharos 1993)

Visser 't Hooft, W.A., ed., *The New Delhi Report: The Third Assembly of the World Council of Churches* (London: SCM 1962)

von Rad, Gerhard, *Old Testament Theology* Vol. 2 (Edinburgh: Oliver & Boyd 1965)

Walsh, W.H., 'F.H. Bradley' in *A Critical History of Western Philosophy*, ed. D.J. O'Connor (New York: Free Press of Glencoe 1964), 426–36

Ward, Keith, *Holding Fast to God* (London: SPCK 1982)

Warnock, G.J., *English Philosophy since 1900* (Oxford: OUP 1958)

Warnock, Mary, *Existentialism* (Oxford: OUP 1970)

Waterhouse, Roger, *A Heidegger Critique* (Sussex: Harvester Press 1981)

Waterhouse, Roger, 'A Critique of Authenticity', *Radical Philosophy* 20 (1978), 22–26

Webb, C.C.J., *God and Personality* (London: George Allen & Unwin 1919)

Webster, John B., *Eberhard Jüngel: An Introduction to his Theology* (Cambridge: CUP 1986)

Webster, John B., 'Eberhard Jüngel' in *The Modern Theologians* Vol. 1, ed. David Ford (Oxford: Blackwell 1989), 92–106

Weger, Karl-Heinz, *Karl Rahner: An Introduction to his Theology* (New York: Seabury Press 1980)

Weiss, Johannes, *Der Erste Korintherbrief* (Göttingen: Vandenhoeck & Ruprecht 1910)

Welch, Claude, *The Trinity in Contemporary Theology* (London: SCM 1953)

Welch, S., *Communities of Resistance and Solidarity* (New York: Orbis 1985)

Wheeler Robinson, H., *The Christian Doctrine of Man* (Edinburgh: T&T Clark 1958)

Whitehead, A.N., *Adventures of Ideas* (Cambridge: CUP 1933)

Whiteley, D.E.H., *The Theology of St Paul* (Oxford: Blackwell 1966)

Wigley, Stephen D., 'Karl Barth on St Anselm: The Influence of Anselm's "Theological Scheme" on T.F. Torrance and Eberhard Jüngel', *Scottish Journal of Theology* 46 (1993), 79–97

Williams, Daniel Day, 'Christianity and Naturalism: An Informal Statement', *Union Theological Seminary Review* 12 (1957), 47–53

Wolin, Richard, ed., *The Heidegger Controversy* (London: MIT Press 1993)
Wollheim, Richard, *F.H. Bradley* (Harmondsworth: Penguin 1959)
Wolterstorff, Nicholas, *John Locke and the Ethics of Belief* (Cambridge: CUP 1996)
Zimmerli, Walther, *Man and his Hope in the Old Testament* (London: SCM 1971)
Zizioulas, John, *Being as Communion* (New York: St Vladimir's Seminary Press 1985)

Index

the Absolute 72–74
adoptionism 154–63 *passim*
agape 63–64
alienation 30–31
anthropological argument for the being of God 136–37
anticipatory resoluteness 19–21
anxiety 17–18
apprehension 109
Aquinas, Thomas 113, 115, 123; *see also* Thomism
Aristotle 148–49
atonement 89
Augustine, St 113, 128–29

Baillie, Donald 144
Baillie, John 82
baptism 90
Barth, Karl 1, 8, 47, 101, 151–53
Being 91–92, 110–13, 134
   concept of 9–11, 58, 70–73
   meaning of 109
   in relation to God 113–17
   in relation to thinking 70
   see also hierarchy of being
Being-with 13–15
Being-in-the-world 15–18
belief and commitment 55–56
Bloch, Ernst 148
Bonhoeffer, Dietrich 1–2, 161
Bornkamm, Günther 147
Bowden, John 147
Bradley, F.H. 2, 43–44, 69–73, 98
Braithwaite, R.B. 54–57, 68
Bultmann, Rudolf 1, 13, 26, 31–36, 43–72 *passim*, 80–84, 117, 122–23, 144, 147, 151–52, 157
   on the church and radical isolation 64–67
   on love as event 63–64
Buri, Fritz 47–89, 97

Calvin, John 101
Camus, Albert 101
care (Heidegger) 17
Celtic heritage 73–74
Christ *see* Jesus Christ
Christ, Faith and History symposium (1972) 160
Christ-event concept 149
Christ-hymn of Philippians 157–58, 164–65
Christian doctrine 87
Christian terminology 29–30
christology 53, 57, 143–67
Church, the
   as the body of Christ 88
   corporate life of 80–90
   memory of 85–86
   task of 65–66
classical theism 124–25
commitment
   and belief 55–56
   of the whole person 131–32
communitas 165
communities of faith 83–85, 88, 90
community, types of 64–65
conative religion 54, 79
conscience 18–19, 131
consciousness 24–25
context of knowledge 26
corporate character of human existence 62–67, 79–80, 122, 129–30

correspondence theory of truth 17
creation
  accounts of 92–93
  doctrine of 125
Cupitt, Don 1

Das Man concept 14–18 *passim*, 31, 65, 67
Dasein 9–21, 24, 30–31, 45, 61–64, 70–73, 91–92, 110
deiformity and deification 127, 135, 163
Descartes, René 8, 101
dialectical theism 125–29, 133, 136–37, 152, 173
Dilthey, Wilhelm 99
Dionysius 126, 128, 136, 152
docetism 154–56
dogma 57, 67, 88
Dunn, James 156–58

egoity 131
embodiment 123
Episcopal Church 82
epistemology 172
equipment (Heidegger) 11–12, 135
Eriugena, John Scotus 74, 126–27, 129
eschatology 65–66, 93, 172–73
evil 137–40
existential-ontological meditation 172
existential-ontological theism 97–98, 103–17, 121–22
  divine pole of 108–17
  human pole of 103–8
existentialism 2–3, 7–9, 13, 15, 18–37, 43–46, 49–51, 62, 71, 79–81, 85–88, 97, 101, 117, 122, 129–30, 145, 151–52
existentiell situation 47, 49, 53, 68
Existenz 10, 123

faith 51–53, 98–99
falling and *fallenness* (Heidegger) 30–31

fate (Heidegger) 21
feeling 72
Fernandez, James 165
Feuerbach, Ludwig 162
freedom 63, 130–32
Fuller, Reginald 156–57

Gnosticism 33, 50, 66, 157
God
  action embodied in Jesus 89
  anthropological argument for the being of 136–37
  concept of 3–4
  and creation 127
  dynamic nature of 127
  existence of 73, 100, 114, 121–26
  function of the word 57–58
  gift of 68
  ground for talk with 27–29
  as a holy being 113–15, 171
  immanence of 73–74, 114, 126, 152
  initiative lying with 26
  kinship with 68
  knowledge of 102–3
  love of 63–64
  ontological and existential meanings of the word 114
  powerlessness of 166
  relationship with Being 113–17
  relationship with the world 114, 124–28, 153
  separation from 31
  treated as an object or hypothetical 102
  ultimate truth about 56–59
  Will of 60–61, 114
  see also transcendence: divine
grace 25, 28, 43–48 *passim*, 63
  and nature 48
grace of being 3, 37, 49, 61–62, 68, 81, 92–93, 97, 114–15, 121–22, 137–38, 143, 146–47, 153, 164, 171–72
Gundry, Robert 34–36, 80

Hegel, G.W.F. 126, 145

hegemonikon 131
Heidegger, Martin 1–2, 7–37, 43–44, 47–50, 57–64, 69–73, 87, 98, 102, 108–14, 126
   Being and Time 7–10, 23, 25, 36, 59, 69–71, 91, 110
Heraclitus 108–9
hermeneutic circle 70
Hick, John 139
hierarchy of being 128, 136, 139
historical continuity 52–53
historical objectivity 36
history, nature of 50–51
Holy Spirit 116
human existence, problem of 27–28
humanistic philosophy 47
Hume, David 101
Husserl, E. 24

idealism 72, 151
immanentist theology 113
incarnation and incarnationism 89–92, 154–58
individualism 62–67
indwelling grace 47
instrumentality 91
inter-subjectivity 62
Irenaeus 148

Jaspers, Karl 14, 47–48, 68
Jesus Christ 21, 51–54, 81–86, 116, 143, 153–54
   body of 88–93
   historical question of 144–48
   humanity of 154, 158–62
   as representative human being 149–50
   see also christology
Jewett, R. 34–35
Jones, Gareth 4, 58–61, 80–81
Judaism 155–56

Kant, Immanuel 101, 145–46, 150
Käsemann, Ernst 2, 157
kenosis and kenotic christology 160–66

kerygma and kerygmatic theology 8, 43–45, 50–54, 58–60, 66–68, 79–80, 108, 129, 146, 151
Kierkegaard, Søren 14, 60–62, 83, 114, 144–45, 152
Knox, John 80–90, 154

Le Roy, Edouard 57
Lehmann, Paul 82
Leibniz, G.W. 61, 126–29, 133–35
Lessing, G.E. 145
liberal modernism 7–8
liberalism 57
Locke, John 12, 18
Lohmeyer, Ernst 157
Lonergan, Bernard 149
love 63–65
Luther, Martin 58
Lutheranism 80–81

Macmurray, John 8
McIntosh, Mark 69
Macquarrie, John, works of
   On Being a Theologian 2, 73
   'Existentialism and Christian Vocabulary' 29
   An Existentialist Theology 7, 30, 36, 43, 50, 62, 72
   'Heidegger's Earlier and Later Work Compared' 69, 71
   'How is theology possible?' 29
   In Search of Deity 3, 74, 121–22, 133, 136, 152, 163
   In Search of Humanity 3, 121–23, 129, 134, 163
   Invitation to Faith 1
   Jesus Christ in Modern Thought 3, 143, 146, 151–52, 154–55, 162
   Kenoticism Reconsidered 162
   'Pilgrimage in Theology' 2, 7, 72
   Principles of Christian Theology 28, 48, 54, 72, 79, 81, 83, 86–87, 91, 93, 97–98, 128, 134, 138, 147, 153, 163
   The Scope of Demythologizing 7, 44–45, 47–48, 56, 146

Studies in Christian Existentialism 7, 51, 54, 146
Twentieth-Century Religious Thought 82
manifestation, concept of 112
Marcel, Gabriel 62, 149
Marcuse, H. 148
Maximos 148
meditation 108, 172
Melanchthon, Philipp 58
memory, communal 85–86
metaphysics 54, 71, 110
microcosm, man as 128–29, 133, 136
mind-matter dualism 134
mineness of existence 37
Modernism 46–47, 56–57
mood 15, 20
Moule, C.F.D. 156
myth 48

natural theology
   as distinct from revealed theology 103, 112, 117, 172
   new-style 27–29, 97–101, 121
   objections to 101–2
   traditional 27–29, 100–101, 124
neo-Platonism 1, 137–40, 152
New Testament 83, 86
Newey, P.S. 112
Nicolas of Cusa 126, 128
Niebuhr, Reinhold 46, 67
Nietzsche, Friedrich 101, 155
nihilism 65

Ogden, Schubert 152
ontology 7–11, 43, 54–62, 68–70, 79, 82, 111–12, 125, 129–30; *see also* existential-ontological theism
openness of human nature 148–49
original sin 31
Otto, Rudolf 113
Owen, H.P. 45

pantheism 2, 113–14, 125–26

Parmenides 108–9
Paul, Saint 32–35, 58, 63–66, 147, 157–58
Pax, Clyde 62
phenomenology 22–26, 71, 121
philosophical basis of theology 8
philosophical theology *see* theology, natural: new-style
Pittenger, Norman 151–52
plenitude, principle of 139
plerosis 163–64
Plotinus 126–27, 137, 152
pre-existence 161
pre-understanding 45
presence, concept of 112
process philosophy 151–52

Rahner, Karl 82, 148–50, 159, 167
Reardon, B.M.G. 56–57
relationality 2
resoluteness 19–21
resurrection 26, 33, 63
revelation 86–87, 110–12
Robinson, James M. 58, 61, 70
Ryle, Gilbert 8, 22–25

salvation 89–90
Sanders, E.P. 147
Sartre, Jean-Paul 28, 43, 70
Schleiermacher, Friedrich 22, 69, 149–50, 154, 159–60
Schweizer, E. 34–35
self-evidence, theory of 23
sin 29–30
social responsibility 123
solipsism 24
soma 32, 35
Sophocles 108–10
Sykes, Stephen 143, 163–65

Teilhard de Chardin, Pierre 133
temporality 20, 37
theism, classical and dialectical 124–29
theological endeavour 60
theological terms 29–30

theology
  aim of 98–99
  scope of 44
  see also natural theology
theophany 128–29, 135
Thielicke, Helmut 45
Thomism 124, 149; *see also* Aquinas, Thomas
Tillich, Paul 7, 58
tradition 87–89
transcendence
  divine 113, 115, 126, 153, 172
  human 90–91, 125, 130, 134–37, 140, 150, 153, 172
Trinity, the 115, 152, 172–73
Turner, Victor 165

understanding 15–16, 20
use, principle of (for religious statements) 55
von Balthasar, Hans Urs 82
von Rad, Gerhard 156

Whitehead, A.N. 122, 126, 132–33, 137, 150
Wiles, Maurice 160, 167
will, divine and human 60–61; *see also* God: Will of
Williams, Daniel Day 82, 122
witness 64
worship 137